Laura A.Victoir

The Russian Country Estate Today

A Case Study of Cultural Politics in Post-Soviet Russia

With a foreword by Priscilla Roosevelt

SOVIET AND POST-SOVIET POLITICS AND SOCIETY

ISSN 1614-3515

Recent volumes

Laura A.Victoir

THE RUSSIAN COUNTRY ESTATE TODAY

A Case Study of Cultural Politics in Post-Soviet Russia

With a foreword by Priscilla Roosevelt

ibidem-Verlag
Stuttgart

Bibliografische Information Der Deutschen Bibliothek

Die Deutsche Bibliothek verzeichnet diese Publikation in der Deutschen
Nationalbibliografie; detaillierte bibliografische Daten sind im Internet
über <http://dnb.ddb.de> abrufbar.

Coverpicture: Derelict country estate, late-1990s. © Priscilla Roosevelt

∞

Gedruckt auf alterungsbeständigem, säurefreien Papier
Printed on acid-free paper

ISSN: 1614-3515
ISBN: 3-89821-426-5

© *ibidem*-Verlag
Stuttgart 2006
Alle Rechte vorbehalten

Printed in Germany

To Nicolas and my parents

Contents

List of Figures

List of Appendics

Acknowledgements

I wish to offer my deepest thanks to Priscilla Roosevelt, Rosamund Bartlett, Olga Sotskaia, and Andreas Umland for their tireless support of this project. In addition I would like to express my gratitude to Ulle Holt and Abbot Gleason for their encouragement over the years.

Foreword

Of Houses and History

The fate of Russia's estate houses is low on the current list of national priorities today, and with some reason. For example, who would place their preservation ahead of the health of Russia's children? Yet a legitimate argument can be made that, even in the turbulent atmosphere of early 21st century Russia, more attention should be paid to this aspect of historic preservation. Dmitri Shvidkovskii, Russia's premier architectural historian, once told me that, according to his calculations, before 1917 about 60,000 substantial estates defined the rural landscape of the 50 provinces of imperial Russia. Of these, less than 5% still exist in any form at present, most of them in Moscow oblast. Russia's crumbling rural estate houses are the sole remaining secular reminder of a flourishing provincial past. These survivors of revolution, civil war, and Nazi invasion served the Soviet state for seventy years in a number of capacities. A small number of manor houses became museums; most were utilized as hospitals or tuberculosis sanatoriums, orphanages or insane asylums, or holiday oases for various unions, agricultural institutes, and state farm headquarters. Many elegant estates in the environs of Moscow became dachas for the Communist elite.

This system of re-use of Russia's grand rural houses broke down in the late 1980s, when the Soviet government ran out of money to pay for its elaborate web of social services. There simply was no cash to repair winter damage to these houses and outbuildings, to pay adequate salaries to their staffs, nor to subsidize the virtually free services they provided. In rural areas, many former asylums and sanitariums simply closed down, as rapidly rising costs for materials and labor made annual upkeep impossible, while inflation wiped out retirees' ability to pay the real costs of formerly subsidized treatment or vacations.

I first glimpsed the dimensions of the historic preservation problem these estate houses pose in 1992, when I accompanied Professor Shvidkovsky and his wife, Katya Shorban, for six weeks, touring the surviving estates around Moscow. For me it was an extraordinary, and disheartening, experience to see so many estates, whose past is well preserved in memoirs or photographs, in their present-day altered, dilapidated, or derelict condition. At Olgovo, the upper floors of the manor house had collapsed upon its foundations in the five years since Shvidkovsky's last visit. Marfino's interior was gutted; huge oak French doors lay precariously across rotting supporting beams. Harsh weather, endemic thievery induced by rural poverty, the inability of caretakers to find means for repairs, or, in some instances such as Marfino, a deliberate decision to abandon an old building for a newly built one, were some of the factors contributing to decay.

Laura Victoir's impressive, groundbreaking case study of estate preservation efforts in Moscow oblast draws together the numerous economic, social, and political factors that are today determining the fate of these old houses. In the decade since the publication of my book, a huge literature on the history and cultural importance of Russia's estates has arisen. Numerous conferences have addressed the preservation situation, and new foundations have been created with the goal of heightening public awareness and support for these houses' continued existence. But, as Victoir's book amply illustrates, while the staggering dimensions and the urgency of the estate preservation problem have become more evident, the obstacles to its resolution may also have multiplied.

Victoir's book, based on a wide spectrum of written sources as well as numerous personal interviews, vividly depicts the impact of the competition for influence and resources between preservationists, developers, and politicians, in the very difficult circumstances of present-day Russian existence. This competition lies at the heart of the problem; its outcome will determine whether or not some of these wonderful sites, silent yet eloquent witnesses to the Russian past, will survive for future generations. The many champions of the rural estates that shaped and defined Russia's cultural and economic past are for the most part academics with little political influence or financial support. They often find themselves at odds with the numerous and contentious governmental bodies claiming jurisdiction over these properties, not to mention with the new real estate moguls and wealthy individuals with their own agendas.

This admirable study will be an asset to all who are actively involved with historic preservation in Russia, and I have no doubt that it will act as an incentive to improve the survival rate of Russia's manor houses.

Priscilla Roosevelt
Washington, DC

Figure 1: The Bakunin Estate

Introduction

The country estate, or *usad'ba*, originally banally defined as a house on a plot of land, was, in fact, a fulcrum of pre-revolutionary Russian culture. Estates were constructed and inhabited by the nobility, often with the ambition of being in harmony with the contemporaneous ideals of humanism and communion with nature.[1] The Russian nobility was not only a social and hierarchical class, but also a unified cultural power; their estates were the linchpins of agriculture, culture, socio-administration and every-day life in rural Russia. The estates were the glue that socially and culturally cemented pre-revolutionary Russia, and, due to their class orientations, immediately became ideologically problematic with the advent of Soviet rule. The estates of imperial Russia suffered greatly at the hands of the Soviet regime; the violent revolutions and civil wars, compounded by the brutal economic policies of utilisation and collectivisation decimated these last vestiges of the Russian aristocracy. Furthermore, those few estates which were fortunate to escape face continual threats to their survival, even in the liberated climate of twenty-first century Russia. These great estates are still susceptible despite currently enjoying governmental protection. Bands of rebel peasants have been substituted for negligence and lax policies of protection as the main threat to their existence. Two great estates recently fell prey to this apathy and negligence; in the winter of 1996 Chicherin's Karaul was razed to the ground, probably due to a fire caused by faulty wiring, as was Nabokov's Rozhdestveno in 1997.[2] Post- So-

---

[1]   Most estates were built between the mid-eighteenth and mid-nineteenth centuries, including throughout the reign of Catherine II (1762-96), a period known as the "Golden Age of the Nobility" in tandem with Europe's Age of Enlightenment. Catherine envisaged the noble class serving as provincial governors, as well as the exporters of culture into the provinces. See P. R. Roosevelt, *Life on the Russian Country Estate: A Social and Cultural History* (New Haven, CT; London: Yale University Press, 1995) 26-27. During this time, focus of life was shifted from the spiritual world to the natural world, which was to be enjoyed for its own merits. The Russian nobles often aspired to embody these ideals through life in their estates.

[2]   Evgeny Pashkin, an expert in mineralogical sciences, commented that another serious threat to estates comes from underground. For instance, near some estates the layer of asphalt can be a metre thick, through which water does not evaporate. The

viet Russia's current methods towards the protection of heritage have been generally unsuccessful; maximum claims of entitlement with minimum investment have frequently led to the ruin of estates. The aim of this book is to cast light on the situation of cultural preservation through detailed consideration of Russia's remaining country estates.

The preservation of Russian country estates serves as an excellent lens through which one may observe the activities surrounding contemporary cultural preservation in Russia. Although an integral part of Russian social and cultural history, estates have received less attention than many of Russia's other secular or religious buildings. Estates have been cast in the shadows; because of this they throw Russia's cultural preservation initiatives into relief. These estates are valuable to study precisely because they are an aspect of Russian cultural identity that has not received support. Russia, in the midst of post-Soviet self-identification, has often sought rational methods of fostering nationhood through protecting famous Russian landmarks.[3] However, despite being charged with cultural symbolism, the country estate has seldom benefited from state-lead preservation schemes.

This book intends to address several key issues; namely, given the commitment pledged by governmental authorities to estate protection, why are these estates not then being adequately preserved? To what extent are these legacies of imperial Russia still subject to the residual prejudices stemming from Soviet ideology? Furthermore, in light of contemporary pride in the cultural achievements of pre-revolutionary Russia, why have these estates, which proved so instrumental in promoting art, music and literature, not been accorded the same level of respect as other monuments? The final

---

wooden foundations of estates become wet and rot, which leads to collapse. Grigorii' Revzin, "Okhrana pamiatnikov: zashchishchat' ne ot kogo - Ostaetsia zashchishchat'sia," *Kommersant-Daily* 13/03/1998. In an interview with Lia Lepskaia from the Ostankino museum, she considered that the road directly in front of the estate has caused such problems with Ostankino's foundations. Repairing the foundations has become a priority for the museum. Interview with Lia Lepskaia, Director of the Theatre at Ostankino Estate, 09/08/2003.

[3] Take, for example, the reconstruction of the Cathedral of Christ the Saviour in Moscow in the 1990's. Another example is the face-lift given to St. Petersburg to prepare for the "City on the Neva's" 300th year anniversary. These acts of reconstruction and refurbishment were undertaken, for various reasons, one of which was to represent a new symbol for a new, cultural and progressive Russia.

point to be addressed is do these estates still have relevance in contemporary Russia and how they may be preserved in the context of Russia's difficult
realities?

This book will focus primarily on the later post-Soviet period. In order to
fully grasp the complexities of the situation, an interdisciplinary methodology
has been employed. As there is very little written on post-Soviet cultural preservation, the basis of research relies heavily on primary sources; notably
newspaper, magazine and journal articles, acts of legislation, government reports and interviews. The methodological framework underlying this work
owes a debt to several disciplines of the social sciences, borrowing exten-
sively from political science, historical and economic theory and even from
the area of heritage management. In other words, this work could be classified as a multi-disciplinary case study of estate preservation, utilising a pleth-
ora of varied, and more importantly, untapped resources.

In order to be able to analyze the cultural and social importance of the
country estate, one needs to place it in its historical milieu. Consequently the
first chapter of this book is devoted to establishing the historical context of the
Russian country estate.

The discrepancy between the government's professed ambitions and its
ability to achieve its aims offers insights into the components of Russia's cultural politics and intra-governmental struggles. The second chapter analyzes
the weakness of the post-Soviet Russian state in the sphere of cultural preservation. With the use of political theory and analysis, the effectiveness of
formal and informal cultural institutions will be explored. A consideration of
federal and regional conflicts, primarily illustrated through the state's clash
with Yuri Luzhkov's Moscow City government, serves as an indication of the
financial and political importance of cultural preservation.

Given the recurrent breach between decision-making and implementation, it is necessary to look at the professed goals of state cultural institutions
and how, in fact, these policies are realized. Russia's wavering institutional
capacity is directly linked to its inability to form a *pravovoe gosudarstvo* or law
governed state. Chapter Three therefore explores how, since the collapse of
Soviet rule, legal efforts to protect Russia's cultural patrimony have not been
effective. The myriad of laws and decrees that establish protocol for the preservation of monuments are outlined and explored. Tracing the path of legisla-

tion can serve to chart the characteristics and the limits of Russia's legal system and societal attitudes over such issues as privatization and restitution of country estates.

Russia's economic prospects as a whole directly affect funding for cultural preservation. The former Minister of Culture, Mikhail Shvydkoi, was cognizant of the fact that the state has been incapable of preserving the approximate eighty thousand monuments of culture of federal value.[4] Chapter Four explores the government's funding of monument preservation primarily through examining governmental documentation and press releases.

In so far as it is emblematic of the post-Soviet period, the disintegration of the central state has not necessarily led to the rise of greater participation in the cultural sphere. Chapter Five discusses the involvement of civil society and the impact of nongovernmental organizations and philanthropy on Russia's country estates. This chapter will briefly analyze civil society in post-Soviet Russia, and then explore what kind of civil society and philanthropic activities are integrated in the preservation of country estates.

This study will conclude by briefly assessing the capacity for cultural heritage to embody collective memories and cultural identities. The issue is not only concerned with the conservation of Russia's historic buildings, but also with exploring ways to make the most advantageous use of these buildings. Efficient economic activity, intelligent investment and viable legal, tax and political systems are all necessary to install a meaningful system of cultural preservation.

Survey of Literature on the Topic

Most extant primary accounts about Russian estates are found in literature and memoirs. Even before the twentieth century, publications about the estate as a traditional and cultural entity were being written, testifying to contemporary concern about the estate's economic decline. Estate culture had already begun to decline after the emancipation of serfs in 1861, although as an economic entity, the estate's decline dates from even earlier. So important

---

[4]   Maiia Bogdanova, "Usad'by v Rossii: zhivye i mertvye," *Mir i Dom* 09/2002.

was the perceived contribution of the estate to Russian culture that these articles were immediately published recounting the enormous cultural value of rural noble estates. Periodicals such as *The World of Art* (1899-1904), *The Russian Tourist* (1899-1913), *Old Years* (1907-1916) *and Capital and Estate* (1913-1917) were intent on studying the role of the estate not only in terms of their aesthetic merit, but also following the estate's contribution to Russian history.[5]

A second upsurge of popular interest in country estates, while not as prevalent as the former, arose amongst those who witnessed the Bolsheviks brutal treatment of the estate. The Society of the Study of the Russian Estate (*Obshchestvo izucheniia russkoi usad'by*, or the OIRU) was formed between 1922 and 1923 by a group of art critics, historians and artists. They felt compelled to engage not only in research activities, but also in public education campaigns for Muscovites from as early as 1923. In addition, they began a series of publications centred on the cultural and artistic value of Russian estates, and presented detailed research papers at various public conferences. From 1925, the cultural-educational work OIRU was extended further: between October and April of each year, the OIRU led thematic excursions to architectural monuments, museums and estates in Moscow and the surrounding region. Moreover, the excursion commission of the OIRU produced five guides between 1924 and 1929. The members of the OIRU also published *The Chronicle of the OIRU* (1927-1929). However, the life of the Society was abruptly curtailed; subject to the repression and terror of the 1930's, it was closed down in 1931 and a number of its members were punished, exiled or executed.

The general literature about estates produced during the Soviet period, excluding the publications of the OIRU, was minimal; the few studies which were published were principally dedicated to the paradigm of art history or were devoted to the handful of existing museum-estates. Estates were generally a taboo subject during various periods in the Soviet Union due to their association with Russia's former aristocratic class. However, after the fall of the Soviet Union, a flowering of interest in Russia's estates occurred. Today, the annual publication of the OIRU's chronicle, *The Russian Country Estate*,

---

[5]   L. V. Ivanova, ed., *Dvorianskaia i kupecheskaia usad'ba v Rossii XVI-XX vv.: istoricheskie ocherki* (Moscow: URSS, 2001) 15.

has been resumed with the resurrection of the Society in 1992. Their work focuses primarily on describing various estates and exploring the historic role of rural noble estates as a united social-administrative, agricultural and cultural centre. The work of the OIRU is less related to pragmatic aspects of preservation, but has provided valuable historical research.

In popular post-Soviet literature, numerous books deal with the history of certain famous estates, principally focusing on those belonging to the fabulously wealthy nobles, such as the Sheremetevs and Yusopovs, or those once belonging to famous writers, artists and composers. However, none of these texts deal with the current situation surrounding the preservation of these estates. There are also periodic journals, such as *Nashe Nasledie* (our Heritage) and *Pamiatniki Otechestva* (Monuments of the Fatherland), which sometimes contain features on Russian country estates. Vladimir Dlugach, the director of the museum-estate at Arkhangel'skoe, has created a magazine, *Life in the Estate*, which takes a broader scope with regard to the history of and contemporary dealings with Arkhangel'skoe and some other estates.[6]

There is a rich collection of works tracing the historiography of the estate, beginning from pre-revolutionary times, but few have dealt with them as special socio-economic and socio-cultural phenomena. However, some specialists are becoming increasingly concerned with the fate of the preservation of estates and the redefinition of the place and the role of estate culture in Russian historical heritage. These analyzes have gradually formed an independent branch of study that some have termed *usad'bovedeniye*.[7] In 1995, *The World of the Russian Estate* was published, compiled by the Institute of Russian History RAN (Russian Academy of Science) and edited by two members of the Institute, Yuri Tikhonov and Ludmila Ivanova, the former president of the OIRU.[8] It considers the history of the noble and merchant rural estates in Russia. V. Shchukin's book *The Myth of the Noble Nest*, published in 1997, explored the life of the Russian noble estate specifically in the nineteenth century. Also in 1997, *The Artistic World of the Russian Estate*,

---

6   *Zhizn' v usad'be* 01/2003.
7   The use of this term has been emerging in popular periodical articles as well as in academic materials.
8   Yuri Aleksandrovich Tikhonov and Ludmila V. Ivanova, *Mir russkoi usad'by: ocherki* (Moscow: Nauka, 1995).

written by T. Kazhdan, examined the historical and cultural evolution of the estate between the nineteenth and twentieth centuries.[9] A recently published a book by Garol'd Zlochevsky provides an excellent overview of publications about country estates from 1787 to 1992. Like the vast majority of works on estates, this survey is concerned with tracing the literature on the history of various estates and architectural and landscape studies. In the book, Zlochevsky acknowledges that "the inventory of works dedicated to the Russian estate, which generalize its history and culture and gives us the possibility to comprehend and evaluate [them]... is very modest."[10] However, a collective composition published by the Institute of Russian History RAN and edited by Ivanova, called *The Noble and Merchant Rural Estates in Russia XVI-XX Centuries: Historical Descriptions*, has been the most important work in this field to date.[11] This book is the most detailed attempt to create a historic overview of the estate's place in Russian culture. The book examines the world of the Russian estate from the sixteenth to the twentieth centuries, and, most importantly, the last chapter and conclusion deal primarily with the Soviet era and contemporary problems of estate preservation.

Outside Russia, very few books have been written about estate culture. The most important book has been Priscilla Roosevelt's *Life on the Russian Country Estate: A Social and Cultural History*.[12] Roosevelt traces the origins of the Russian country estate as an important social and cultural phenomenon, and uses a wide variety of source material, including diaries, memoirs, letters and cultural works. She provides an extensive account of the social, political, economic and cultural history of noble country life. In her conclusion, Roosevelt briefly described the contemporary deplorable condition of most estates, but there is no other English-language literature which focuses directly on this subject. Nor is there any in Russia which deals specifically with estate preservation.

---

9   T. P. Kazhdan, *Khudozhestvennyi mir russkoi usad'by* (Moscow: Traditsiia, 1997).

10   G. D. Zlochevsky, *Russkaia usad'ba: istoriko-bibliograficheskii' obzor literatury, 1787-1992* (Moscow: Institut naslediia, 2003) 259.

11   Ivanova, ed., *Dvorianskaia i kupecheskaia usad'ba v Rossii XVI- XX vv.: istoricheskie ocherki*.

12   Roosevelt, *Life on the Russian Country Estate: A Social and Cultural History*.

An Overview of the Problems Facing Russia's Country Estates

The extant country estates today are theoretically protected by the government of the Russian Federation. There are three levels of protection afforded to Russia's historic buildings. The first is for buildings of local significance, which fall under the responsibility of municipal government and organizations. Commonly, monuments of this category are less historically and culturally valuable and, consequently, are permitted to be sold to private individuals. Estate complexes of this category generally lack main houses and sizeable territories. The second level of protection is for buildings of regional importance, for which regional committees of culture and property and the government are designed to oversee protection. Included in this category of protection are some estates with preserved main houses, particularly in the Tver, Riazansk, Smolensk, Vladimir and Kaluga provinces. The third and most important grouping of historic buildings falls under federal protection but may be governed through regional authorities. Estates under federal protection include the greatest quantity of those with preserved main houses.[13]

The gravest threats that most estates face are those of fire and negligence. The majority of the estates are made of wood and tend to be quite fragile. Over time, numerous estates have been lost to fires, caused by preventable measures, such as faulty wiring, and general habitual neglect. An absence of action has left estates not only vulnerable to the elements but also to other encroachments. Estates have been, and still are being picked apart for construction materials by local residents. Their territories are being divided as illicit construction has been taking place within estate parks.[14] Estates are

---

[13]   G. Anni, "Sud'ba rezidentsii," *Salon" nedvizhimosti* 12/02/2003.

[14]   Even the land of the famous Moscow-area Arkhangel'skoe estate, which today is a museum, is under serious threat. On 9 December 2003, the Minister of Ecology and Wildlife Management of the Moscow area, Alla Kachan, signed the order in which 46 hectares of the estate's grounds could be leased on a competitive basis, including the area where the Gonzago Theatre is located. This move became possible because the State Duma had approved an amendment to the Wood Code in the summer of 2003, which allowed the lease of woods to private companies. The land surrounding Arkhangel'skoe was officially classified as "wood-land", without any mention of the protected or reserved zone or that hypothetically should surround Arkhangel'skoe. The Wood Code, in this case, directly contradicted the 2002 Federal law "On Objects of Cultural Heritage (Monuments of History and Culture) of the Peoples of the Russian Federation". Having learned about the plan, the director of

being sold to or taken-over by private individuals without any official over-sight. Privatization of estates could alleviate many of these menaces, how-ever there is the risk that some the problems that plagued previous privatisa-tion initiatives could again prevail. Individuals are often tempted to buy es-tates purely for the real-estate value of their land. Already, less than legal methods have been developed for eliminating unwanted historic buildings, which are often seen as costly burdens by the investors. This has been done by finding ways to lower the official status of the estates (i.e. by reducing the significance of monuments from federal to local or regional importance) or by intentional destruction, or *ruinirovaniia*. The latter was the case for the Trubetskoi estate in Moscow. Aleksey Komech, an art historian and director of the State Institute of Art History, stated, "Most likely, they burnt it down in order to make a copy in concrete. They create a copy but do not understand the value of the original. We devalue the concept of authenticity. The city ceases to be attractive for tourists, even with Moscow's well-tended parks and cleanliness. For the cultured foreigners, there is nothing new in the stores on Tverskaia [Street]. They do not come to Moscow for them. But that which

Arkhangel'skoe, Vladimir Dlugach, wrote in protest to the head of the Central Ad-ministrative Board of Natural Resources and Environmental Protections MPR of the Russian Federation, Nikolai' Garankin, in October, 2003, but to no avail. On 15 January 2004, a bidding competition resulted in 49-year rent contracts for three lit-tle-known private companies: *"E'rlikon grup"*, *"Oblstroi'universal"* and *"Park 'Ark-hangel'skoe"*. It is widely speculated that once the wood-land has been rented, the companies will construct upon it, later to lay claim to the ground underneath the buildings.

One reason that it was possible to rent this land was because there is a lack of clar-ity about who actually owns the land. Amongst the groups which control parts of the Arkhangel'skoe territory are the State Wood Fund, the Ministry of Defence, the Min-istry of Culture and agricultural and private holders. Also, the price of land generally in north-west Moscow, and specifically around Arkhangel'skoe, is at a premium. This provides a major incentive for the construction of luxury housing sites in this area.

This situation calls into question the future of the rest of the land of Arkhangel'skoe, and possibly other estates in desirable areas. See Ninel' Shcherbina, "Usad'ba 'Arkhangel'skoe' v osade," *Rossiiskie Vesti* 16/06/2004., Oleg Kashin, "Zemel'nyi vopros. Park v Arkhangel'skom priniali za les i sdali v arendu," *Kommersant-Daily* 01/06/2004., Natalia Granina and Natalia Kochetkova, "'Arkhangel'skoe' zastroiat kottedzhami," *Izvestiia (Rossiia)* 03/06/2004., Tatiana Rostova, "Usadebnoe khoziai'stvo," *Versiia* 24/05/2004., Anna Viktorova, "Nasledie. Unichtozhitel'nyi' krai'," *Kul'tura* 15/04/2004., Tatiana Sei'ranian, "Konflikt. Kto spaset Ark-hangel'skoe," *Gazeta* 08/06/2004.

is unique rapidly disappears."[15] There are further challenges that threaten the survival of the remaining estates; the current museum network is starved of financial assistance and many museums exist and function purely by the enthusiasm of local museum workers. However, enthusiasm can not serve as the sole means of protection. As in the Soviet period, official protection of estates today is minimal.

---

[15]   Nikolai Ol'gin, "Nasledie: privatizatsiia istorii," *Itogi* 18/02/2003.

Figure 2: Arkhangel'skoe, courtesy of P. Roosevelt

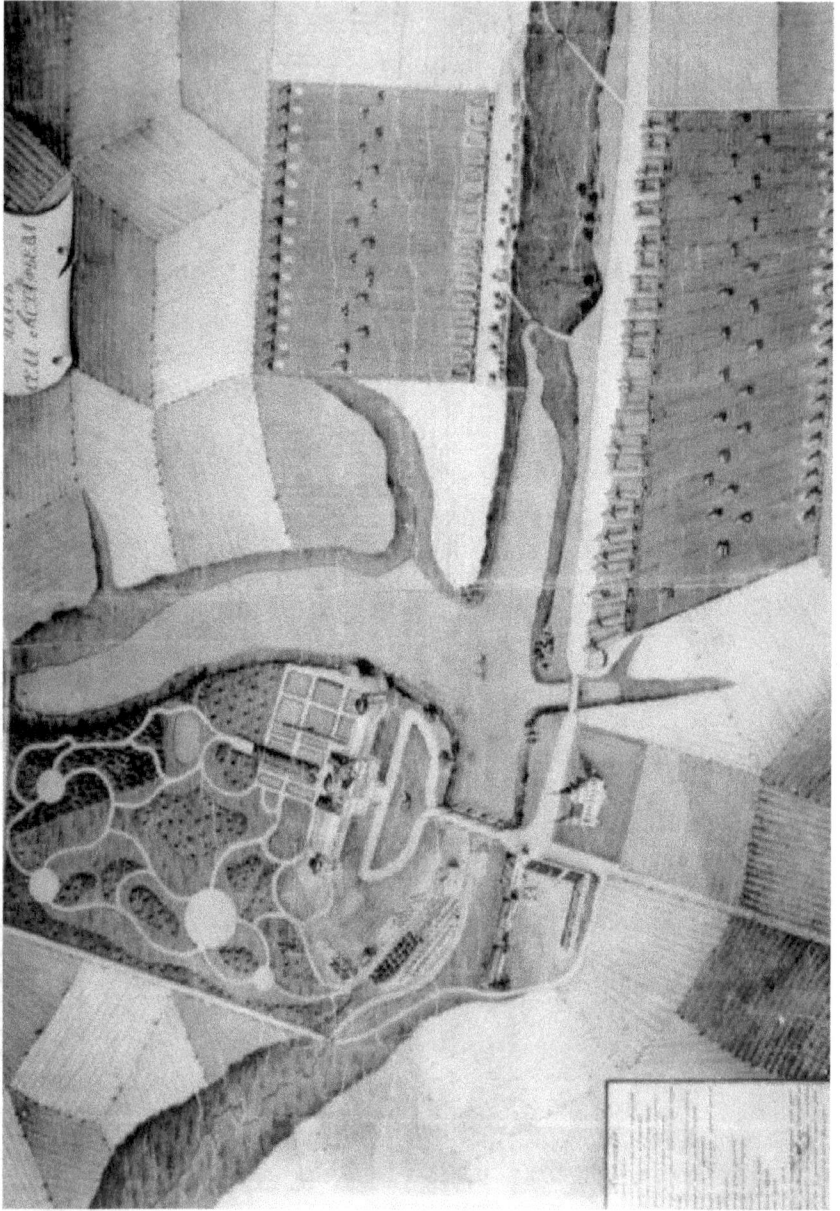

Figure 3: 1805 plan of Ostafievo Estate, Moscow province

I   The History of the Russian Country Estate

This chapter will provide a definition of the Russian country estate and an overview of its history. This analysis will explain why the estate has been considered to be the cradle of Russian high culture and the centre of administration and agriculture in the countryside. The fate of the estate will be traced through the revolutionary and Soviet periods, when the vast majority of estates were destroyed.

There are two principal complications with the historical study of estates. Firstly, it is difficult to actually define what an "estate" is, as it has been subject to historically divergent meanings. In addition to the word *usad'ba* there were different terms for estates: *votchina i pomest'e* (inherited estate), *vladenie i imenie* and *derevnia*.[16] Secondly, the definitions of "estate" have undergone in the course of time remarkable changes. The word *usad'ba* is thought to be a derivative of the verb "to sit" or "to plant". Vladimir Dal', the author of the first dictionary of the Russian language, described *usada* or *usad'ba* as "a manor house in a village, including the buildings, garden and vegetable-plot."[17] The first edition of the Great Soviet Encyclopaedia of 1936 provides two entries for the word; the first is a historical description of the noble estate, and the second, in a manipulation of its original meaning, also used the label of *usad'ba* to delineate Soviet collective farms. In this second entry, the Encyclopaedia defines a *usad'ba* as a Soviet state farm (*sovkhoz*) or a collective farm (*kolkhoz*): "A large agricultural enterprise at the centre of the concentration of control, management and organization of the new, socialist production and way of life."[18]

---

16   Ivanova, ed., *Dvorianskaia i kupecheskaia usad'ba v Rossii XVI-XX vv.: istoriche-skie ocherki, Introduction.*

17   Vladimir Ivanovich Dal', *Tolkovyi' slovar' zhivago velikoruskago iazyka*, 2 ed., vol. 4, 4 vols. (St. Petersburg; Moscow: 1882) 524.

18   O. Iu. Shmidt, ed., *Bol'shaia Sovetskaia E'ntsiklopediia*, 1st ed. (Moscow: Gosudarstvennyi Institut "Sovetskaia E'ntsiklopediia", 1936).

An Early Print of Izmailovo

The definition is symptomatic of early Soviet ideological bias; due to their aristocratic origins, country estates were not tolerated in the new political regime. However, with the passing of time and the subsequent tempering of ideological commitment, in the second and third editions of the Great Soviet Encyclopaedia of 1956 and 1977, the definition of an *usad'ba* was reduced to simply a description of the architectural elements of the former noble estates, with all references to Soviet farms excluded: "A Russian architecture complex of habitable, economic, park, and other buildings, which compose a united economic and architectural whole."[19]

Secondly, there is a lack of demarcation of the concept and role of the estate. For the convenience of typology, Russian estates can be divided into three categories: those in the city, village (*derevnia*), and countryside. There are significant difficulties with the terminological, methodological and historical character of estates as well, especially as historiography in this field lacks definition. In addition, the role of the rural estate was complex and covered a wide multiplicity of duties; simultaneously it fulfilled agricultural, socio-administrative, and cultural functions and greatly affected daily life (*byt*). Moreover, estates belonged to hosts of different classifications of owners; there were those belonging to tsars, nobles, *raznochinets* (nineteenth century non-aristocratic intellectuals) and later merchants. For each of these stratifications, and even within each subgroup, wealth and status differed enormously. The estates of the extremely affluent landed gentry (for example, the Sheremetev, Golitsyn and Yusopov families) tended to be opulent and grand, even exceeding those of the tsars. In contrast the estates of the minor gentry were frequently more reminiscent of peasant farmsteads.

Although the exact numbers were never recorded, estates were wide-spread in Russia's countryside, particularly in fertile lands. According to the calculations of the Institute of Russian History RAN, there were between sixteen to fifty thousand noble estates in the mid-eighteenth to the mid-nineteenth centuries.[20] Today experts estimate that only seven to fifteen percent of pre-

---

[19]   B. A. Vvedensky, ed., *Bol'shaia Sovetskaia E'ntsiklopediia*, 2nd ed., vol. 44 (Moscow: Gosudarstvennoe nauchnoe izdatel'stvo, 1956).

[20]   Ivanova, ed., *Dvorianskaia i kupecheskaia usad'ba v Rossii XVI-XX vv.: istoricheskie ocherki* 650.

revolutionary estates remain.[21] Specifically, according to the data of the Fund of the Revival of the Russian Estate, there are 652 estates in the Moscow region. Of those, only 190 have preserved main houses. In the remaining regions of central Russia there are about 250 vacant estate complexes with preserved main houses.[22] Hundreds more exist with preserved minor buildings, including wings or annexes (*fligeli*), agricultural buildings and churches.[23] Generally, experts also conclude that although the exact number of historic monuments in Russia is not known, the country loses between 110-115 each year due to neglect. Others claim that the actual numbers destroyed annually are, in reality, double these figures.[24]

Although archaeological findings have shown that large dwellings in the cities already existed in the ninth and tenth centuries, rural estates were a later phenomenon, linked to the military.[25] Soldiers were under obligation to serve the great Moscow prince (and since 1547, the tsar) and were rewarded for military merit with land either in the form of hereditary possessions (*votchina*) or personal occupancy (*pomestie*). It is partly for this reason that the greatest concentration of rural estates was found in the region of the old Muscovite principality, and to the south and west. Soldiers could transfer estates through inheritance only on the condition that their sons continued military service. Thus, individual estates' fates were reliant both on the will of sovereigns, who set the conditions of donation, and on that of the actual owners. This rather arbitrary tenure lasted until land ownership was legally established with the Land Code (*Ulozhenie*) in 1649.[26]

The heyday of estate culture began in 1762, when the noble class was released from the obligation of state service by Peter III, and continued until 1861, with the abolition of serfdom. After the nobles' liberation from the state and release from residence in the proximity of the Tsar's court, thousands of

---

[21]   A. Tolstikhina and V. Mach, "Privatizatsiia v istorii," *Ezhenedel'nyi' zhurnal* 01/09/2003.

[22]   T. Iur'eva and S. Zharkov, "Novye pomeshchiki," *Vedomosti* 14/04/2003.

[23]   Elena Rudometkina, "Novye russkie bare: Poselit'sia v dvorianskoi usad'be ne tak uzh slozhno," *Russkii fokus* 20/01/2003.

[24]   "Nuzhno li privatizirovat' pamiatniki kul'tury?" *Ekho Moskvy* 25/07/2003.

[25]   Much of the historical background on Russian estates was found in Ivanova, ed., *Dvorianskaia i kupecheskaia usad'ba v Rossii XVI-XX vv.: istoricheskie ocherki* 650.

[26]   P. R. Roosevelt, *The Russian Estate on the Eve of the 21st Century: Problems of Preservation and Survival* (Khmelita Estate, Smolensk Oblast: 2000).

nobles departed to the countryside. They constructed or renovated their own personal palaces, often with the ambition of being in harmony with the contemporary ideals of the enlightenment and in communion with nature. At this time, the Russian nobility was not only a social and hierarchical class, but also a unified cultural power; their estates were centres around which culture, socio-administration, agriculture and daily life revolved.

Between the end of the eighteenth century and the first half of the nineteenth century rural estates served as an important link between the capitals and provincial towns (see Figures 4 and 5). Additionally, rural estates were the centre of agricultural and industrial production, and aided the diffusion of agricultural technology and use of natural resources. Throughout Russia's history, the estate life was clearly different from life in the major cities, where the noble class was subject to stringent rules of the court and high-society. In the country estate, nobles were able to shed the restrictions of public protocol and re-define their surroundings according to their desires; estates were the manifestation of particularly personal character reflecting individual tastes and needs.

Figure 4: A view of a rural town in Russia, Volokolamsk' - the Moscow Road

Figure 5: Volokolamsk' - view of the trading rows (market place)

Estate culture was the fulcrum of artistic activities outside major cities from the late eighteenth century until the twentieth century; it served as a foundation of Russian high culture. In many cases, the world view of Russian intelligentsia, artists, scientists and statesmen was moulded through exposure to this estate culture. Estate owners tended to be patrons of the arts and were responsible for bringing culture to rural Russia. Theatres, picture galleries, libraries and village schools were established in or by estates. In her informative book on the history and significance of Russian country estates, Roosevelt identifies three different varieties of estate life which greatly affected Russia's social and cultural development. The first type, the estate served as an "aristocratic playground," in which the owner's fantasies and luxury played centre stage. The lavish spending needed to maintain this way of life proved to be unsustainable and was replaced by more simple refinement. The second concept, that which stressed the estate owner's patriarchal role, highlighted the landowner's commitment to his villagers and Russian tradition and lasted until the advent of industrialization. The third version was of an idyllic and bucolic refuge and inspiration for Russia's educated and artistic elite.[27]

The emancipation manifesto signed by Alexander II on 19 February 1861 triggered deep changes within Russia's society and economy. With the abolition of serfdom, landowners were deprived of the serf labour upon which many estate economies were dependent. They were forced to find different ways to exploit their estate's economy. In spite of the changes, the daily life and many old traditions within estates were often little affected. As in previous times, the estate continued to be the ancestral "noble nest" (*dvorianskoe gnezdo*), where Russia's elites continued to dwell.

Numerous social changes of the late nineteenth century evoked a general reminiscence of the "golden century" of Russian and estate culture. Estate culture, in spite of everything, began its slow decline with Russia's nascent attempts at modernisation and the advent of capitalism and industrialisation. With the increasing importance of industry, the estate economy declined and the social composition of owners of rural estates began to change. After the emancipation, merchants entered into the league of estate owners. Previously, social constraints prevented the merchant class from owning land, par-

---

[27]   Roosevelt, *Life on the Russian Country Estate: A Social and Cultural History* xiii.

ticularly land which belonged to the noble class. The rural and urban estates entered into the hands of the industrial and financial classes. Bringing with them business skills and economic savvy, the merchants often modernised the estate economy and reconstructed estate complexes, frequently drawing from among the best architects of that time. In spite of the social changes, the "*kupecheskii*" (merchant) period in the history of the rural estate tended to be a positive and productive phase for estate architecture.

Another general trend in the nineteenth and twentieth centuries was the conversion of rural estates into the summer residences, or "dachas".[28] According to Stephen Lovell, a dacha, distinct from an estate, is usually defined as a "country house" or "cottage" in English and as a vacation house or second home in Russian. The distinction between the two lies in the fact that dacha residents did not consider the dacha properties as money-making assets, as did estate owners.[29] From the mid-eighteenth century, with the advent of a relatively prosperous layer of non-noble society, the demand for out-of-town summer residences induced a manifestation of "dacha fever" in Russia. Dachas, which included subdivided estate buildings available for rent, became havens for summer leisure for the ever increasing stratum of landowners who began to spend the major portion of the year in the city. Increasingly, estates began to be rented out to city-dwellers for the summer.

The beginning of the twentieth century proved to be cataclysmic for rural estates. The reforms of 1861 were inadequate for the development of a healthy peasant economy. From that time until the turn of the century Russia's population had grown dramatically and land prices had continued to rise. These conditions fostered massive agrarian disturbances. Between 1905 and 1907 revolutionary agitation amongst the peasants swept a number of provinces. Often, peasants rebelled against landowners, and in doing so, hundreds of noble estates were burnt to the ground. Similar events occurred during World War I, when conditions of life in Russia declined in tandem with the moribund war economy.

---

[28]   An excellent analysis of the emergence of the dacha as a Russian phenomenon can be found in Stephen Lovell, *Summerfolk: A History of the Dacha, 1710-2000* (Ithaca, NY: Cornell University Press, 2003).

[29]   Lovell, *Summerfolk: A History of the Dacha, 1710-2000* 1.

Figure 6: Neo-classical estate building plan

The popular revolts beginning on 8-11 March 1917 would prove to be the beginning of the end for Russian country estates. The abdication of Tsar Nicholas II, the creation of the Provisional Government and its ensuing downfall helped pave a crooked and unlikely path leading to the October Revolution and the rise of the Bolsheviks. The role and significance of country estate in Russian history and culture were not palatable to Soviet ideologues; these physical remnants of the "exploiting class" of Imperial Russia could not be tolerated by the new regime. Few estates survived the brutality of the advent of Soviet power, and the subsequent years of Soviet rule witnessed the destruction of more.

Estates and estate culture were physically shattered with the fatal blow, the Bolshevik's *Decree About Land*, passed on the 26 October (8 November) 1917. The Decree dictated that the estate, as a land and juridical establishment, was to be liquidated. In addition, Russia's civil war proved to be very effective in destroying estates. And in the regions of central and western Russia, the course of World War II (1941-1945), with the invasion of the Nazi army, devastated many of the remaining estates. In the subsequent decades of Soviet rule, many estates which had survived upheavals, revolutions and wars were purposefully destroyed or fell into ruin as a result of neglect. During this time, there was little interest in calculating and recording the number of preserved estates; therefore today there is a lack of data about what still remains. Unfortunately, when many estates, including even some of the most renowned, had been rediscovered, they were frequently found in ruins.

Figure 7: A. T. Bolotov watercolour of Bogoroditskoe in Tula province. Bolotov was one of the most renowned estate architects in Russia

Figure 8: Derelict Estate, 1990's. Picture courtesy of P. Roosevelt

In the early days of Soviet rule, two tendencies existed with respect to estates. The first was initiated by certain factions of scientists, cultural workers and enthusiasts. These groups did what they could for the physical retention of estate ensembles. In order to illustrate the historical and original roles played by estates in Russian culture, they began initiating the creation of estate-museums. They also launched research projects and proposed to the Soviet government that hundreds of estate-monuments be granted state protection. About this time, about five hundred estates were recognized by these groups as deserving protection.[30]

The second tendency, in opposition with and more pervasive than the first, was the conventional disregard of the Russian estate as a historical and cultural phenomenon by the Soviet government. Soviet historiography was completely subjected to the ideological framework of Marxism-Leninism. The study of estates and estate culture, hence, was directed by a one-sided class approach. Soviet historians highlighted the conservative and reactionary nature of noble landowners and the economic stagnation caused by estate economies. Namely, they deemed landowners and their estates as "obstacles for public progress."

The exception to this prevalent concept was found in the Museum Division of the People's Commissariat for Public Education (*Narodnyi' komissariat prosveshcheniia* or *Narkompros*) first headed by the literary critic Anatoly Lunacharsky between 1917 and 1929. In the 1920's *Narkompros* sometimes became involved in the protection of estates. This was essentially because members of the former intelligentsia worked in the division, many of whom understood the value of the Russian estate. *Narkompros* was able to compile a significant number of sources, and helped create policies of state involvement in the protection of monuments. However, the measures taken during this fortunate period for the estate were not enough. The state's financial difficulties led to the under-financing and poor custodianship of those newly created estate-museums. The majority of museums were eventually eliminated in the middle of the 1920's. In addition, the Bolsheviks' penchant for modernity and urbanity led to the removal of historical-cultural valuables from the countryside and doomed many rural estates to oblivion.

---

[30]   Ivanova, ed., *Dvorianskaia i kupecheskaia usad'ba v Rossii XVI-XX vv.: istoricheskie ocherki* 646.

Estates were assigned new and diverse functions. Estate churches, for example, were inactive and regularly served as storage houses. Often only the main houses of estates were guarded, while wings and other agricultural buildings or parks were not protected or utilised. Many estates were transformed into sanatoria or hospitals for the Ministry of Defence, while others into dachas, general hospitals, club-houses, communal farms, schools, houses of recreation (*dom otdykha*), and so forth. Only a handful of estates escaped this outcome and were converted into museums, usually commemorating certain famous personages. Others were destroyed for their building material, and yet others were forgotten and left to decay. Even with the Soviet state's support, cultural preservation funds were often irrationally or ineffectively used. Furthermore, as the estate was not valued, those that were preserved as museums rarely received the necessary funding from the state. Of those that did survive, artistic valuables were moved to the cities or relocated in the dwellings of high officials. Family collections were depersonalized and dispersed. As Ivanova noted in the book *Noble and Merchant Rural Estates in Russia*,

> There were abundant examples of general negligence towards estates, even in years of a 'developed socialist society,' when the authorities loudly declared their respect for cultural heritage. Not only were there numerous instances of the dismemberment of estate complexes, of their irrational use and merciless operation of aging buildings, but also the fact that half of all inspections of estates between the 1960's and 1980's, even in the Moscow region, which had always had more economic and cultural importance than other region of the country, revealed that estates were still declining in condition many decades after the revolution.[31]

---

[31]   Ivanova, ed., *Dvorianskaia i kupecheskaia usad'ba v Rossii XVI-XX vv.: istoricheskie ocherki* 637.

Figure 9: Derelict Estate, 1990's. Picture courtesy of P. Roosevelt

The estate-cum-museum did not account for many of the existing estates, and even those estates under "protection" were still under great danger. Local collective farms rapidly damaged several estates. For instance, Ivanova described the case of the poet Mikhail Lermontov's house in Tarkhany (later renamed Lermontovo by the Soviets). *Narkompros* decided to take this estate under its protection "by placing the responsibility for its spoiling or destruction on those establishments or private individuals who occupied the estate". A local collective farm was established in the premises. Details from the inspection of 7 July 1924 reported that the estate was almost reduced to ruin (wrecked fields, walls covered with smoke and crumbled plaster) and had become unfit for habitation, with the exception of two rooms repaired for the manager of the state farm. The park was neglected, the mausoleum opened, its doors and windows broken, and the sepulchral marble board commemorating Lermontov's grandmother was torn away.

If preservation was to be achieved, the onus was upon local cultural workers themselves. A certain A. I. Khramov (1901-1958) described to the All-Russian Congress of the Cultural Workers about his findings at Tarkhany. Through his efforts, restoration works began in 1934, and the Lermontov state museum was founded in 1939. The museum was modest, encompassing only nine hectares, with poor roads as the only access routes. On 30 July 1969 Tarkhany was turned into a museum-preserve, and in 1973 significant restoration works began. Again, it was only in the beginning of the 1980's that enough resources were pooled to bring Tarkhany up to the standard of a significant museum dedicated to Lermontov: its territory was expanded to one hundred hectares, lost monuments were reunited at the estate and Lermontov themed holiday-trips were conducted there.[32] The creation of the museum-estate of the great national poet took many decades and was thus built upon the initiative of an individual; estates once belonging to lesser-known personages did not have such good fortune.

Particularly from the end of World War II, historic monuments as a whole, including the country estates, did not rank high amongst the priorities of the Soviet organs of authority. The newly-created government cultural

---

[32] Ivanova, ed., *Dvorianskaia i kupecheskaia usad'ba v Rossii XVI-XX vv.: istoricheskie ocherki* 635-6. See also the Takharny Museum website at http://www.sura.ru/tarhany/eng/museum.htm

plans did not include estates. If estates were mentioned in popular publications, it was mostly about the few existing museum-estates with no consideration paid to the condition of the remaining estates.

Some hope for certain estates remained, again not through state initiative, but through the efforts of individuals. In 1965, the All-Russian Society for
the Protection of Historical and Cultural Monuments, VOOPIK (*Vserossii'skoe
obshchestvo okhrany pamiatnikov istorii i kultury*) was formed.[33] The Society
was created with the intention of including the participation of the community
in the preservation and maintenance of monuments. Michael Urban, in his
book *The Rebirth of Politics in Russia*, describes post-Stalin expressions of
popular demand as the first embryonic forms of a civil society.[34] In this sense
VOOPIK could be considered such an institution, in opposition to an unre-
sponsive state, it served as an expression of a popular will working towards
the preservation of cultural heritage. Ivanova estimated that VOOPIK had approximately twenty million members at its peak, and had significant means
through voluntary contributions made by citizens and enterprises. VOOPIK
aided in the restoration numerous estates. Under their auspices the estate-
museums of Spasskoe-Lutovinovo, Tarkhany, Ivanovka, Bernovo, and Bo-
goroditsk were created in the 1970's. Added to this list in the 1980's were
Gremiachka, Nikol'skoe-Pogoreloe, Permukhino, Izvara, Petrovskoe and
some others.

Some estate territories, parks, and buildings were restored through pa-
tronage and "volunteerism." For example, in 1982 approximately three hundred students worked on the estates in the Orel region. The Machine Building
Plant undertook the restoration of the estate house of Leo Tolstoy in Nikol'skoe-Viazemskoe. The Podol'sky Machine Building Plant and the Professional Technical School #27 restored the estate house in Ivanovskoe (Moscow *oblast*). In the 1980's, the public club "*Veche*" helped with I. A. Bunin's
estate Ozerki in the Lipetsk *oblast*, where he spent his childhood.[35] During
this period, the Ministry of Culture and local Soviet organs received hundreds

[33]   For more information on VOOPIK, you can visit their website at
http://www.voopik.ru/today/

[34]   Michael E. Urban, *The Rebirth of Politics in Russia* (Cambridge: Cambridge University Press, 1997) 35.

[35]   Ivanova, ed., *Dvorianskaia i kupecheskaia usad'ba v Rossii XVI-XX vv.: istoricheskie ocherki* 634.

of similar proposals, and the lists of the newly revealed estate monuments rapidly grew. Yet progress remained slow. While these examples prove that there were those who were interested in the survival of estates, the government and the general public remained unmoved. The state and Soviet specialists still disregarded the value of the Russian estate as a historical-cultural phenomenon.

In a state-sponsored programme of cultural protection at this time, the concept of the "Golden Ring" was created, which included hundreds of restored and refurbished monuments of architecture and history, including Old-Russian Kremlins, monasteries, churches and museums around Moscow. However, the restoration of estates did not receive the same priority as more ancient monuments. The creation of a similar "Pushkin Ring" (1968-1976), which was much more focused on estates where the poet once resided or visited, died out because of lack of funding and cooperation.

In the 1970's work began on an All-Russian Code for Monuments of History and Culture, which was an attempt to gather information about monuments, including estates. In 1997 the Institute of Culture published the materials from this *Code of Monuments of Architecture and Monumental Art of Russia* (collected between 1975 and 1985) and combined this material with contemporary data. Their findings show that in the Kaluga and Vladimir provinces, regions once rich in estates, only a fraction of the original numbers remain. Today the Vladimir region has 38 estates, including those in ruins, and Kaluga has 82, of which only 14 are protected. Fewer estates remain in other central regions: Ryazan has six and Tula nine. It was from these two provinces, besides the Moscow *oblast*, that the greatest amount of looting occurred after the revolution. Of those estates recognized by the Code in the late Soviet period in the regions of the "Black Earth" Centre (Belgorod, Voronezh, Lipetsk, Orel, Tambov) very few are completely preserved: in Voronezh 11 estates were protected by the state and only five preserved, in Lipetsk, 20 were protected and five preserved, Tambov ten were protected and two preserved, in Orel 74 were protected and 36 preserved. These areas were most affected by the Civil and World Wars.[36]

---

[36]   Ivanova, ed., *Dvorianskaia i kupecheskaia usad'ba v Rossii XVI-XX vv.: istoricheskie ocherki* 644.

There have also been other post-Soviet state efforts to aid in the preservation of culture in broader ways. The *Constitution of the Russian Federation* of 1993 guarantees access to cultural activities and objects for all citizens. Additionally, in June 1993, the government created the *Federal Programme for the Development and Preservation of Culture and the Arts (1993-1995)*. In this programme the state anticipated that its support of culture would be supplemented by the activities of cultural organizations and sponsors with investors picking up the slack. The programme was continued with the *Federal Programme for Culture of Russia (2001-2005)*, adopted by the Government in December 2000, designating the Ministry of Culture responsible for its implementation. A specific goal of the programme is to oversee the effective use of monuments with the intention to harmonise their historical and cultural importance with economic pursuits. The drafting of a *Federal Programme* for 2006-2010 is taking place at this time.

On 20 February 1995, a presidential decree affirmed "The list of objects of historical and cultural heritage of federal (all-Russian) value," which outlined all monuments guarded by state laws of 1960-1993. Included on this list were 38 monuments connected with estates: 17 museum-preserves, 17 annexes, three museum-estates, and one preserve. Of urban architectural monuments 58 estate objects were named: one noble-estate complex, 52 estates, one park, and four estates houses. In whole, only 96 estates were incorporated on the list.[37] Some estates (the number is unknown) are under local protection. Nothing is documented about estates without any kind of state protection.

The principal tasks of these programmes are to provide state support for professional creative activity and cultural participation, to preserve the cultural heritage of Russia ensuring its effective use, to develop and strengthen cultural infrastructure providing access to cultural goods and information resources of state museums, libraries and archives thus joining the global information space, to develop the role of culture in strengthening civil society institutions, to raise people's social awareness, to protect socially vulnerable groups, and to concentrate funding on priorities of cultural development. The general cultural policy objectives are in accordance with the Council of

---

[37]   Feodosii' Ustinenko, "Chto imeem, ne khranim. Prikliucheniia 'milanskoi' kolonny'," *Parlamentskaia gazeta* 22/10/2002.

Europe priorities with a special emphasis on national cultural values and traditions, preservation and protection activities, social cohesion and national integrity of Russia. The most widely used political notion today is preserving heritage while finding acceptable means of usage.[38] It is positive that these programmes exist, but their effectiveness in implementation is less encouraging. Chapters Two and Three will analyze why state institutions are often incapable of realising their stated cultural goals.

Ministries and other parties are engaged in the specific realm of preservation of monuments. Efforts are being undertaken to make known the grave problems facing Russian patrimony. Shvydkoi, the Minister of Culture until March 2004, recounted, "We recently published a three-volume edition dedicated to monuments. It consists of a black book, in which are assembled the lost monuments, a red book, monuments which are in a stage of destruction, and a white one, of preserved monuments. The thickest, unfortunately, is the black volume. We live in the country of the disappearing monuments."[39]

---

[38]   For more information on the details of these programmes, visit the Ministry of Culture of the RF's website at http://www.mincult.ru or its information centre at http://www.cpic.ru or http://www.russianculture.ru

[39]   Aleksei' Karakhan and Grigorii' Revzin, "*Pokazatel'noe vystuplenie. 'Podozrevat' menia v zhelanii zarabotat' na pamiatnikakh glupo',*" *Kommersant-Vlast'* 22/09/2003.

Figure 10: Example of a Russian Estate: Olgovo

II   A Weak State with Weak Institutions

This chapter will explore the formal state institutions involved with cultural preservation. Identifying continuity and change in the field of Russia's cultural politics is a way to grasp the relationship between institutions and the transformation of their capacities and objectives. This will by done by examining state institutions' intended functions and assessing their ability to achieve these goals. The first task will be to define the theories underpinning the evaluation of the overall effectiveness of governmental institutions in Russia. Then there will be a brief outline of some of the problems of institutional enforcement in Russia's regions. Finally, the interactions between the Moscow city government and the federal government will be examined in order to illustrate cultural dealings gone awry.

It is first imperative to define what is meant by an institution. As Neil Robinson has written in his book *Institutions and Political Change in Russia*, "institutions can be defined formally, as the products of constitutions, laws etc., and informally, as the result of values that are more diffuse in origin, springing from culture, historical practice and repeated interactions between actors that produce equilibrium and stable expectations over time. Formal and informal institutions can, of course, exist in tandem, reinforcing, subverting or reshaping each other."[40] As a whole, Russian formal institutions have not proved adept at ensuring the preservation of culture in Russia; their weakness is a primary cause. Institutional effectiveness is directly linked with the state's overall facility to command. According to the political scientist Michael McFaul, state power has two principle components: autonomy and capacity. The degree of a state's autonomy is gauged by its ability to define its preferences independently of other actors. Capacity measures a state's capability to implement these preferences. The extent of consensus and effectiveness of state institutions determines a state's ability to define and imple-

---

[40]   Neil Robinson, "Introduction," *Institutions and Political Change in Russia* (Basingstoke: Macmillan, 2000) 1.

ment its preferences.[41] This institutional effectiveness can be achieved with the "institutionalization of agency," meaning that "the rules according to which political and distributional conflicts are carried out" are impervious to conflict.[42]

Cultural preservation is included amongst state preferences, as indicated by the numerous laws, codes and ministries involved in this very matter. Preservation may not be a state priority, but it is seen as a desirable outcome. Even the President of the Russian Federation, Vladimir Putin, has often spoken in favour of culture and the preservation of Russia's patrimony. For example, in the summer of 2000, when Putin chaired a meeting of the presidential council of cultural advisors, he acknowledged, "The influence of Russian culture is diminishing each day like shagreen leather," a reference to a disappearing piece of leather in Balzac's *The Magic Skin*.[43] However, as the state has not been capable of implementing this preference of preservation, the Russian government can be considered weak in this sphere. The rules that have been established over cultural preservation are mired in conflict or are simply disregarded. If another measurement of state power is its ability to counter leading interest groups in society, again, agency has not been institutionalized within formal cultural institutions. Robinson resumed that there has been no thorough institutionalization of agency in Russian and state autonomy remains low.[44] In general, the erosion of formal institutional influence and capability has allowed dominant individuals and groups to directly influence decision-making. This can be seen as historic monuments have been subject to illicit sales and alterations throughout the post-Soviet period. Nor have de facto seizures of estates been uncommon.

---

[41]   Michael McFaul, "State Power, Institutional Change, and the Politics of Privatization in Russia," *World Politics* 47.2 (1995): 214.

[42]   Ulrich Klaus Preuss, Claus Offe and Jon Elster, *Institutional Design in Post-Communist Societies: Rebuilding the Ship. Theories of Institutional Design* (Cambridge: Cambridge University Press, 1998) 27-34.

[43]   Celestine Bohlen, "After the Chaos, A New Day for the Cultures of the Soviet World," *New York Times* 19/08/2001.Perhaps the most visible example of Putin's supposed commitment to Russian culture is the government support given to the refurbishment of St. Petersburg to commemorate the 300th anniversary of the founding of the city in 2003.

[44]   Robinson, "Introduction," 4.

The weakness of the Russian state has been acknowledged even in the highest corridors of power. On the eve of gaining the presidency on 31 December 1999, Putin declared his doctrine of reversing the "weakening of state power" that had occurred in the 1990's. The question is, then, from where does this weakness stem? The survival of Soviet informal and formal institutions into the post-Soviet period has provided some historical roots of contemporary state weakness. Briefly, the Soviet system supported a pervasive structure of informal relations and connections through which actors were able to achieve certain ends. Means were largely attained through contacts, *blat* and coercion and not through the adherence to the rule of law.[45] These client-like relations provided an undercurrent of activity, which have continued to exist in Russia today.

In the rebuilding of the Russian state, Soviet formal institutional agencies also survived. There were a multitude of Soviet institutions with diverse interests and overlapping competencies which influenced and interfered with Russia's newly created institutions. In the following years Russian formal institutions were still "dominated by social units constructed according to the organizing principles in the Soviet regime."[46] These organizing principles, however, proved to be disorganized and ineffective. The institutional problems of cultural preservation today derive not from the lack of state organs charged with this responsibility, but from the lack of *effective* culture-supporting institutions. In other words, Russia's efforts to preserve its culture have been stymied by residual Soviet formal and informal institutions.

In addition to the problems resulting from the Soviet state's institutional legacy, many institutional problems were created in the post-Soviet period. Through the combination of poor attention to institutional design and suspect methods of ruling, President Boris Yeltsin largely promoted the creation and embedment of overlapping state institutions with undefined roles and functions. Moreover, cultural institutions were not immune to these overlapping

---

[45]   For an in depth analysis of *blat* , please see: Alena Ledeneva, *Russia's Economy of Favours:* Blat, *Networking, and Informal Exchange* (Cambridge: Cambridge University Press, 1998). According to Ledeneva, *"blat* is the use of personal networks and informal contacts to obtain goods and services in short supply and find a way around formal procedures." p. 1.

[46]   McFaul, "State Power, Institutional Change, and the Politics of Privatization in Russia," 220.

competencies. Vladimir Tolstoy, the director of Yasnaya Polyana, Leo Tolstoy's former estate, and of the Association of Russian Museums, commented that his efforts, and those made on behalf of Yasnaya Polyana, have
been hampered by government control, predominantly by the overlapping in-
tervention of endless government commissions.[47]

Pervasive corruption is both symptomatic and a cause of weak formal
institutions in face of ubiquitous informal functions. Weak state institutions
and norms, inherited from Russia's Soviet past, coupled with a very imperfect
transition, have fed the institutionalization of corruption. In an assessment of
corruption in countries undertaking transitions by the World Bank the countries of the Commonwealth of Independent States (CIS), including Russia,
had the highest levels of corruption.[48] According to Louise Shelley, rent seek-
ing and corruption were extremely evident at the end of Yeltsin's tenure.
"When he resigned from office there was institutionalized corruption at all levels of government and possibly irreversible damage to key Russian institutions."[49] Corruption is manifest in preservation affairs primarily through the si-
phoning off of funding intended for conservation and the misuse of monuments. This matter will be discussed in more detail in the next chapter.

II.1   The Players

It is important to be aware of the various predominant federal state institutions
involved in the field of cultural preservation and to have an understanding of
their supposed functions.[50] To begin with, the President of the Russian Federation has substantial significance in deciding cultural matters as he is
charged with determining the direction of internal policy, appoints members of
the federal government and can issue decrees (which can be especially ef-

---

[47] Roosevelt, *The Russian Estate on the Eve of the 21st Century: Problems of Preservation and Survival.*

[48] The World Bank, *Anticorruption in Transition: A Contribution to the Policy Debate*
(Washington DC: 2000), xiv.

[49] Louise Shelley, "Crime and Corruption," *Developments in Russian Politics 5*, eds.
Zvi Y. Gitelman, Alex Pravda and Stephen White (Basingstoke: Palgrave, 2001)
244.

[50] See Appendix I for a diagram of the Federal institutions involved with culture before
the 2004 reforms.

fective in situations where the legal groundwork is inadequate). The President is also responsible for including cultural policy on the national agenda. An advisory body, consisting of cultural administrators, artists and representatives of the artists' unions, called the Council on Culture and the Arts, aids the President in this realm.

The State Duma together with the Federation Council make-up the Federation Assembly, Russia's legislature. These institutions, through their responsibility of adopting the federal budget, which includes the annual allocation for culture, have a large capacity to affect federal cultural policy and funding. The legislature also passes federal laws both on general policy issues and on more distinct cultural issues. Particularly relevant is the State Duma's Committees for Culture and Tourism which readies laws for parliamentary debate.

The Ministry of Culture, which existed as a single entity until March 2004, was responsible for the implementation of federal policy on the protection and use of historical and cultural heritage. The Ministry executed state control over Russia's heritage and supervised other state institutions (such as libraries, museums, cultural centres, research and education units, etc.). The Ministry also managed and financed federal cultural organizations, provided funds and technical assistance to cultural organizations, including regional cultural institutions. Additionally, the Minister of Culture was the president of the Co-ordinating Council for Culture and Cinema, composed of the heads of regional cultural administrations, and was a member of the Council of Ministers.

Throughout much of the Soviet period the Ministry of Culture's role in national life had been poorly played. More often than not, it served as a "rubber stamp" ministry without any significant means or influence, filled with party bureaucrats without any explicit knowledge of culture. It was not until Mikhail Gorbachev's appointment of Nikolai Gubenko, one of the former Soviet Union's more influential cinema directors of the 1970's and '80's, that a member of the intelligentsia was handed the post.[51] However, even in the 1990's, Russia's Ministry of Culture has followed largely along the path laid forth by its Soviet predecessor.

---

[51]   Gubenko served as the Minister of Culture during the final years of the USSR (1989-1991).

Putin has boosted federal support for culture in general over his tenure. Shvydkoi, a former theatre critic who worked for state television throughout the 1990's, was appointed as Minister of Culture in February 2000. While often unrefined in his actions, Shvydkoi was the first Minister of Culture of the post-Soviet period to attempt to implement change. Komech had noticed a difference after Shvydkoi took the reins, as the Ministry before 2000, "had been asleep for ten years."[52] In August 2000 Putin oversaw the overall restructuring of the Ministry of Culture.

With Putin's ministerial overhaul of March 2004 a merger of the Press Ministry and the Culture Ministry took place. The Press Minister Mikhail Lesin and Culture Minister Shvydkoi have been replaced by Alexander Sokolov, who will now serve as the Culture and Information Minister.[53] Three agencies were created under the new ministry: one to deal with archives, one for culture and cinematography, and one for mass communications. Sokolov, a professor of music theory, was the rector of Moscow State Conservatoire. Within a week of his appointment and in the aftermath of the incineration of Moscow's Manezh[54], Sokolov stressed, "It is necessary to urgently create proper conditions for safeguarding the priceless monuments of Russian architecture."[55] He, unlike Shvydkoi, however, is less of a proponent of privatization of monuments. "What is now happening is, in fact, an outright abuse of the existing situation. To declare it inevitable would mean to give temporary leeway for actually robbing everything," he said.[56]

The reorganization of the Ministry of Culture has resulted in conflict, which cumulated in 2005, when Shvydkoi brought allegations of corruption against Sokolov to the judiciary for defamation. Sokolov had previously publi-

---

[52]   Kevin O'Flynn, "Heritage Champion Battles City Hall," *Moscow Times* 03/02/2004.

[53]   Shvydkoi has been transferred to a deputy ministerial post in the newly created Culture and Press Ministry

[54]   The Manezh was built in 1817 in honour of Russia's victory over Napoleon as an equestrian school for military officers. From 1918 it was used as a garage after and was later transformed into the Central Exhibition Hall, the country's biggest exhibition hall. It resumed its original name in the early 1990's. It was burnt down on 14 March, 2004. Moscow's Mayor Luzhkov has promised to rebuild the Manezh.

[55]   Igor Veksler, "Russia's monuments of architecture must be saved--Sokolov," *Itar-Tass Weekly News* 16/03/2004.

[56]   Sergei Mingashev, "Saving of national treasures - culture ministry's priority task," *Itar-Tass Weekly News* 11/03/2004.

cally accused Shvydkoi of taking bribes.[57] This personal conflict may also stem from an overarching institutional discord. Under the new organizational scheme, in effect Sokolov is responsible for policies and Shvydkoi oversees the funding. Shvydkoi then accused Sokolov of trying to tarnish his reputation to gain control of the agency's budget and make up for failing to convince the government to significantly increase spending on culture. The situation was alleviated on 2 September 2005, there is a very public reconciliation between the two men. It will be left to be seen how Sokolov functions as the Culture and Information Minister, and what changes will be made to this new extended Ministry.

Until the government restructuring of March 2004 the Ministry of Property Relations was officially designed to conduct state policy in the region of property and land relations. The Ministry dealt with privatization and managed state assets; specifically it regulated the activity of the real estate markets and land resources. This Ministry tended to be more powerful than the Ministry of Culture. Additionally, the Federal Agency for the Management and Utilization of Historical and Cultural Landmarks was created by the Ministry for the Management of State Property and the Ministry of Culture to enforce the regulations throughout the regions. Today, the Ministry of Property Relations, which was headed by Farit Gazizullin, has been incorporated into the renovated Ministry of Economic Development and Trade, which is lead by German Gref.

Several other ministries are involved in the domain of culture and their functions tend to overlap. For example, the Ministries of Finance and Economy and other relevant ministries and departments also help draft the federal budget, create lists of major projects to be financed through the federal budget and define forms of state support to the social sphere. Additionally, from 1992 the State Committee of the Russian Federation for Architecture and Construction has been charged with the overview of the preservation of

---

[57] Sokolov, speaking on the "Postskriptum" news programme, said the floors of the agency's building were filled with visitors carrying cash for bribes as part of an agency "kickback" system. He also said the Culture and Press Ministry had a similar system in place before he succeeded Shvydkoi in March 2004. Shvydkoi's agency manages 25 billion rubles ($875 million) of the 41.5 billion rubles that are earmarked for culture in this year's federal budget. Under the 2006 draft budget, spending for culture will slightly increase to 44 billion rubles, it said.

architectural heritage. It also regulates activities in architecture and city planning, participates in the elaboration of legal norms in the preservation and use of historical and cultural monuments and oversees the establishment of museums and memorial objects of federal importance.[58] Additionally, certain research bodies have traditionally been involved with Russian heritage. There is a special division in the Russian Institute for Cultural Research which deals with historical monuments and national cultural heritage. The Russian Research Institute for Cultural and National Heritage is also involved in this arena. The Russian Architects' Union, with 11.5 million members as of 1995, lobbies for architectural purposes.

II.2   *"Kem skhvacheno chto?"*: Who Has Grabbed What in Russia's Regions

According to the Federal Treaty, Russia's March 1992 multilateral treaty concluded with its constituent territories, protection of cultural heritage is under joint jurisdiction of the federal authorities and the subjects of the Russian Federation. However, in practice, this sharing of responsibilities is difficult to coordinate, often leading to conflict. Vague separations of power are also found in Russia's region-centre interaction. 89 regions are included in the Russian Federation, and their inter-relationships are distinguished by sundry economic and political conditions. The diversity and vastness of the Russian Federation complicates central governance of the regions. Here, power has been largely consolidated by republic, regional and territorial elites in such a way that allusions to these elites as "rulers of personal fiefdoms" may not be far from the truth. Thus, even if meaningful laws about cultural preservation are created by the federal government, it is often difficult to persuade regional and local elites to implement them, especially if the laws run against their interests. Another difficulty is in monitoring adherence to and compliance with centrally established protocol due to bureaucratic limitations.

---

[58]   Kirill Razologov and Tatiana Fedorova, *Cultural Policies in Europe: A Compendium of Basic Facts and Trends* (Strasbourg, Bonn: Council of Europe/ERICarts, 2003), 6-7.

With the disintegration of the Soviet Union and Russia's transformation into a federation, regional government institutions have acquired greater political and legal autonomy. With decentralisation and diluted vertical controls, the relocation of resources and funding to the regions has augmented regional institutional muscle. During the post-Soviet period, regional political regimes have been greatly criticised. According to Vladimir Gel'man, regional political regimes are "mostly determined by the nature of actors and their strategies for dealing with uncertainty, rather than by institutions *per se*. The arrangements of government institutions in Russia's regions do not so much influence the characteristics of political regimes, as these characteristics themselves determine formal and informal institutional arrangements and the significance of regional authorities. Diversification means this influence takes different forms across Russia."[59] Most of Russia's regions have their own Ministries of Culture. Furthermore, territories (*krai*) and localities also have governmental units, with their own budgets, which deal with cultural affairs. The Ministry of Culture and Information, in theory, implements its policies through the regional Ministries and special administrative units. Financial support for non-federal cultural institutions comes from regional budgets.

However, this decentralisation has had its drawbacks due to poor institutional implementation. Relations between the regions and the centre have been fraught with inconsistency and discord on many more issues than just cultural ones. In general, local government bodies are dependent on the provinces for budgetary incomes, and this dependence has reinforced the dominance of the regional governors and republic presidents. As Darrell Slider depicts, all of Russia's regions show signs of major deficiencies, which are attributable to the actions of the regional leadership. During Russia's initial privatization of industrial enterprises, local officials regularly distorted procedures in order to become more advantageous to the local elite. In cooperation with local courts, regional elites became even more capable of taking over,

---

[59]   Vladimir Gel'man, "Subnational Institutions in Contemporary Russia," *Institutions and Political Change in Russia*, ed. Neil Robinson (Basingstoke: Macmillan, 2000) 104.

controlling, or pilfering bribes from the local economy after the 1998 crisis.[60] As the potential for economic exploitation and manipulation tends to be great in the regions, one would argue that the same holds true for the treatment of Russia's cultural patrimony located in the regions. The environment of corruption is analogous for culture as it has been for law, economics and politics. Furthermore, Bill Bowring deems that the Russian regions seem to be building their own separate legal spaces, incongruent with those of the federal government.[61] There has already been evidence of illicit privatization and misuse of historic buildings, particularly in the regions. Here again, elite interests hold enormous sway over the fate of country estates. Several governors, often having taken estates as their own residences, can greatly influence the privatization process of other estates.[62]

In spite of the poor results, the trend in the 1990's has been to reallocate cultural administration from the centre to regional authorities. The redistribution of responsibilities among the levels of administration has led to the growing diversity of challenges regarding policies within particular regions or municipalities. The Ministry of Culture established new relationships between powerful inter-regional associations ("The Urals", "Central Russia", "North-West", "Northern Caucasus", "Siberian Agreement" and "Far East") at the end of 1990's. Here, the former Ministry of Culture signed special agreements with inter-regional associations and with other "subjects" of the Russian Federation. In this context, regional authorities are supposed to supply the Ministry of Culture and Information with a list of objects of cultural heritage within the region recommended for federal ownership. The Ministry of Culture and Information then passes on their suggestions to the Ministry of Economic Development and Trade. Again, the success of this decentralisation remains to be observed. The adoption of the federal law *On the Protection of Cultural*

---

60   Gordon Smith, "Russia and the Rule of Law," *Developments in Russian Politics 5*, eds. Zvi Y. Gitelman, Alex Pravda and Stephen White (Basingstoke: Palgrave, 2001) 161.

61   Richard Sakwa, "State and Society in Post-Communist Russia," *Institutions and Political Change in Russia*, ed. Neil Robinson (Basingstoke: Macmillan, 2000) 70.

62   Mr. Chizhkov, the former Vice President of the Fund for the Revival of the Russian Estate asserted that, "If two to four years ago the privatization or lease of an estate complex was easily solved on the level of the leader of committees on property or the culture, today an estate cannot be obtained without having gained the influence of the governor." Iur'eva and Zharkov, *"Novye pomeshchiki."*

Heritage of 2002, which demarcates the responsibility for cultural protection between the different levels of government, has been a necessary step for beginning an effective mechanism of cultural management. In addition, the former Ministry of Culture has prepared an individual chapter of the law *On State and Municipal Property*, which was developed by the former Ministry of Property Relations. This chapter was designed to define the lawful status of monuments.[63]

II.3   Ownership Issues, the Moscow Example

In no other part of the country has there been such a vehement dispute over the protection of historical architecture such as there has been between Moscow city government and the federal government. Battles have been waged over the control of Moscow's monuments by these two governmental authorities. There are more than 4,000 historical and cultural monuments in Moscow which are classified as being federally significant.[64] Moscow's elected mayor, Yuri Luzhkov, took advantage of the poorly defined cultural relations in the sphere of control over state and city property, privatization, tax incomes and budgets. According to Slider, "the Moscow city government constantly sought and won the right not to implement a number of Yeltsin-era policies in privatization and tax policy. The city government maintains tight control over the Moscow economy, which is heavily regulated and taxed, and it is assumed that the construction projects for which Luzhkov is famous are rife with corruption."[65] In the cultural sphere, Luzhkov and his associates have chosen to ignore the federal government's *modus operandi* so as to gain control of lucrative monuments (and the land upon which they stand).[66] Most of the dealings in this area tend to be shrouded and disjointed, thus this analysis covers only the major occurrences.

---

[63]   A. Bochkarev, "Istoriia ne prodaetsia. No ob usad'be stoit podumat'," *Elit Dom* 2003.

[64]   "State Council considering priorities of Russia's cultural policy," *Itar-Tass Weekly News* 16/06/2003.

[65]   Smith, "Russia and the Rule of Law," 160.

[66]   For example, Moscow city collected rents from such profitable buildings as the *GUM, TsUM,* and *Gostiny Dvor* retail centres.

Luzhkov joined the Moscow city council as a deputy chairman in 1987, rising to head chair in 1990 and to the position of vice mayor from 1991 to 1992, when he became the mayor and head of city government with the resignation of Gavrill Popov, the first mayor of post-Soviet Moscow. Since then he has overwhelmingly been re-elected as mayor three times: in 1996, 1999, and 2003. Luzhkov's reign over Moscow's monuments began much earlier, but it was not until the beginning of April 2001 that the Moscow government officially became involved with the protection of federal monuments that the city created a ten-year work plan for the protection of threatened national heritage found within Moscow's territory, gaining not only the right to restore, but also over the use of the monuments. In accordance with the Russian Constitution (art. 72), monuments classified as federally significant are under the joint jurisdiction of the federal authority and the subject of the Federation where the monument is located. Thus, ownership of these monuments should have been shared between the federal and the Moscow governments under the aegis of the Administration of Government Control for the Protection and Use of Monuments of Culture (UGKOIP).

Under the Soviet Union, the division of administrative clout between the Ministry of Culture and the UGKOIP was considerable; however, today the gap has largely closed. Since the dissolution of the Soviet Union, the Moscow government had been gradually assuming control over various monuments, as there was a severe shortage of funds within the Ministry of Culture. In general, the Ministry of Culture tended to off-load superfluous monuments onto local budgets. Often, in other regions of Russia, this tendency led to the abandonment and destruction of numerous monuments. (Churches and monasteries were spared as they were transferred to religious institutions.) However, in Moscow, Luzhkov recognized the value of Moscow's monuments, many of which, located in the city itself, became succulent morsels.[67]

The UGKOIP contemplated the introduction of a new law about the protection of monuments in Moscow, and in 2001 the Justice Department registered all monuments in Moscow as municipal property. At this time the Moscow City Duma passed the law *On the Privatization of State and Municipal*

---

[67]   Grigorii Revzin, "Pervaia Polosa. Iuriia Luzhkova lishaiut pamiatnikov pri zhizni," *Kommersant-Daily* 12/05/2001. See also Grigorii Revzin, "Kul'turnaia politika. Doloi' pomeshchikov, kapitalistov i ikh usad'by," *Kommersant-Daily* 27/11/2002.

Property of Moscow City.[68] According to the authorities, Moscow's benevolent privatization policies for monuments were fashioned so as to increase the effective use of these properties. Included, also, was a particular article about the standards by which the owners must maintain privatized buildings, as well as a description of the rights to the land surrounding the privatized objects. The law appointed all income earned from leases and sales to go to the UGKOIP. It was also conferred upon the UGKOIP to act as a contractor and assume functions of control over the monuments. This arrangement proved to be very lucrative; it is doubtful that the UGKOIP, or the Mayor's office, had the best intentions for the monuments in mind.

Another organization has become involved in the dispute. The Federal Agency for the Management and Utilization of Historical and Cultural Landmarks, headed by Vladislav Klimchenko, created a list of roughly 900 federal monuments registered as Moscow city property (40 of which, according to Klimchenko, the city has already sold off). This Agency vowed to fight Moscow in the courts in order to regain control.[69] If successful, the Agency hopes to receive the rents for the use of national landmarks and use these funds specifically for their restoration, in addition to the limited appropriations from the federal budget. Evidently, the Moscow government will have to fend off those who also wish to have their finger in this historic pie.

Much earlier than the creation of the law *On the Privatization of State and Municipal Property of Moscow City*, Yeltsin had signed an edict demanding the transfer of monuments from Moscow's control back to that of the federal government, but this was never enforced. It was not until a new minister arrived in the State Committee for Construction that a strategy for overcoming Moscow's determined procurement of monuments was initiated. The Ministry of Culture and State Committee for Construction teamed up take back control of the city's monuments once again. Moscow kept the upper hand until Putin passed a Presidential Decree in 2001 which stipulated that Moscow's monu-

---

[68]   "Why do you think the city took on such a liability - to maintain and restore historical and cultural landmarks? Because it is painful to see fine buildings fall into disrepair and run the risk of destruction. All because the federal government never has time for them while the RF Ministry of Culture is short of funds..." reported Alexander Krutov, deputy chairman of the Moscow City Duma. Tatiana Andriasova, "Moscow Monuments Will Be Divvied Up," *Moscow News* 26/06/2002.

[69]   Andriasova, "Moscow Monuments Will Be Divvied Up."

ments of federal value were to be unequivocally transferred back into the control of federal structures. The capital still maintained its rights to Moscow sites of federal significance, arguing that the city has already spent great amounts of money on restoration work. In a criticism of the situation, Shvydkoi commented,

> In the capital there are rather aggressive seizures of the monuments of federal value, the registration of the monuments of as [belonging to] Moscow or there some others through privatization... federal authorities can do something [now]... Indeed, the desire of city authorities to lower the value of monuments is very dangerous... For example, Moscow authorities sold the estate Nikol'skoe-Uriupino to Vladimir Bryntsalov. For three years the owner did nothing, he only proposed some strange projects, and we insisted that he return the monument back into the property of the state.[70]

The essence of the Ministry of Culture's claims against Moscow was not only based on the juridical aspect of the rights of property. It claimed that the Moscow government was guilty of objectionable use of historic houses and dilettante restoration of buildings. According to the Ministry of Culture, almost every month letters came into the Ministry from Moscow's prominent cultural experts requesting the Ministry to bring to an end the ruin of architectural monuments by those leaseholders who gained leases from Luzhkov through political favour and bribery.[71] Komech, in his role as a member of the city's Architecture Council, felt that the problem stemmed from the city authorities' complete lack of respect for history and heritage.[72] Komech explained that the city had all the laws it needed to protect its historical buildings, but the problem was with the authorities' attitude, illustrated by Luzhkov's typical response to censure, "Well, that is theory - we do things in reality."[73]

---

[70]   Karakhan and Revzin, "Pokazatel'noe vystuplenie. 'Podozrevat' menia v zhelanii zarabotat' na pamiatnikakh glupo'."

[71]   Nikolai' Golobkin, "SOS! Kuvaldoi' po istorii," *Rossiia* 23/10/2003.

[72]   According to Komech, "In the centre there are already very little [space] left... There is a search going on for what can be knocked down. The city is interested in receiving so much [from construction] that it pushes the architecture council to allow anything... It has to allow them to destroy, to start anew, to build underground garages at the price of the historical part of the city... It's all at the expense of the city's history" O'Flynn, "Heritage Champion Battles City Hall."

[73]   O'Flynn, "Heritage Champion Battles City Hall."

If the institutions of the federal government, such as the Ministry of Culture and Information, suffer from under-funding and the lack of political means, the question remains as to what they will do with the monuments they have regained? In 2003 Shvydkoi commented that the situation was much more difficult for the Ministry, which cannot resort to the same economically viable methods vis-à-vis those employed by Moscow. "Moscow, as do a number of other municipalities, restores monuments through an economic method from private investments... In principle I approve, but as a rule, it is an unacceptable means for the Ministry of Culture, which works with unique monuments of culture and history."[74]

The debate still continued, although as of 2002 the conflict took a different form. According to the *Moscow News*, in order to keep control of certain monuments, the Moscow government had attempted to barter with the Ministry of Culture over the control of certain monuments. In this case, Moscow offered to restore the Pashkov House, through the means of investment contracts, if the federal government would release their claim to the former Lenin Museum on the Red Square.[75] Moscow claims that, having issued an appropriate order more than a year ago, the museum is rightfully theirs.[76]

Today, the relations between the federal government and Moscow may be improving. Historic urban buildings, as of January 2004 are now affected by the law *On the Differentiation of the Government Ownership of the Objects of Cultural Heritage*. This was brought about through the efforts of the Conciliation Committee, with included representatives from the Ministry of Culture, the Ministry of Property of the Russian Federation and the Moscow City government. In effect, this law distinguishes between federal and municipal property amongst monuments of history and culture. As a result, three lists

---

[74] Karakhan and Revzin, "Pokazatel'noe vystuplenie. 'Podozrevat' menia v zhelanii zarabotat' na pamiatnikakh glupo"."

[75] About this, Shvydkoi commented, "Our task is to preserve the cultural heritage... What is important for us is that reconstruction should not diminish the significance of a landmark or change its original functions. At present we are doing the work at the Pashkov House that is invisible to an outsider - draining the basements and strengthening the foundations and load-bearing structures. The building will remain the core of the Rumiantsev Library whose 175th anniversary will be marked next year." Andriasova, "Moscow Monuments Will Be Divvied Up." He contended that private investment is not appropriate for such unique landmarks.

[76] Andriasova, "Moscow Monuments Will Be Divvied Up."

were agreed upon: the first of monuments which would fall under the jurisdiction of Moscow, the second of federal property and the third of religious monuments. A fourth list, comprising 123 disputed monuments, still to be settled at the time this work was written, is the inventory of monuments to be conjointly controlled by both Moscow and the federal authorities.[77] With the inauguration of a clear demarcation of ownership, the privatization campaign within Moscow can resume, but possibly this time with the imposition of firmer regulations.

In a sense, Moscow's monuments have been used as an ideological showcase representing two popular options on cultural preservation. On one side, Luzhkov's stance has been emblematic of capitalistic and progressive activity. Luzhkov has been a significant political figure in Russia largely due to the popular standing of his aggressive revitalisation of Moscow. Although Moscow's economic *renaissance* has resulted in the destruction or misuse of Moscow's historic buildings, this is not unusual. The weak voices of the federal agencies and the handful of specialists have not proven to be an effective impediment to Luzhkov's campaign. Moreover, those of Luzhkov's policies which affect monuments underline the limits of the federal government's ability to enforce its will in this arena and raise questions regarding preservation prospects for Russia as a whole.

[77]   Found at Culture Portal News, "Property rights to the monuments of Moscow are demarcated" 25/10/2003 http://www.russianculture.ru

Figure 11: Example of a Russian Estate: Pokrovskoe

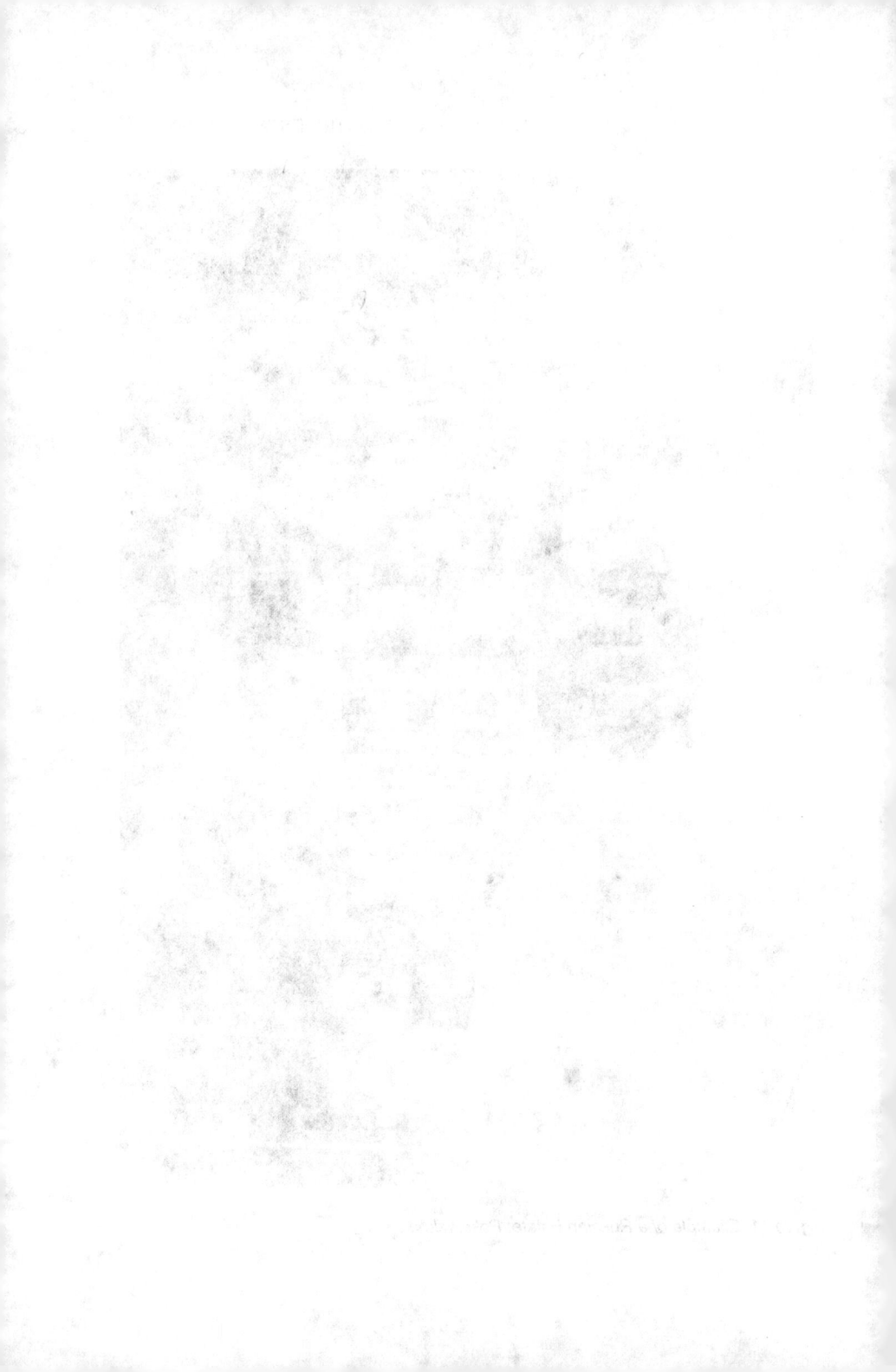

III   Cultural Preservation Law

This chapter develops the second political theoretical argument of the work, elaborating on how the lack of the rule of law in Russia hinders cultural preservation. For various reasons, the norms of the "rule of law" in the Soviet Union were minimal; post-Soviet Russia has inherited this general disregard for law. And in spite of major efforts to attain a *pravovoe gosudarstvo* (law-governed state), Russia has not yet achieved this goal. This chapter will provide an overview to the laws, drafts and bills which regulate cultural preservation. It will also explore the legal framework surrounding the privatization of monuments, land ownership and restitution to pre-revolutionary owners and their heirs.

This chapter will begin by discussing the rule of law as it applies to Russia. Juan Linz and Alfred Stepan, scholars known for comparing political transitions, a field known as transitology, include the "rule of law" amongst the five interrelated and crucial factors necessary for the creation of a consolidated democracy. The rule of law is needed "to ensure legal guarantees for citizens' freedoms and independent associational life" by which "all significant actors – especially the democratic government and the state – must respect and uphold the rule of law."[78] In Russia, many of the formal foundations have been laid to create a law-governed state. However, informal relations operating outside of the law still play a major role in political, social and economic dealings. Until the rule of law is realized, state institutions will remain weak, the consolidation of democracy will remain unobtainable and monuments will remain unprotected.

The process of developing norms of rule of law in Russia involves overcoming the Soviet legacy which has largely deflated the importance of law. Russia, in its attempt to reinforce the status of law, has accomplished many necessary undertakings; new legislation and codes of law, new judicial and

---

[78]   Juan J. Linz and Alfred C. Stepan, *Problems of Democratic Transition and Consolidation: Southern Europe, South America, and Post-Communist Europe* (Baltimore; London: Johns Hopkins University Press, 1996) 110-11.

enforcement agencies have been created and fundamental reorientations of previously existing legal institutions has been attempted. However, the rule of law cannot be created merely through the issuance of laws and creation of new institutions; implementation and enforcement play the key roles. Unfortunately, implementation is still being hampered by shortages of personnel, equipment and funding. But this is not all. Gordon Smith notes, with some exaggeration but with a core of truth, that in the 1990's there was an erosion of power of the state and a lack of consensus about the proper boundaries of state activity. "The transition from communism experienced in Russia, rather than expanding the state's capacity to make and implement policy, has resulted in the creation of political malaise, chaos, and lawlessness."[79] On coming into the presidency, Putin declared the imposition of a "dictatorship of law" as a measure to acknowledge and counter this lack of control. It is unclear at this time whether any actual significant progress has been made in this arena since his coming to power, although he has made several attempts at centralizing the federal government.

III.1 Overview of Russia's Cultural Legal Environment

If law has not played a leading role in Russian politics, this generalization holds true for cultural politics as well. Often, those with power or wealth are able to shape certain outcomes regardless of presiding law; this state of affairs has helped fuel a general apathy to and disregard of legality. Yet, the laws governing cultural matters, while sometimes pliable, still provide a valuable foundation upon which precedence and protocol can be set. Here, we will provide an overview of the laws which specifically affect the preservation of country estates. While an analysis of legislation is helpful to point out the direction in which Russia is moving, in many instances the effects of these laws have been ambiguous in dealing with Russian realities.

The post-Soviet Russian cultural legal environment is an assortment of surviving Soviet code and doctrine mixed with presidential decrees and new legislation. The legal and normative underpinning for cultural heritage, spe-

---

[79]   Smith, "Russia and the Rule of Law," 112.

cifically dealing with the problems surrounding estate preservation, has been determined by the following laws: *Law of the RSFSR On the Protection and Use of Historical and Cultural Monuments* (1978); *Basic Law of the Russian Federation on Culture* (1992); *On Specially Preserved Natural Territories* (1995); *Law on the Museum Fund of the Russian Federation and the Museums of the Russian Federation* (1996); *On Objects of Cultural Heritage (On Monuments of History and Culture) of the Peoples of the Russian Federation* (2002). A *State Code of Particularly Valuable Objects of Cultural Heritage of the Peoples of the Russian Federation* also exists, as well as the *Acts of the Federal Government* which regulates licensing, restoration, trade, conservation and usage of Russia's patrimony. In spite of the numerous laws regulating cultural preservation, deficiencies within the framework still exist. For instance, the *RSFSR Law on Protection of Historical and Cultural Landmarks*, from 1978, is still legitimate but is inadequate in the contemporary context.

The *Basic Law of the Russian Federation on Culture* (1992) established the state's cultural responsibilities and partitioned jurisdiction over culture between federal, regional and local authorities. It stipulated that cultural institutions should be established at each of these levels and they should be financed by the respective authority. In the breakdown of tasks as specified by the *Basic Law*, the federal level is responsible for: guaranteeing cultural rights and liberties; determining principles of national cultural policy; adopting federal laws and other regulations and programmes; establishing, financing and maintaining federal cultural institutions; coordinating cultural policy cooperation; determining the National Code of Historical and Cultural Monuments; and maintaining the national statistical system and background information on the cultural sector.

However, with the ensuing chronic scarcity of resources in the post-Soviet period, it has been necessary to jointly finance certain cultural institutions through both federal and regional budgets. Those responsibilities which fall under joint federal and regional cultural jurisdiction are guaranteeing cultural rights, property rights, liberties and the preservation of the national cultural heritage and monuments included in the National Code; financing monuments of particular value; and elaborating and implementing federal state cultural policy and programmes. The regional level is responsible for elaborating principles of regional cultural policy and regional and local cultural development and heritage preservation; implementing interregional cultural co-operation; establishing laws on culture and related matters and develop other regulations; founding territorial administration and institutions for cultural activities; allocating funds for culture in the regional budget and determining general principles for taxation; and organizing staff education and training, information and statistics. Finally, the local level is accountable for implementing cultural policy; forming local budgets and funds for cultural development; establishing local cultural administration and institutions; regulating property relations within local competence; and managing and maintaining municipal property.[80] As we can see, many responsibilities overlap on all levels of government.

Due to developments in federal and regional legislation and economic and social changes, the need to adapt the *Basic Law on Culture* has been recognized by cultural authorities. Draft laws are being submitted which aim to reinforce governmental obligations in the cultural sphere. Additionally, the problem of the lack of coordination between federal and regional cultural legislation will need to be resolved in the future.

In light of certain fissures, numerous drafts of federal laws pertaining to cultural heritage were recommended before the *Federal Law On Objects of Cultural Heritage (On Monuments of History and Culture) of the Peoples of the Russian Federation* was adopted in 2002. The *Federal Law*, which is planned to be completed by 2010, will theoretically provide a fully established system of legal regulations in the cultural sphere. Here, some problems that affected estate preservation in previous legislation should be addressed. For example, there was a lack of bona fide "zones of protection" encircling estates; the previous laws were unclear as to what should be done to the territory surrounding estates. Often this ambiguity has led to the selling-off of valuable pieces of estate land for commercial or private construction. To address this deficiency, the law has established that the territory of any monument must enter into the composition of monument itself. Komech, who was involved in the drafting of this law, explained, "According to the new law such territories fall under the concept of 'an object of protection' and must respectively take shape. This provides a last chance to gather the territories of urban

---

[80]   Razologov and Fedorova, *Cultural Policies in Europe: A Compendium of Basic Facts and Trends*, 9-10.

estates and to avoid the division and crushing of estate monuments every-
where. The organs of the protection of cultural heritage must perform work on
the development of the territories of monuments and their assertion as guarding units."[81] Importantly, the law also incorporated provisions for privatising of
cultural heritage, and delineated the rights and obligations of its owners. This
topic will be discussed in more depth later in the chapter.

III.2 The Issue of Land

Another legal situation that has a great effect on the world of the estate is the
quandary surrounding land ownership, which is particularly salient in rural
Russia. Often, country estates are surrounded by agricultural land which, in
the Soviet Union, was generally partitioned off to the local collective or state
farm. Land reform is revolutionary for Russia's countryside, especially for the
rural population. Collective farms were the focal point of Soviet and even
post-Soviet rural local life; farmers' economic and social network depended
upon the farms.[82] Thus, to change the means of ownership implicitly changes
society in rural Russia. Communist influences had previously made the issue
of the sale of land taboo and evoked Russia's historical notion of land as a
communal asset. Today, those people wishing to purchase country estates
are faced with problematic issues dealing with land.

There is little scholarly consensus on the achievement of land reform,
but regardless, significant changes have taken place since 1991. According
to Stephen Wegren and David O'Brien, experts on Russian land reform, the
early reforms were not based on an understanding of institutional and social
organization arrangements of the Soviet period. Yeltsin largely ignored administrative details, and "at best" had a *laissez-faire* attitude regarding land
and agrarian reform.[83] The legal basis for land reform and privatization was

---

[81]   Ol'gin, "Nasledie: privatizatsiia istorii."

[82]   While in the early years of privatization, when the market for land was constrained,
this did not inhibit farm directors from selling land to local elites, which have left residual grievances amongst local populations.

[83]   Stephen K. Wegren and David J. O'Brien, "Introduction, Adaptation and Change:
Old Problems, New Approaches," *Rural Reform in Post-Soviet Russia*, eds. David J.

centred around a government resolution of December 1991, presidential decrees of October 1993 and March 1996, Article 27 in the 1993 Constitution,
which secured private landownership rights, and the 1994 Civil Code (articles
260 and 261). However, the legal milieu was disordered, and this led to much
confusion. The elusiveness of authority regulating transfers of ownership and
the insecurity of land tenure plagued reforms for years. However, in spite of
impediments, land was sold. After a tumultuous period, by 1999, 83 percent
of agricultural land was in private hands and only 17 percent remained as
state property.[84]

Moreover, from 1998-2001 the legislation regulating land issues improved with a set of federal laws that established a liberal basis for land tenure. These laws were the *Law on the Registration of Real Estate Rights and
Transactions* (1998), the *Law on the State Land Cadastre* (2000), the *Law on
Land Management* (2001), the *Law on State and Municipal Land* (2001), the
Land Code (2001), the *Law on the Enactment of the Land Code* (2001) and
the *Law on the Transfer of Agricultural Land* (2002). The *Land Code* has clarified what is permissible for the use and sale of 406 million hectares of agricultural land throughout Russia. Additionally, and especially pertinent in matters
of restitution, which will be discussed later, as foreigners have been restricted
from ownership but can lease properties for up to 49 years.

Today, considerable improvements in land tenure have been made. According to the Land Administration Review of the Russian Federation, produced by the UN Economic Commission for Europe (ECE), the new *Land
Code* clearly recognizes the role of land in society. The regulation of land use
and protection is now based on the notion that land is both a natural resource
and an object of ownership. According to the legislation, protecting land is a
priority because it is a vital component of the environment and a means of
production in agriculture and forestry. The legislation also specifies the use of
land as real property, which can be freely possessed, disposed of or used by
its owners unless it harms the environment and the interests of other par-

O'Brien and Stephen K. Wegren (Washington, DC: Woodrow Wilson Center Press,
2002) 11.
[84]   A. Petrikov and V. Uzin, "Zemel'nii otnosheniia: problemy i reshenia," *APK: Ekonomika, upravlenie* 6 (1999): 9. quoted in Wegren and O'Brien, "Introduction, Adaptation and Change: Old Problems, New Approaches.."

ties.[85] Viktor Pleskachevsky, a member of the pro-Kremlin Unity party and the chairman of the Duma's Property Committee, has been responsible for all legislation involving property in Russia, from the Land Code to laws on privatization. "Of course there are still a lot of holes in this bill, and it won't be easy to again build the [land] culture that was lost so many years ago," Pleskachevsky said. "But what is most important is that the bill finally sets the rules for the turnover of land."[86]

The definition of a land cadastre in the *Land Code* includes land and buildings as data components of the unified registration system.[87] Importantly for both rural and urban estates, this means that the land and all objects permanently attached to it are considered inseparable units; thus it has theoretically terminated the separation of land from its buildings. Both the *Land Code* and the *Law on the Enactment of the Land Code* provide incentives for owners to acquire the land parcels which accompany their buildings. These laws will supposedly ensure the much needed "guarded zones" around estates and help protect the land from contemporary construction. At present, however, the discovery of unsanctioned building is still encountered regularly. And, as a rule, there very little one can do to inhibit this illicit construction; red tape can last of up to two years and in the meantime, the new buildings continue to be built.[88]

The ECE's report has acknowledged the fundamental changes in Russia due to privatization, development of land markets and the creation of new system of agricultural holdings. They consider that through these efforts, the foundation of an effective land policy has already been established. However, the existence of several competing agencies involved in land administration, "undermines the effectiveness of the system and leads to conflicts of interests." The report also contended that the mixture of public law and private-law functions within one state authority is controversial. "An obvious conflict of in-

---

[85]   UN Economic Commission for Europe, *The Land Administration Review of the Russian Federation* (Geneva: UN Economic Commission for Europe, 2004), 3.

[86]   Victoria Lavrentieva, "State Duma Puts Business on Hold," *Moscow Times* 02/07/2002.

[87]   A cadastre is a public record of the value and ownership of land as a basis of taxation.

[88]   *Dimitrii' Pisarenko, "Podmoskov'e. Kazhdoi' usad'be - po pol'zovateliu!," Argumenty i fakty 30/08/2000.*

terest arises when decisions on land and other real property are taken by the agency that also has the authority to represent the interests of the owner of the property." In addition, the state's influence "reduces the confidence of other parties in the reliability of the market infrastructure and the real property market in general." Finally, an aspect which is extremely problematic for rural estates, is that the registration of agricultural and other rural land is in disarray. Rural properties have often not been recorded in cadastral maps.[89] Until cadastral identifier and an owner are entered in the unified register of real estate rights and transactions, land cannot be privatized or restructured.[90]

III.3   Privatization – How Have Estates Been Affected?

In 1992, a massive scheme of privatization, the process which brings fundamental changes to property ownership, was initiated by the Yeltsin government. It was considered to be a necessary step in Russia's transition from the invasive government-ownership of Soviet socialism to a system of capitalism with private ownership. The timing was also deemed critical. A rapid course of privatization was seen to be necessary to help limit the possibility of a Communist resurgence. Also, it was in the state's interest to reduce the number of enterprises dependent upon state subsidies and halt illicit privatization. However essential this step may have been, privatization had caused great difficulties in Russia. The initial form of privatization, implemented as a voucher programme, was inefficient and proved disappointing for the general public. The goal of the programme, to build up a large number of share-holders and property owners, actually did not financially benefit the large percentage of citizens. Furthermore, the 1995 "loans-for-shares" debacle was the even more discouraging. Here, a number of Russia's enormously wealthy busi-

---

[89]   The classification and ownership of forests is a case in point. Forests often do not fall under the jurisdiction of a specific authority and are not even recorded as a forest on the cadastral map. The land within and around the forests still remain in limbo until the type of classification of the land and an authority are decided upon. See the footnote 14 in the Introduction, which outlines the problems which the estate Arkhangel'skoe has had in protecting its woodland from developers.

[90]   UN Economic Commission for Europe, *The Land Administration Review of the Russian Federation*, 15.

nessmen lent the government money in return for ownership of and administrative control over Russia's most valuable and profitable industries and assets at artificially low prices. The programme resulted in a wholesale reallocation of state property to an advantaged few and led to the entrenchment of the oligarchic class.

It was not only the process of privatization that was controversial; the result was also damaging. Briefly, state revenues gained from the sale of state enterprises and property were negligible. Furthermore, corrupt privatization was partially the cause of Russia's unstable economy in the 1990's and took a high toll on society. Those in strategic positions exploiting their knowledge, assets and contacts, abounded in what was termed "Nomenklatura privatization". The efficiency of the privatized enterprises tended to decline due to pervasive "insider" control and firms did not become more market-orientated. Asset stripping and rent-seeking, in this case, were considered more profitable than enterprise restructuring. Russia's gross domestic product declined, as did state revenues. Much of the failure of privatization arose from ineffective fiscal and political controls and corruption. As Richard Sakwa explains, "The vast majority of the population had been lumpenised, deprived of property, and in these conditions the attempt to conduct a radical economic reform and privatization without strict controls by the executive and judicial authorities allowed a small group of economic managers and nomenklatura capitalists to seize the lion's share of state property."[91] Needless to say, privatization can be easily identified with corruption and is regarded with suspicion by many Russians today. In addition, many fear that if the controls of the executive and legislature are inadequate, as they had been, privatization of Russia's monuments may result in a similar outcome.

In the case of historical monuments, privatization can be viewed as a double-edged sword. For, on one hand, it offers tremendous opportunities for retaining and re-using historical buildings by selling them to responsible investors. On the other hand, it could just as easily lead to their destruction and loss. This latter scenario is particularly likely if necessary measures of control and surveillance are not instated. For instance, Dlugach, the director of Arkhangel'skoe, recounts how he had repeatedly witnessed "new Russians"

91   Richard Sakwa, *Russian Politics and Society,* 2nd edn. (London: Routledge, 1996) 242.

making propositions which would have turned estates into "genuine *bordellos*".[92] Also, a tendency had developed in which historic buildings on valuable pieces of real-estate are destroyed by investors. Historic buildings can be perceived to be more problematic than valuable. Komech explains that, "If an investor takes an estate, he signs an obligation. It is not surprising that the investors perceive monuments as headaches. They take the object because of its location and very rarely because of the monument itself. Maintenance is an optional product in the way of the extraction of profit."[93]

Experts at many agencies are convinced that privatization should be permitted, in light of the fact that the state lacks the funds to maintain and restore historic buildings. The topic of privatization of cultural heritage is also discussed within the corridors of power, especially in periods of retracting national assets. And, despite general hesitation, debates have become increasingly common. Shvydkoi, in an interview in *Kommersant-Vlast'* in September 2003, shed some light on his, and the Ministry of Culture's, attitude towards privatization. "No one is considering privatising the Bolshoi theatre nor the Kremlin nor the Hermitage, but it is completely obvious, for example, that the tens of thousands of rental housing units in Petersburg are possible [to privatize] and it is necessary to try to transmit them into particular hands. Of course with one condition – that the state is left with the most severe control of the buildings' restoration and use..."[94]

If the state is struggling to finance its programmes of maintenance and restoration of monuments, this holds particularly true for Russia's country estates. Rural estates are off the honing screen of national politics and funding, and in many cases, they remain uncared for and forgotten. Privatization would give these estates, at any rate, a chance for survival. Additionally, a sort of informal privatization has been taking place for years, unobserved and unregulated. It is estimated that between 1994 and 2003 the state has supervised about two-hundred applications concerning the privatization of unique landmarks across Russia. Independent experts believe, however, that the

---

[92]   Pisarenko, "Podmoskov'e. Kazhdoi' usad'be -po pol'zovateliu!."
[93]   Ol'gin, "Nasledie: privatizatsiia istorii."
[94]   Karakhan and Revzin, "Pokazatel'noe vystuplenie. 'Podozrevat' menia v zhelanii zarabotat' na pamiatnikakh glupo'."

number of such buildings actually surreptitiously privatized is much higher.[95] At least an official programme of privatization, which would theoretically furnish strict guidelines for local authorities, could help bring some of this spontaneous privatization under federal guiding principles of protection. In the best case, "guarding obligations" would become universal in all cases of privatization.

To comprehend the overall effect of a privatization programme is difficult. However, it is clear that privatization would need to be monitored. If the essential structures of surveillance and control are in place, then privatization seems to be the best solution in face of chronic shortages of funds and the lack of effective non-governmental organizations dealing with the protection of Russian heritage. Special organizations, under the aegis of the federal government, could be created to investigate and assesses the restoration and reconstruction done by the owners of privatized historic buildings. In addition, they would need to monitor the budgets and cash-flows of the organizations that oversee the sale and leasing of such properties. Yet if these state controls are not inaugurated, privatization of monuments could lead to a free-for-all devastation of much of Russia's heritage.

In this context, the government must take precautions before agreeing to privatize monuments. Hasty action could be extremely harmful. "Before concluding the agreement about the lease, we must ascertain that they can repair and renovate this monument," recounted Sergei Guzhayev, Chairman of the Committee on the Culture of Moscow Region. "The first thing that we tell investors is that we must be informed about their finances in recent years. We must know if they are affluent enough to undertake the restoration of the monument. And for us even to create working papers for the monument is an expensive matter. Scientists are consulted, whom we must pay, and calculations estimate that we pay four to six thousand rubles [per monument]."[96] However, Vissarion Aliavdin, the president of the National Fund for the Revival of Russian Estate, considers the danger small of new owners destroying or completely reconstructing estates.

95   Ol'gin, "Nasledie: privatizatsiia istorii."
96   Pisarenko, "Podmoskov'e. Kazhdoi' usad'be - po pol'zovateliu!."

If a person purchased an estate or any other house-monument, they cannot decide that they will go around the controls of the protection of monuments, the courts of law, the penalties... There are estate-ensembles where fifty to seventy percent of the buildings are destroyed. It is possible to restore everything, including with the use of contemporary technologies, but it is compulsory to stay within the limits of the surviving foundations. It is simple to monitor this construction activity. Privatization is more reliable than leases, which the authorities prefer today... Those who lease have very little incentive to actually restore objects, to develop projects. There are also the fears that, with a strong enough desire, bureaucrats would be able to find a way to dissolve the lease agreement.[97]

Another crucial issue to contend with is the need to establish a system of positive discrimination towards those who undertake the renovation and maintenance of estates. Undertaking the restoration of an estate is much more expensive and time-consuming than constructing a new building. Consequently, the government must establish incentives for those who conduct proper renovations of estates. Tax breaks, educational programmes and support for owners of privatized monuments are necessary to create a favourable environment for investment. For, if an investor is unable to manage the estate within the framework of law, there is the threat that they will simply discard the guidelines set before them. In this regard, Komech declared, "Do not take too much from the investor when they took a monument in emergency condition, but create privileged conditions for the investor."[98] It is essential that an agreement is struck between investors and the government if the privatization programme is to be productive. The lack of tax incentives for investment is discussed in Chapter five.

III.4   The History of Privatization Laws for Historic Monuments

In the heady first years after the dissolution of the Soviet Union, President Boris Yeltsin passed a decree which stipulated that monuments of federal value

---

[97]   Ol'gin, "Nasledie: privatizatsiia istorii."
[98]   Ibid.

were not suitable for privatization, the *Decree of the President of the Russian Federation No. 2121 of November 26, 1994 on the Privatization of Immobile Historical and Cultural Monuments of Local Importance in the Russian Federation*. This decree was backed up with the *Order of the State Property Management Committee of the Russian Federation No. 2920-r of December 28, 1994 on the Privatization of Stationary Local Monuments of History and Culture in the Russian Federation*. However, this restriction of privatization did not affect monuments classified as only locally significant. Due to these restrictions and classifications, manipulation with the status of estates became a rather regular occurrence; properties catalogued as holding federal or regional importance were often furtively reduced in stature, and thus local officials were able to sell them off. Often during this time, estates were sold for personal interests, and no guidelines regarding renovation were ever imposed.

Voices urging privatization of certain monuments became louder; for instance, in 1998 Viktor Chernomyrdin championed the privatization of monuments. Yet it was not until April 2000 that the Duma accepted in its first reading the new law *On the Objects of the Cultural Heritage of Peoples of the Russian Federation*. It stipulated that citizens of the Russian Federation have the right to buy and to lease monuments of history and architecture. The law was written by cultural professionals and attempted to combine experience of Western Europe with the realities of Russia. One of the developers of new law described that, on the insistence of the Communist Party faction in the Duma, it was necessary to include the stipulation that, although it is possible to privatize monuments, it would only be applicable when the buildings are "worn" by forty percent. They even created an algorithm to calculate the percentage of wear on monuments.[99]

Around the same time a bill was introduced in the Duma, which supplemented the law *On the Objects of the Cultural Heritage*. It was entitled *On the Limits of the Right of Property of Monuments of Architecture*, and introduced by Grigori Tomchin, a member of the Committee of the State Duma on Property. About the law, Tomchin commented, "With the transfer of monument to another owner there will be an agreement which would prescribe the

---

[99]   Iurii Arpishkin, "Pamiatnik arkhitektury smozhet kupit' kazhdyi," *Vremia MN* 28/04/2001.

operating conditions of the monument, including repair and restoration. In this case, those responsible for the safety of the monument will not only be the owner, but also the state."[100] The law provided the opportunity for the federal government to benefit from the gains made through investment in the monuments under federal protection, for, as mentioned above, the 1994 presidential decree permitted only the privatization of monuments of local importance. This new bill would optimistically slow the "downgrading" in status of many monuments from federal to local importance, so as to qualify for sale. Thus, this bill theoretically would curtail illicit privatization and would give experts a bigger role in determining the conditions which would limit the actions of owners. The draft determined that the organ responsible for the protection of specific monuments must enter into a "guarding agreement" with the new owners. However, the bill was not an absolute solution. For example, the zones surrounding an architectural monument lost the status of "separately guarded territories," which, according to the land code, indicates the impossibility of establishing regulations of land tenure along the boundaries of the monuments. This still left the land surrounding estates unprotected and susceptible to modern construction.[101]

On 25 June 2002 a law tolerating the privatization of all classifications of monuments was accepted. The State Duma accepted the law *On the Protection of Historical Heritage (Monuments of History and Culture)*, which permitted privatization, but a moratorium of privatization was superimposed on it. The law details the protocol involved with the transfer of objects and the obligations of both the state and the owner. It stipulates that "objects of cultural heritage independent of the category of their historical cultural value can be situated under federal ownership, ownership of the subjects of the Russian Federation, municipal ownership, private ownership, and also in other forms of ownership, if another order is not established by federal law." Thus, according to the new law it is possible to privatize monuments not only of local, but also federal value when the rights for the federal or municipal properties are clearly established. The law also provides that public access to the estates must be made available and that a room must be dedicated to the his-

100   Aleksandra Tolstikhina, "Ia pamiatnik sebe kupil...," *Segodnia* 11/03/2000.
101   Gleb Lebedev and Georgii Fursei, "Sud'ba kul'tury mestnogo znacheniia," *Nezavisimaia gazeta* 19/03/97.

tory of the estate. Additionally, this new law deals with the territorial issues that the other laws failed to adequately address. It unites the concept of a "monument of history and culture" with the territory upon which it is located.

About this Shvydkoi commented, "The new law *On the Protection of Monuments* assumes that it is possible to sell, to privatize, all monuments independently of the level of protection, with exception of those monuments which are not permitted. In Russia there are in the order of ten to twelve thousand monuments which can be transmitted quietly to particular owners. You will see, what will occur with noble estates, which are being destroyed under our eyes, but the Ministry of Culture simply does not have money to save them, and the same can also be said about rental housing units."[102] Additionally, this new law addresses the territorial issues that the other laws failed to do adequately.

Privatization is generally being supported by the government. During a May 2003 session of the State Soviet in St. Petersburg, President Putin concluded that privatization was the solution to the woes surrounding most of Russia's monuments. Boris Nemtsov, the leader of the Union of Right-wing Forces, echoed this need for privatization.[103] Earlier, Shvydkoi stated at the session of the Council of State for Culture, which was held in connection with St. Petersburg's 300th anniversary, that privatization was as necessary as the air we breathe. He was in favour of abolishing the moratorium to this article of federal law *On the Objects of Cultural Heritage.*[104] "We do not intend to reduce the level of protection. And, conditionally speaking, work on the monuments of federal value must be conducted only under the absolutely indefatigable control of specialists."[105] Evgeny Bogatyrev, the director of the Pushkin Museum at Prechistenko, believed that the state is incapable of ensuring the quantity of monuments of history and architecture of federal value, which he estimates to be close to 25 thousand. He declared, "It is important that the state develop an effective mechanism to control and monitor objects which would be transferred to private individuals. This mechanism of control is

---

[102]   Karakhan and Revzin, "Pokazatel'noe vystuplenie. 'Podozrevat' menia v zhelanii zarabotat' na pamiatnikakh glupo'."
[103]   Ibid.
[104]   Golobkin, "SOS! Kuvaldoi' po istorii."
[105]   Karakhan and Revzin, "Pokazatel'noe vystuplenie. 'Podozrevat' menia v zhelanii zarabotat' na pamiatnikakh glupo'."

worked out in the West... [and] since it is logical and effective, it can be included into our Russian law. I would support the adoption of this law."[106]

Throughout the succession of laws, the role of public organizations in
the arena of cultural protection has remained ambiguous. Duma debates
have discussed the need to determine the position of such public organizations in the paradigm of state protection.[107] Several members of The Central
Council of the All-Russian Society of the Protection of Monuments of History
and Culture (VOOPIK) feel that the 2000 federal law *On the Objects of Cultural Heritage* left very little place for the participation of public organizations
in the sphere of protection of monuments. Galina Malanicheva, chairman of
the Central Council of VOOPIK, signalled that the community should be involved in the area of state historical-cultural examination, the creation of state
list, deciding the zones of protection and managing museums preserves. She
considered the moratorium on privatization of federally important monuments
should be used to help change societal values and instate workable monitoring systems. "[Investors] will not buy ruins, but the prestige that comes with
objects of cultural heritage. Let the moratorium act while a lawful mechanism
is developed which will guarantee the scientific restoration of monuments and
their safety. Finally, certain monuments must be segregated, which under no
condition would they be subject to privatization."[108] The well-known restorer
Saveli Yamshchikov, who is also a governing member of VOOPIK, is an open
opponent to privatization of monuments. He said that perhaps businessmen
could raise the question of buying monuments, but in no way should the Minister of Culture be suggesting such a thing. He recalled Russia's previous attempts at privatization with negativity, baptized by the people as "snatching
up" (*prikhvatizatsiei*), which he fears would happen to Russia's patrimony if
privatized.[109]

In the eyes of many experts, there have already been examples of the
successful privatization of historical estates, for example, Korallovo, an eighteenth century estate not far from Zvenigorod. At one time the estate housed a

---

[106]   E. Vasenina and N. Basiunin, "Obstoiatel'stva. Tol'ko ne stav'te v mavzolei' dzha-
kuzi," *Novaia gazeta* 19/06/2003.

[107]   Lavrentieva, "State Duma Puts Business on Hold."

[108]   Golobkin, "SOS! Kuvaldoi' po istorii."

[109]   "Nuzhno li privatizirovat' pamiatniki kul'tury?"

sanatorium and a house of recreation, but after the dissolution of the Soviet Union, the estate was abandoned. Eventually, Minatom and YUKOS took over the estate and completely restored and renovated it and have used it as a boarding house.[110] Also, Vympelkom possesses the estate Ivanovo-Kozlovskoe on the Istrinsky reservoir and RAO YEES has the estate Mikhailovskoe near Moscow and Karacharovo in the Tver region.[111]

Corporations are not the only targeted investors. Wealthy individuals may be interested in creating either a private residence or to use the estates for other investment opportunities. Adaptive re-use of estates as hotels, restaurants, offices, conference centres and resorts may be promising solutions. According to Aliavdin, estates must find a purpose. "If the owner lives there - all the better, if it is a manager, this is a little bit worse, but if no one lives there, the estate will be pulled apart. In France, as in other Western countries with rich histories, there is an old method of maintaining chateaux in superb condition. They host weddings, holiday events, forums, films, auctions, and antiquarian salons. Many chateaux serve as bases for hunters, fishermen, or provide simple leisure in nature. This experience is useful, since it is not possible to convert each estate into a museum."[112]

Yet, there have also been failures. Nikol'skoe-Uriupino, a Moscow area estate once belonging to the Golitsyns, was leased for three years by Vladimir Bryntsalov, a pharmaceuticals magnate. In spite of the restoration and protection agreements signed by Bryntsalov, he failed to undertake even the most basic tenets of the contract. The territory was not fenced in and as a result, crowds of vacationers destroyed the park, and smoke from the *shashlik* stands and the night bonfires caused irreparable damage to paintings and the moulding of the buildings.[113] Nikol'skoe-Uriupino was taken away from Bryntsalov in 2003 by the Ministry of Culture on grounds of breaching the "guarding" agreement.

However, not only must new purposes be found for estates, but erstwhile attitudes towards legality must also improve. Even for those who wish to

---

[110]   Rudometkina, "Novye russkie bare: Poselit'sia v dvorianskoi usad'be ne tak uzh slozhno."

[111]   Anni, "Sud'ba rezidentsii."

[112]   Ol'gin, "Nasledie: privatizatsiia istorii."

[113]   Anni, "Sud'ba rezidentsii."

acquire an estate in good faith, their experiences have shown, in Russia to-day, as in the past, connections, money and *blat* seem to be the prevalent way of accomplishing one's means. If, in spite of the numerous laws regulating the privatization of monuments, informal influences continue to reign over Russia instead of the rule of law, this dire prediction may come true.

III.5 Restitution

The idea of restoring property to the heirs of pre-revolutionary owners may be a more difficult case to rectify than privatization. As Alexander Solzhenitsyn observed, "You cannot draw up a restitution law on the principle of returning everything to everyone. In that case, you will be causing new injustices."[114] In the Soviet Union, many of the surviving estates were divided into multi-family dwellings or communal farms, and thus have housed generations of people other than the pre-1917 owners. In 1998, the Moscow Times editorialised against restitution, claiming that, "Russia simply cannot afford the instability that would result if the courts were to decide in favour of the descendants of robbed nobles. Where would it end?"[115] Moreover, Oleg Scherbachev, an expert at the Nobility Assembly, calculates that "It's unlikely in the near future [that] any way can be found to get property back. If our state considered itself the successor to the Russian Empire, things would be easier. But this state is a direct successor to the Soviet Union."[116]

In spite of the prevalent controversy, there have been attempts at passing restitution bills through the Duma, namely by Vladimir Lisichkin in 1998. This was also attempted in 2000, initiated by deputy Alexander Chuyev, entitled *On the Restoration of the Rights of the Physical Persons to the Immovable Property, Forcedly Alienated by the Organs of the Authority of the RSFSR, the USSR and by Other Organs of Authority in the Extrajudicial Order After 7 November of 1917 (By the New Style), That is in a Improper Eco-*

---

[114]   Quoted in Carol Matlack, "Homecoming for the Erstwhile Elite," *Business Week* 26/10/98.

[115]   "It's Too Late to Restore 1917 Losses," *Moscow Times* 13/02/1998.

[116]   Daniel Williams, "Palatial Ruin is Russian Heir's Dream House," *The Washington Post* 23/03/98.

nomic Condition, Reconstruction of Which the State Did not Take Up. This unsuccessful draft stipulated that both Russian citizens and foreigners would be sanctioned to claim back their property. The key phrase of this draft was that the property available for restitution had to be in "improper economic condition," and could not be targeted for restoration by the state. The draft was rather ambiguous as to which properties this law would have applied. At that time, Chuyev emphasised that, "The return of objects that are registered as monuments of history and culture to their former owners entails their duty to comply with legislation on monuments, including the coordination of restoration and modernisation plans with corresponding authorities."[117] He believed that when the properties were returned to their former owner's heirs, they, in turn, would promptly begin restoration work. Although these drafts were not accepted, there are continued efforts within the State Duma to create legislation permitting restitution.

In addition, according to the 2000 draft law, the period within in which a claimant would have been able to file for the return of property was brief; twenty years from the date of the hypothetical acceptance of the draft. For many of those to whom the draft would have applied, time is a luxury which most do not have. According to Prince Obolensky, he felt as though he was too old to enter into a morass of legal battles to regain his family's former estate. He indicated that amongst others he knows in his position, they felt similarly. His children did not have the same connection to Russia as he did as a first generation émigré, and for this reason they show less interest in entering the contest for the family's former possessions.[118] Similarly, Georgie Shtruk, who was ninety-five years old in 1998, having filed a claim two years previously for his familial home outside of Moscow, felt that he was not going to live to hear the court's decision.[119] Age is an uncertain condition affecting many possible claimants.

Yet, some families are taking up the gauntlet to regain ownership. According to Alexei Firsanov, chairman of the League of Property Rights Protection, as of 1998 at least five families have filed claims for the restitution of

---

[117] Anna Kozyreva, "Po kakim zakonam zhit' budem. Na grafskikh razvalinakh," *Rossiiskaia gazeta* 20/10/2000.

[118] Interview with Prince and Princess Obolensky, 10/12/2003.

[119] Matlack, "Homecoming for the Erstwhile Elite."

family property, none of which had succeeded.[120] In Russia, the most infamous of these cases surrounded the efforts of Prince Alexei Meshchersky, who attempted to gain claim over Alabino, a former family-owned estate outside Moscow. Meshchersky, earlier an engineer in Nikolayev, Ukraine, prompted by the new legal environment of the Russian Federation, decided to move his family to Alabino in 1997 to stake his claim for the estate. He moved into the estate's gate-house, one of the only remaining habitable structures of the once-grand estate, because Russian law dictated that, to claim property, one must reside in it.

Here, Meshchersky explains his motivation.

> It is necessary for someone to begin the march for his rights. Here I reserve patience; I will go to the end. My example will inspire other hereditary Russian citizens. And we already have a not-so -bad document in our hands... the Constitution of the Russian Federation. You will find in article thirty-five: 'The right to private property is guarded by law... No one can be deprived of their property otherwise based on a court decision. The eminent domain of property for state needs can be produced only with the condition of preliminary and equivalent compensation. The right of inheritance is guaranteed.' It seems that we now proclaim to live in a civilized state. Here I want the court of law to affirm: the hereditary citizens of Russia with the surname Meshchersky in no way misbehaved before the fatherland but, on the contrary, served it faithfully and truthfully for a period of eight centuries. Rehabilitation of this kind is necessary. Let it be heard that our disappearance during the Soviet regime was pursued incorrectly and that our property and, in particular, the estate of Alabino, was confiscated illegally, which means that it is subject to recovery... But not the estate itself, alas, but its ruins.[121]

Alabino belonged to the State Committee of Culture. The ruins, which were the only surviving vestige of the once-majestic estate, were classified as a historical monument in 1964. In spite of this classification, the protection of the estate was minimal at best. Meshchersky noted, "It's ironic that anyone

---

[120]   Ibid.
[121]   Ruslan Armeev, "Kniaz' Meshcherskii: U menia est' ruki i golova, chtoby vernut' slavu nashego roda," *Izvestiia* 21/02/1998.

can come along and take it to bits, brick by brick, and the Committee of Culture doesn't lift a finger, but when someone actually wants to restore it, they're up in arms and putting every stumbling block they can think of in your way."[122]

Meshchersky's plans for the estate included creating a technical club for local children, a small hotel and a museum dedicated to Ivan Vsevolodovich Meshchersky. Additionally, he planned to build a bath house around a medicinal spring he had found on the property. Amongst the ruins of the estate, which he proposed to leave in the same state as an *aide mémoire* of the atrocities of the Communists, he intended to host concerts and artistic exhibitions.

The local authorities were immediately hostile to Meshchersky and his campaign. He tried his case in the local court, which refused to hear Meshchersky's contention, so he moved to various levels of the legal system. The court rulings filed both at the local level and in the Supreme Court, have declined Meshchersky's claims, asserting that, as the estate was a classified historical monument it could not be conceded to a private individual at that time. Due to his continual failures in the Russian legal system, he passed his case to Strasbourg, to seek aid from international courts. Nothing came from his efforts.

The Prince and his family were evicted in September 2001. A local resident, having disappeared several years beforehand, reappeared with the registration card for the gate-house of the estate in which the Mershcherskys had been, in effect, squatting. This man maintained that he had been registered there since 1973, and was thus entitled to the house. This man stated, "I completely understand that in the next hundred years, and maybe even the next two hundred years, there will be not be any money to restore this estate. The main house, to be more precise, what remains of it, as it fell, so too will it fall. I, of course, will try to not let mountain climbers enter here with their hooks. But I cannot guarantee that they will listen to me."[123]

---

[122]   Juliet Butler, Ignatiev, Nikolai, "Prince Returns to Family Palace," *Moscow Times* 10/03/1998.

[123]   Elena Egorova, "Moskoviia. Khrias' po kniaziu," *Moskovskii komsomolets* 16/09/2002.

In other scenarios, local governments are occasionally restoring ownership and returning property to legendary families.[124] Take the Nabokov family,
for instance. The officials in the Gatchina region wanted the Nabokovs to
build a Nabokov memorial and conference centre in return for restoring ownership of the Vyra estate to the family. Dmitri Nabokov, son of the famous
writer, had visited his father's former estates during the centenary celebration
of his father's birthday. At that time, there were discussions regarding the restitution of one of the three Nabokov estates to V. V. Nabokov's surviving
heirs. Dmitri Nabokov stated that he would not consider spending the funds
necessary to restore the other two estates. "I cannot take this expenditure
upon myself, because I must leave something of the Nabokov funds." Instead
he planned to draw in sponsorship. "I know the main person at Chrysler well...
It is possible that I will turn to Coca-Cola - there is the division which deals
specifically with the restoration of old houses. It is possible, through my friend
Leonid Parfenov that I will toss up a hint to the banker who manages company NTV."[125] Dmitri Nabokov planed to recreate the house which once stood
on the bared foundations of Vyra through use of photographs and convert the
new house into a cultural centre. "I would want concerts to be held there, exhibitions; writers could arrive and work in special apartments. I would get
great pleasure to stay there from time to time, for example in winter. I would
travel a little on a troika..." However, the lack of laws stipulating what would
be done with the land surrounding the estate was problematic at that time.
Anatoly Ledovsky, a representative from the Gatchina region, stated, "We intend to lease this land to Nabokov for fifty years or to create a long term-less
lease. We are prepared to even leave this question to the legislative assembly of the region, but it is compulsory to solve this question."[126] In the opinion
of some, even if Vyra were not to be restored, the very fact that the estate
was returned to the Nabokovs would be seen as an excellent advertisement
for the entire region.

Another successful tale of restitution is that of estate Serednikovo,
where the writer, Mikhail Lermontov, spent the summers between 1829 and

---

[124]   Lavrentieva, "State Duma Puts Business on Hold."
[125]   Svetlana Smetanina, "Restitutsiia: belye nachinaiut i vyigryvaiut," *Kommersant-Daily*
28/02/98.
[126]   Ibid.

1832. It is here that he composed seven poems, two dramas and about a hundred poetic verses. Although Serednikovo was not the ancestral seat of the Lermontov family, it is most famous for its connection with Lermontov. Also contributing to the estate's distinguished history, Serednikovo was acquired by the Major General Dmitri Alekseyevich Stolypin in 1825, the brother of Mikhail Lermontov's grandmother. Serednikovo was expropriated after the revolution and initially used as "Tishin's health resort" for the members of the All-Russian Central Executive Commission (*Vserossiiskii Tsentral'nyi Ispolnitel'nyi Komitet* or VTsIK) (1917-1936), and then as a neurological sanatorium, and from 1946 as an anti-tubercular sanatorium. In 1991 an organization called "Lermontov Heritage" was created, with the goal or reuniting the Lermontov descendants, many of whom were scattered throughout the world. The organization became involved with Serednikovo when the Ministry of Culture of the USSR offered to lease Serednikovo to them in 1992. In the same year, the group organized the National Lermontov Centre in Serednikovo and became the leaseholder of estate. At that time, the government pledged significant aid but this was revoked almost immediately afterwards.

The current Mikhail Lermontov, the great-grandson of the cousin of the poet, spearheaded the project and moved into the estate with his family in 1996. Today, his daughter Marina Lermontova is the executive director of this centre. The Lermontovs undertook the restoration of Serednikovo without aid from the state. As Marina Lermontova recounted,

No, [the state] did not help. Although it promised to. The state is obligated first of all to check the performance of guarding obligations by each leaseholder or the owner. And in the case of their non-observance, the state is simply obligated to assign the leaseholder or owner on the responsibility. Our estate is one of few where the protected zone was affirmed, which included the zone of the monument, the guarding zone and the zone of the guarded landscape. And here we cannot wait for the state to provide assistance with protection. Forests are cut down, cottages are constructed. But even with signs of land seizures (*zemleotvody*) the same state is shutting its eyes to the fact that this is a protected zone. As far as I know, the same problems occur in Shakhmatovo, Muranovo, and Abramtsevo.[127]

In spite of some problems, Serednikovo's future looks bright. The main house, wings, courtyard and park are mostly restored. Lermontova reported that that the guest wings are already ready to be used as a small bed and breakfast and a conference centre. Also, Lermontov recounted, "We have a joint project with the Committee of Tourism of the Moscow region to create a tourist industry around Moscow estates... it is possible to gradually prepare each object, each estate, for investment expectations."[128]

In other situations, the local governments have allowed former owners to live on the estates without claiming official ownership. Count Alexei Kamensky reported in 1998 that local officials in his ancestral village had permitted him to repossess the ruins that were once his family's estate.[129] Similarly, in 1993, Platon Afanas'ev obtained a forty-nine year lease for 708 hectares of land of his grandmother's former estate in the Opochkinskeyeo region of the Pskov province. "This proved to be improbably simple. I arrived at the Head of Administration of the Opochkinskeyeo region, showed them the certification of my noble ancestry and asked them to give me the land. And they did." The collective farm that previously inhabited the estate's land unanimously decided to return the land to "new nobleman."[130]

It is also important to analyze those former-owners who do not seek restitution, but instead, an involvement with their family's former seat. Consider, for instance, one branch of the Obolensky family. The Obolensky estate, Berezichi in the Kaluga province, today houses Internat #6 Boarding School for Special Children (for disabled and/or abused children). The family decided that the best course of action would be to provide aid and support to the school. The Kaluga government had been cordial towards the Obolensky's initiatives, often matching funds donated by the family. Since the Obo-

---

[127]   Svetlana Bogdanova, "Lermontovy: khotim, chtoby usad'ba sebia okupala," *Dom gazeta* 30/05/2003.

[128]   Leonid Smirnov, "Mikhail Lermontov, potomok poeta: Vodochnymi butylkami byli zabity vse dymokhody," *Izvestiia* 08/08/2002.

[129]   Mitchell Landsberg, "Legally or not, Russian aristocrats moving back to ancestral estates," *Milwaukee Journal Sentinel* 15/03/1998.

[130]   Smetanina, "Restitutsiia: belye nachinaiut i vyigryvaiut."

lenskys' involvement at Berezichi, the government designated the estate as a Heritage Property of the Russian Federation. In addition, the school has been renamed "The Prince Aleksei Dmitrievich Obolensky School", in memory of the current Prince's grandfather. For the Obolenskys, their endeavours were aimed to instil a spiritual and historic meaning at Berezichi rather than a financial or material gain. The Obolenskys' efforts are rather unique amongst the former nobility of Russia. According to them, most families do not take the initiative or are not interested in being involved with former family estates; for the Obolenskys, the school provides the motivation.[131]

[131]   Interview with Prince and Princess Obolensky, op. cit.

IV   Funding

Although the estate has now been liberated from the Soviet's prejudiced and idiosyncratic one-sided class approach, the sensitive issue of funding for estates has not changed much since Soviet times. Still, a lack of financial transparency stands out, which has made research on this subject more difficult. This chapter will examine the financial aspects of cultural preservation in Russia through an investigation into the amounts of state funding allotted for culture, and more importantly, for the area of state investments in buildings and reconstruction. There will be an overview of the federal budget allocations for culture throughout the late 1990's until today. Additionally, in a quest to evaluate the Ministry of Culture's ability to use the available funding efficiently, the reports of the State Auditing Chamber of the Russian Federation and the Duma's Committee of Culture and Tourism will be examined. Finally, certain attempts made by directors of museum-estates at garnering enough financial aid to ensure survival will be discussed.

General funding for culture during the post-Soviet period, and for estates specifically, has been inadequate. During a radio broadcast the summer of 2003, Shvydkoi acknowledged that there is very little money for monuments, and this was especially true in the provinces. He did not envision any changes in this situation in the near, or even distant, future.[132] In the 1990's, with the exception of the special funds available for the bi-centenary of the Russian poet Alexander Pushkin in 1998-1999, the cultural budget had been reduced several times. The budget for culture, while recognized as important, has not been deemed vital, especially when Russia was preoccupied with financial and monetary difficulties; considered expendable, the budget was often drastically cut. Competition between cultural institutions for the exceedingly scarce resources became the foremost priority. Cultural institutions' hands were tied as the lack of funding inhibited action. In the words of Svetlana Anokhina, the head of the Administration of the Protection of Monuments

---

[132]   "Nuzhno li privatizirovat' pamiatniki kul'tury?"

of Committee for the Culture of the Moscow region, "Many reproach us for poor quality work... But that we can do? Our specialists huddle in four rooms, and they have absolutely no control."[133] The achievement of many of the state's professed goals has been greatly hampered by economic crises and general under-funding.

The period between 1996 and 1998 proved to be the most modest years in the public financing of culture in Russia. At this time institutional funding was limited only to the payment of workers' salaries, the payment of which was nevertheless delayed by several months. In 1997, the actual funding was reduced to only twelve percent of the approved budget for culture. Most cultural budgets fell below the acknowledged minimum level, and practically all restoration works and other activities were brought to a standstill. After the August 1998 economic crisis, some consistent funding was reestablished to select establishments, but the general dearth of funding continued.

The alleviation of the funding crisis for Russia's culture began in 1999, when the state cultural budget was fully paid for the first time in years. However, even this achievement fell short of the tenets of the *Basic Law on Culture*, which stipulated that cultural funding should equal two percent of the entire federal budget and six percent of regional budgets. As in 1999, the state's financing of culture was fully allotted again in 2000, although the situation remained volatile. The *Culture of Russia Programme (2001-2005)* was implemented with the sanguine allegation that a new chapter for the cultural sector has been opened.[134] Here, a new financial scheme was introduced calling for multi-level co-funding of cultural projects.[135]

[133]   Bogdanova, "Usad'by v Rossii: zhivye i mertvye."

[134]   As indicated in the Introduction, the federal programme of *Russia Culture 2001-2005*, is the third of such programmes. The first began in 1993, and the second was completed in 1999. Only approximately 29 percent of the funding for the first programme was actually delivered, and for the second programme it was only about 40 percent. Mikhail Shvydkoi, "Press Briefing on Results of Government Meeting," *Official Kremlin International News Broadcast*, 2000.

[135]   Razologov and Fedorova, *Cultural Policies in Europe: A Compendium of Basic Facts and Trends*, 24.

The budget allocations for culture were kept over the level of 0.5 percent of the federal budget in both 2001 and 2002.[136] Shvydkoi reported that Russia's culture received approximately seven billion rubles in 2001, an amount that exceeded the 2000 level by 30 percent.[137] In addition to the overall expenditure of the state budget in 2000 on "Culture and Arts", a windfall of 289 million rubles of supplementary funding was allocated. Of this sum, certain estate-related works were included on this list of recipients, including the restoration of the museum-estate Ostaf'evo (which received one million rubles), the estates of the town Saratov (which received three million rubles), the restoration of the Vasil'chikov-Lansky-Goncharov estate in the town of Chekhov (which received two million rubles), and the restoration of Arkhangel'skoe (which received five million rubles).[138] Again in 2001, due to additional federal income, 100 million rubles were awarded in addition to the original sum. Of this amount, some of the funding for estates included the restoration of the estate of N. A. Yaroshenko, "Pavlishchev Bor" (which received one million rubles) and the restoration of Arkhangel'skoe (which also received one million rubles).[139] In both years, smaller amounts were allotted for other estate restoration works and for the restoration of objects within the estates.

According to a report by the Committee of Culture and Tourism of the State Duma, in 2003 the division of "Culture, Art and Cinematography" was supposed to receive just under 14 billion rubles, or 37 percent over the amount of 2002 (the amount from 2002, roughly 10.3 billion rubles, was a 61 percent increase on 2001).[140] This expenditure equalled 0.59 percent of the entire federal budget. Of this amount, just under 12 billion went to the subsection "Culture and Art". 2.1 billion rubles had been marked for the area of state

---

[136]   See Appendix II for a more detailed breakdown of Federal spending in 2000 and 2001.

[137]   Igor Veksler, "Russian culture to get about 7 billion roubles in 2001," *Itar-Tass Weekly News* 02/08/2000.

[138]   "Raspredelenie dopolnitel'nykh assignovanii' iz federal'nogo biudzheta na 2000 god po razdelu 'Kul'tura, iskusstvo i kinematografiia' funktsional'noi' klassifikatsii raskhodov biudzhetov Rossiiskoi' Federatsii," *Rossiiskaia gazeta* 20/01/2000.

[139]   "Neizvestnaia usad'ba," *Moskovskaia pravda* 12/10/2000.

[140]   This amount allotted for 2003 included the major restoration works conducted in St. Petersburg for the celebration of its 300th anniversary. Although I have not found details on the amounts spent for this event, I would imagine that it took the vast majority of the federal funds allotted for culture.

investments for buildings and reconstruction, up from almost 1.9 billion in 2002. In spite of the increases, the financing for capital investment in 2002 was deemed vastly insufficient by the Committee; in their opinion this sum could not cover the major renovation works needed on federally significant buildings, many of which, they had recognized, were in a state of emergency. The Committee considered that at least 70 percent of the entire budget for "Culture and Arts", not just the 2.1 billion rubles, was needed to be spent on such renovation works. In the report, the estates of Arkhangel'skoe, Tsarskoe Selo and Peterhof were noted as being priorities in 2003.[141] In 2002, the estate Yasnaya Polyana was singled out as a recipient of federal funding for renovations.[142] The Committee of Culture and Tourism, in its 2002 report, testified, "The means set aside in the budget for the restoration of monuments of history and culture is 450 million rubles, which will make it possible to ensure the restoration of not more than five percent of monuments, and in the Russian territory more than 80 thousand monuments are found."[143] Sokolov reported that the Ministry of Culture and Mass Communication's affirmed budget in 2005 was 38.5 billion rubles, which was 18 percent higher than the budget of 2004. He went on, "But I did not begin to be glad. First, this number only temporarily exceeds the percentage of inflation, in the second place, the very order of the chosen sum does not completely correspond to the real needs of society. Recently we acquainted journalists with the forecasts of the development of Russian culture, made by one very respectable western agency. They gave us three scenarios - poor, satisfactory and good. So here, the means put aside for us are even less than the figures depicting the worst scenario which were provided by this organization."[144]

---

141   *Conclusion of the Committee on Culture and Tourism on the Draft of the Federal Law "On the Federal Budget for 2003"* (Moscow: Committee of Culture and Tourism of the State Duma of the Russian Federation, 2002).

142   *The Expenditures of the Federal Budget for 2002 for Culture Will Exceed the Level of the Present Year by 61%* (Moscow: State Duma of the Russian Federation, 2001).

143   N. N. Gubenko, *Conclusion of the Committee on Culture and Tourism on the Draft of the Federal Law "On the Federal Budget for 2002"* (Moscow: Committee of Culture and Tourism of the State Duma of the Russian Federation, 2001).

144   Sergei Biriukov, "Ministr kul'tury i massovykh kommunikatsii rossii Aleksandr Sokolov: Pora vspomnit' o chesti," *Literaturnaia gazeta* 23/03/2005.

To compound the problems resulting from a sever lack of funding, there is the added complication that the funding which is allotted is not always used efficiently. The State Auditing Chamber of the Russian Federation carried out an examination between October 2001 and January 2002 to determine whether those federal funds directed towards restoration and preservation of monuments as decreed by the federal law *On the Federal Budget in* 2000 were used effectively and purposefully by the Ministry of Culture. In 2000, 497.5 million rubles were provided for measures for the protection of immovable monuments of history and culture, up from 329.7 million rubles in 2001. Several cases of mismanagement of these funds by the Ministry of Culture were cited. For instance, in accordance with an order of 26 March 2001, the Ministry of Culture created the Central Competitive Commission (TsKK) which was to conduct competitions for firms to win governmental contracts for renovation projects. However, the State Auditing Chamber found that these competitions were, in actual fact, often not conducted at all. In addition, from 2000-1 the Ministry of Culture's specialized restoration agency, *Gosrestavratsiia*, used 2.8 million rubles, or 5.8 percent of its total budget allotted for restoration works for internal, extra-budgetary uses. None of this money should have been draw on by *Gosrestavratsiia* for such matters. The report also highlighted that restoration works, paid for in advance by the Ministry, were often not completed by the contractors, and were left half-finished.[145]

In spite of gradual increases in overall funding for culture, the levels are still inadequate. In the words of Shvydkoi from September 2003, "If we calculate [the amount of funding spent by the Ministry of Culture, itself, on monuments], then on the average will come out about billion of rubles per year. One billion for the entire country, but about half of this sum remains in Moscow and Pieter... In principle the state can effectively restore 500 to 600 monuments per year, while in other situations, 200 to 250."[146] Moreover, in addition to a lack of general funding for monument preservation, most country estates are not priority funding projects. Alexander Kudryavtsev, the Presi-

---

[145]   Iu. M. Voronin, "Otchet o rezul'tatakh proverki polnoty finansirovaniia i tselevogo raskhodovaniia sredstv federal'nogo biudzheta za 2000 god i istekshii period 2001 goda, napravlennykh na vosstanovlenie i restavratsiiu pamiatnikov istorii i kul'tury," *Biulleten' Schetnoi palaty Rossiiskoi Federatsii* 5 (2002).

[146]   Karakhan and Revzin, "Pokazatel'noe vystuplenie. 'Podozrevat' menia v zhelanii zarabotat' na pamiatnikakh glupo'."

dent of the Academy of Architecture, commented on the specific plight of estates in an environment lacking adequate funding for estates.

According to the classification used by the Academy of Architecture, Russian museums are divided into several groups. First, are the literary and artistic estates, in which famous Russians lived and stayed. Such estates are easily restored: with approaching anniversaries associated with these famous people, the directors of the museums inform the media about the estate, they obtain budgetary (or non-budgetary) money and restore the museum quickly, in time for the approaching anniversary. The role of the directors of these museums is very important; it is they who convert the estate, as a rule, into the financially viable entity. Such examples exist: Yasnaya Polyana, Khmelita, the Pushkin State Museum-Preserve. The second category are destroyed estates with interesting histories or impressive artistic value, which become the project of initiative-taking people These people attract society's attention to such estates, attempt to find funding from different sources, obtain international grants, which is the starting capital for the revival of these estates. There is a third category of estates: those which can be returned to their legal owners or acquired by private individuals. Koralovo, in the environs of Moscow, is such an estate. The owner finances all work on its restoration and reconstruction.[147]

Yevgeny Bogatyrev, the director of the Pushkin State Museum, elaborated on his museum's fight for survival:

How we do survive today in the very complex times? Balls, musical evenings, concerts and children's holidays are hosted in the estate. This gives us the possibility to earn small amounts of money, but in essence the museum exists on payments from the state budget. In Russia only two museums independently earn enough money to be self-sufficient due to the enormous flow of visitors - Peterhof and Saint Isaac's Cathedral. Everything else survives on... the support of the state. Our museum earns five to seven percent of the total volume of budget financing; we plan to increase this portion to 15-20 percent. When rich people visit the museum, are en-

---

[147]   "Russkaia usad'ba s paradnogo pod"ezda," *Rossiiskaia gazeta* 15/09/2000.

raptured by it and some make personal gifts, and small sponsor aid is given. We are ready get involved with joint business collaboration... but thus far business solutions, unfortunately, have not been found.[148]

Cultural preservation could intrinsically serve as a show-case signalling Russia's economic revival and portraying the government as lasting partners in promoting national culture. However, issues of funding directly obstruct the capabilities of and general esteem for government involvement in cultural preservation. For Russia's estate-museums, the responsibility for finding enough funding lies almost entirely on the shoulders of the directors. Many museum directors today began their careers under the Soviet system; they are often reluctant to change the way they have run their museums for the past decades. However, even those forward thinking directors who would embrace change, do not have many avenues of recourse. As the next chapter will illustrate, while charitable donations are sometimes made to the sphere of culture, general public participation in cultural preservation is minimal.

---

[148]   Ibid.

Figure 12: Example of a Russian Estate: L'ialichi

V   Civil Society and Philanthropy

This chapter will draw attention to the activities of Russia's civil society and the role of philanthropy in the sphere of estate preservation. Russians' overall apathy with respect to preservation projects offers interesting insights into the components of Russia's contemporary culture. Firstly, the task will be to define civil society and explore its role in post-Soviet Russia. To do this, the effect of the Soviet Union's legacy on Russia's civil society will be considered. Secondly, an assessment of philanthropic practices amongst Russia's citizens and businesses will help discern non-governmental activities in the sphere of culture. Thirdly, an analysis of Russia's taxation policies for non-profit organizations and philanthropic activities will provide the context of the government's relations with these sections of civil society. Finally, this chapter will look at those organizations which work specifically for the preservation of Russia's country estates.

Civil society is a generally contested concept; there is no single correct definition.[149] For the purpose of this work, we will use Jean Cohen's explanation, in which civil society is explained as

> a sphere of social interaction between economy and state, composed above all of the intimate sphere (especially the family), the sphere of associations (especially voluntary associations), social movements and forms of public communication. Modern civil society is created through forms of self-constitution and self-mobilization. It is institutionalized and generalized through laws, and especially subjective rights, that stabilise social differentiation. While the self-creative and institutionalized dimensions can exist separately, in the long term both independent action and institutionalization are necessary for the reproduction of civil society.[150]

---

[149] For another precise description of the concept of civil society see also Larry Diamond, "Rethinking Civil Society: Towards Democratic Consolidation," *Journal of Democracy* 5.3 (1994).

[150] Jean Cohen and Andrew Arato, *Civil Society and Political Theory* (Cambridge: MIT Press, 1992) ix.

Russia had inherited a chronically weak civil society from the Soviet Union, where extra-governmental organizations were not accepted. Matthew Wyman, the author of *Public Opinion in Post-Communist Russia* explained that, "in the mature communist system, intermediate institutions through which ordinary people were able to communicate their views to government, and via which government could seek to develop a sense of legitimacy to underlie its actions, hardly exists. Trade unions and interest groups had, in the classic description, merely acted as 'transmission belts' for regime policies."[151] Society tended to be underdeveloped and atomised. Steven Fish elucidated the notion that groups' capacity for aggregating interests, the possibility of representation of those interests, the articulation of interests into concrete political claims, access to political arenas and control over outcomes, and groups' autonomy from the state all indicate the institutional health of civil society. Independent organizations did not score high on any of these indicators in the late Soviet period.[152] Although a nascent civil society was forming during the late period of *perestroika*, Russia has had very little experience with vigorous civic action.

With the end of the Soviet Union came the end of much of the government organization and funding of social and cultural activities. However, from that time a network of non-profit and non-governmental associations and organizations to fill those functions has not emerged fully, leaving a vacuum of activity. The infrastructure of civil society in Russia, according to Bruce Parrott, has not yet approached the density and durability of such social networks in other established democracies.[153] Its civil society is less institutionalized and is thus more vulnerable to outside influences. Again, Fish asserted that with the collapse of the Soviet Union and the ensuing economic, national

---

[151]   Matthew Wyman, "Public Opinion and Political Institutions," *Institutions and Political Change in Russia*, ed. Neil Robinson (Basingstoke: Macmillan, 2000) 173.

[152]   M. Steven Fish, *Democracy From Scratch: Opposition and Regime in the New Russian Revolution* (Princeton: Princeton University Press, 1995) 53-60.

[153]   Bruce Parrott, "Perspectives on Postcommunist Democratization," *Democratic Changes and Authoritarian Reactions in Russia, Ukraine, Belarus and Moldova*, eds. Bruce Parrott and Karen Dawisha (Cambridge: Cambridge University Press, 1997) 25.

and political problems were thrust at the top of the agenda, at the expense of attention paid to civil society.[154]

Marc Howard, author of the book *The Weakness of Civil Society in Post-Communist Europe*, provided three explanations for the low levels of public participation in Russia: firstly, due to residual experiences, most people mistrust and avoid joining formal organizations, secondly, a deep network of friendships and personal support hampers desires to join organizations, and thirdly, widespread disappointment with the post-communist transitions has led to popular avoidance of the public sphere.[155] Another critical problem with the formation of a strong civil society in Russia today is that most reforms have been determined from the summit of power, with few prospects for initiatives to be taken at a grass-roots level. In a system where public confidence in Russia's state institutions has remained low, popular apathy towards government initiatives is common. Sakwa explained that "the public shows little loyalty to public institutions, national identifiers or political parties. There is an extraordinary indifference to the political institutions of a modern state."[156] Corruption and the lack of the rule of law directly contribute to these views. Furthermore, in face of popular inertia, the government has failed to provide many venues in which to actively engage civil society. Additionally, the economic crises and hardships endured by the general population also been an effective inhibitor of popular participation. Irina Boutenko, a Russian cultural expert, maintains that volunteerism "is almost a new idea" to Russians, many of whom resented the forced "volunteerism" under the Soviet system.[157]

The formation and functioning of non-profit organizations has also been mired by the recalcitrance of the state. In the opinion of Olga Alekseyeva, a researcher in the Moscow office of the Britain's Charity Aid Foundation, nongovernmental organizations have to compete with the state for business do-

---

[154]   Fish, *Democracy From Scratch: Opposition and Regime in the New Russian Revolution* 214-15.

[155]   Marc Morjé Howard, *The Weakness of Civil Society in Post-Communist Europe* (Cambridge: Cambridge University Press, 2003) 26-29.

[156]   Neil Robinson, *Institutions and Political Change in Russia* (Basingstoke: Macmillan, 2000) 194.

[157]   John J. Monahan, "Russian Researcher Visits Local Nonprofits," *Christian Science Monitor* 01/04/98. See also Robert Wuthnow, ed., *Between States and Markets: The Voluntary Sector in Comparative Perspective* (Princeton, NJ: Princeton University Press, 1991).

nations. With such a contest for funds, federal authorities seldom promote the formation of such nongovernmental organizations. Additionally, non-profit status effectively bears no benefits and can even result in harsher tax regulations.[158] And for those non-profit organizations that do exist, they too harbour certain inefficiencies. S. Frederick Starr, a historian of Russian culture, said that what are still missing in Russia are American-style boards of trustees which can call directors and sponsors into account. "With the waning of state control and the emergence of private institutions, you have individual cultural entrepreneurs with huge power. In the end, you have to ask the question: Who are the permanent guardians of culture?"[159] In order for meaningful societal change to occur, Howard defines three factors that need to coincide: first, new civil society institutions should be authoritative and binding; second, they should be constructed upon existing tendencies, traditions or cultures; and third, significant time will be needed for the foundations to settle.[160] Until these changes are implemented, civil society in Russia risks remaining weak and divided.

As non-profit organizations, by definition, cannot be in the business of making money, they are dependant on either grants or money from private individuals and legal entities. Currently, organizations operating in Russia are not required to register with the government, however, if they do so, they do so as an option that provides certain tax benefits, as well as a degree of legal protection. Recently, the Federal government has implemented a renewed and vigorous attempt to marginalize and reign in the activities of non-profit organizations in Russia. The State Duma approved the initiatives in the first reading on August 5, when 332 parliament members voted for the bill "On amendments to chapters 23 and 25 of the second part of the Tax Code and some other legislative acts on taxes and levies." Russia's lower house of parliament supported "in principle" the idea of reforming the taxation system of non-profit organizations and charities. This bill would give government officials greater control over the operation of both foreign- and local-funded groups, allowing authorities to oversee their financial flows and activities.

---

[158]   Masha Gessen, "The Rebirth of Russian Charity," *The American Benefactor* Spring (1997): 126.
[159]   Bohlen, "After the Chaos, A New Day for the Cultures of the Soviet World."
[160]   Howard, *The Weakness of Civil Society in Post-Communist Europe* 20.

Non-governmental organizations already face a myriad of government-imposed restrictions, especially when making and accepting charitable contributions, which act as substantial barriers to fundraising, especially onerous for organization not run by the state or which do not have "Friends of" affiliates abroad.

Even before this current legal initiative, organizations have been only receive such deductions in Russia if they have been registered as tax residents here, and usually such deductions have been restricted and carefully scrutinized due to the government's ongoing struggle against tax evasion.[161] In addition, a draft Federal Law "On the Introduction of Amendments to Certain Legislative Acts of the Russian Federation" which was adopted by the State Duma at its first reading on 23 November 2005, is an attempt to rationalize the mechanisms for the registration of non-profit and non-government organizations and charities, and monitor the compliance of the activity of these organizations with their supposed aims. Moreover, the legislation would require local branches of foreign non-governmental organizations to reregister as de-facto Russian entities, which would give the government the power to subject groups to stricter financial and legal restrictions. Justice Minister Yuri Chaika described one Federal Registration Service objective as follows: to get rid of "dead soul" NGOs. According to Chaika, Russia has over 40,000 of these.[162]

As to from where the government's apparent hostility to non-governmental organizations, there are several theories. Mark Urnov, chairman of the Expertiza think tank, stated, "I call this a culture of distrust. No one believes that you can work in a civil group without pursuing your personal interests. Together with the old culture of fear, this distrust kills civil society here."[163] Foreign criticism about the pending legislation has claimed that it is

---

[161]   According to Olga Boltenko, a tax lawyer at Haarmann, Kemmelrath & Partners, to qualify as a tax resident and thus be eligible for a deduction, a potential donor must spend more than 183 calendar days a year in Russia. If that is the case, a tax-resident donor is exempt from paying thirteen percent in income tax on the amount of the donation, and the deduction cannot be bigger than twenty-five percent of the annual income of the donor. Kimberly O'Haver, "Philanthropists Get Little Pay Back," *Moscow Times* 13/10/2004.

[162]   Anastasia Kornia, "The Justice Ministry Cleans Up Civil Society," *Nezavisimaia gazeta* 06/04/2005.

[163]   Dmitry Babich, "Will Civil Society Fly?" *Russian Profile* 23/08/2004.

symptomatic of the Russian government's gradual drift toward authoritarian-
ism. Critics place the blame for tightening restrictions for organizations and
freedom of speech on the *siloviki* Putin has positioned in places of power.
Some pundits allege that the people in power feel threatened by that which
they can not control, and are using this bill as a method by which to "divide
and appropriate" what they perceive as their opposition.

As to the number of organizations these draft laws may affect in the future, it is not clear. The exact number of NGOs in Russia is unknown. The
Justice Ministry has registered more than 300,000 NGOs and others estimate
that there are up to 450,000. In actuality, the true number of NGOs is likely to
be much higher than those officially registered with the state, because not all
groups of active citizens decide that it is necessary to register. Lev Po-
nomarev, head of the For Human Rights organization, explained, "Some
groups deliberately decline to seek registration, due to the bureaucratic red
tape involved In Moscow, for example, any organization with a zero balance
in its bank accounts only needs to report once a year."[164]

In analyzing the public's role in cultural preservation, philanthropy must
also be considered. According to I. M. Snegirev, a historian specializing in
nineteenth century Russia, charity was customary amongst the nobility: giving
of the *desiatina*, or "one-tenth", akin to the tithe in the West, survived until
1917.[165] Today, while philanthropy does not uniquely apply to the wealthy elites and businesses, until standards of living have improved for the general
population, it will generally be this elite class which will give to culture.[166] Philanthropy in Russia plays an important role, although is almost fully based on
the activities of business rather than individuals. According to Andrei Verbit-
sky, the publisher of a Moscow newsletter, *Socially Responsible Business*,
approximately two-thirds of all Russian businesses and almost all Russian
banks contribute to charities. Banks generally give in three realms: the arts,
the media and the poor.[167] To date, many big corporations are supporting culture. Donations from business make an estimated ten percent of the consoli-

---

[164]   Kornia, "The Justice Ministry Cleans Up Civil Society."
[165]   Gessen, "The Rebirth of Russian Charity," p. 125.
[166]   This generalization would exclude, naturally, donations given to religious institutions.
[167]   Gessen, "The Rebirth of Russian Charity," 124.

dated budget for culture, estimated Shvydkoi in 2004. "Earlier, people brought money to us and asked not to say from whom it came, and this was ubiquitous, because they were afraid that the tax service, bandits or somebody else could crack down on them," Shvydkoi said. "And these people do it absolutely unselfishly, as they do not get any tax privileges for that."[168] Pavel Zhuravlyov, the vice president of the Union of Charitable Organizations of Russia, clarified this point. He explained that because the knowledge of businesses' philanthropic activities was often exploited by the tax police or criminal elements in the 1990's, many companies gave clandestinely. "Now corporations publicize their philanthropy to improve relations with the government," Zhuravlyov said.[169] There are no statistics on businesses' social contributions as there is not a system to record the amount of donations given. It is clear, however, that increasing support is being given to religious institutions today, as they are seen as being more trustworthy than other organizations. The most popular charitable cause in post-Soviet Russia has been the reconstruction of the largest cathedral in Russia, the Cathedral of Christ the Saviour in Moscow. In addition to businesses wishing to project a positive corporate image, foreigners, especially those of Russian decent, have been playing an important role in creating and sustaining the nascent non-profit sector.[170]

---

[168]   Vladimir Kikilo, "Patrons of arts emerging in Russia - culture minister," *Itar-Tass Weekly News* 24/02/2004.

[169]   Maria Levitov, "Corporations Flaunt Their Social Conscience," *Moscow Times* 01/04/2004.

[170]   John Varoli, "In Russia, Charity Rides on Corporate Shoulders," *New York Times* 07/07/1999.

V.1 Taxation

Taxation is a key instrument with which to encourage private involvement in the public sphere. Russia's philanthropic community has the potential to be further strengthened and channelled if nurtured. Nurturing, in this sense, could take the form of excluding non-profit organizations, trusts, foundations and charities from taxation. It is important to foster these organizations as they are capable of performing functions which the government is often not. As seen in this excerpt of a report by Semyon Mikhailovsky, St. Petersburg Academy of Arts, written to the World Monument Fund (WMF), Russia's archaic taxation laws are problematic for non-profit activities. Mikhailovsky's report intended to update the WMF on the progress of the works at Arkhangel'skoe, including how the funds provided by the WMF were spent:

> Taxes are unavoidable, since the Russian law is completely ignorant of categories such as 'non-commercial', 'non-profit-making', etc. In other words, any money you transfer to Arkhangel'skoe will be subject to heavy taxation. It is not only the well-known philanthropist Mr. Soros who comes up against this severe and ugly system, but all who unthinkingly send money through banks without preliminary consultation with beneficiaries and without taking account of all the peculiarities of the Russian tax system. It was only thanks to a directive issued by the Russian government, for instance, that the palace at Tsarskoe selo was able to escape paying crippling taxes on the money it received from Rurhgas for restoration of the Amber Room.[171]

Tax policies and taxation in the field of culture are directed by two principal entities: the Ministry of the Russian Federation for Taxation and Payments and the Ministry of Culture. The *Taxation Code* and other laws which control economic activities are applied to the realm of culture and various other laws dictate the formation of charitable and non-governmental organizations. The federal law *On Charitable Activities and Charity Organizations* was

---

[171]   Semyon Mikhailovsky, *Report on a Visit to the Country Estate at Arkhangel'skoe* (Moscow: World Monuments Fund, 2000).

adopted in 1995 and was followed in 1996 by the law *On Non-Commercial Organizations*, which bestowed tax exemptions to private and semi-private organizations. However, with the ensuing financial crises, the state limited and later even abolished tax exemptions for cultural organizations. This occurred even though the legal regulations of state financing for culture were never enforced.[172] Thus, the financing of culture was left in a state of limbo; not enough was provided by the state, but the state blocked public efforts by reinstating taxation for non-profit organizations.

As exemplified by the short lives of the aforementioned laws, legal incentives for public-private partnerships remain at a very low level. Even with the government's demands on business to invest in social programmes, the tax breaks that encouraged corporate philanthropy were eliminated on 1 January 2002. Before this, companies could deduct their spending on social programs and charities up to three percent of their taxable income. "In an effort to make all companies equal under the law and combat tax evasion, the 2002 changes to the tax legislation cancelled all write-offs for social investments," said attorney Alla Tolmasova, author of the book *Problems of Taxation of Non-profit Organizations*.[173] The overarching fluidity of laws in the taxation sector had obstructed fundamental reform, including reforms for culture. To correct this imbalance, a new *Law on Maecenas and Maecenat Activities* is presently being reviewed.

Although the experience and policies of other countries cannot simply be transferred to another without adaptation to that country's historical circumstances, local situations and traditions, they can still provide useful guidelines. For example, the government of the United States of America has provided federal tax incentives for those who rehabilitate historic buildings since 1976. The programme defines rehabilitation as, "the process of returning a property to a state of utility, though repair or alteration, which makes possible an efficient contemporary use while preserving those portions and features of the property which are significant to its historic, architectural and cultural val-

---

[172]   Razologov and Fedorova, *Cultural Policies in Europe: A Compendium of Basic Facts and Trends,* 27.

[173]   Levitov, "Corporations Flaunt Their Social Conscience."

ues."[174] Currently, the federal income tax credit equals twenty percent of the cost of rehabilitating historic buildings, but these tax incentives apply only to certain buildings: it must be listed on the National Register for Historic Places or certified as a significant historic building, following rehabilitation the building must be used for income-producing objectives, the works conducted on the building must be substantial and the National Park Service must approve the completed renovation. Therefore, the goal of the tax credit is to convert these historic buildings into housing, commercial and retail units. In this sense, the programme is aimed at rehabilitation and not at restoration.

The standards used to evaluate the project must meet the Secretary of the Interior's Standards for Rehabilitation, which are based on the preservation principles enumerated in the UNESCO Venice Charter. These tax credits offered by the United States government are held in tandem with an accelerated annual depreciation awarded to all income-producing buildings; their values are reduced more quickly, allowing for greater tax write-offs.[175] Since 1976, the Historic Preservation Tax Incentives have produced the meaningful benefits: more than 31,000 historic properties have been rehabilitated and saved, the tax incentives have stimulated private rehabilitation of over $31 billion, more than 181,000 housing units have been rehabilitated and 137,000 housing units created, of which over 70,000 are low and moderate-income units.[176] The gains reaped by the programme has allowed for the creation of new construction jobs and housing for new businesses. Moreover, the rehabilitated buildings have led to substantial increases in state and local property tax revenue

This tax programme has been much more successful than targeted grants or federal subsidies. In this case, tax incentives have been more compelling than direct grants and are less expensive to the government. Government oversight helps ensure the preservation of the historic character of the building. The proposed project for a historic building must be economically viable. The government also must take on the task of promoting the tax credit

---

[174] *Definition of "rehabilitation"*, 2004, Available: http://www2.cr.nps.gov/TPS/tax/incentives/standards_1.htm, 14/04/2004 Access.

[175] H. Ward Jandl, *Preservation Tax Incentives in the United States* (Prague, Olomouc, Banská Štiavnica and Bratislava: World Monuments Fund, 1992), 38-39.

[176] *Federal Historic Preservation: Tax Incentives*, 2004, Available: http://www.cr.nps.gov/hps/tps/tax/index.htm, 13/04/2004 Access.

programme and provide direct assistance to investors. Using tax credits as a tool to aid the preservation of historic buildings is made more imperative because preservation work often is more costly than new construction.

Tax incentives, as seen in the context of the United States, have served as an effective tool in stimulating private investment in historic buildings; according to H. Ward Jandl's presentation at the World Monument Fund's Conference of Architectural Conservation in the Czech and Slovak Republics, over eighty percent of investors specified that they would not have undertaken the projects without the tax incentives.[177] Tax incentives therefore may be an inexpensive and politically feasible tool for Russia. However, particularly in Russia's case, tax incentives would need to become institutionalized, for if not, they risk being cut back in economically difficult times. This need has been recognized amongst the Russian authorities. In 2003 Shvydkoi commented, "We must create privileges for the people who take monuments and assume the very burdensome conditions for their operation."[178]

V.2   Organizations

Although we have discussed the shortage of non-governmental organizations in post-Soviet Russia, there are three organizations which deal specifically with estate preservation. These organizations are: the Society for the Study of the Russian Country Estate (OIRU), the Fund for the Revival of the Russian Estate, and the "Russian Estate" Fund. These organizations have, in various ways, played a meaningful role in research and estate preservation. Their actions have been especially salient in face of the government's incapability to effectively protect estates. Additionally, there are other organizations which are involved with general cultural preservation, such as VOOPIK.[179] Today VOOPIK is a lobby organization with a mix of cultural workers and amateurs with several territorial branches across the country. It is involved with the

---

[177]   Jandl, *Preservation Tax Incentives in the United States,* 41.

[178]   Karakhan and Revzin, "Pokazatel'noe vystuplenie. 'Podozrevat' menia v zhelanii zarabotat' na pamiatnikakh glupo'."

[179]   See a description of VOOPIK's creation and actions under the Soviet Union in the first chapter.

preservation of cultural and historical heritage.[180] This section, however, will focus on those organizations exclusively specializing in country estates.

The OIRU

The OIRU (*Obshchestvo izucheniia russkoi usad'by*), as presented in the introduction of this work, was re-established in 1992 after six decades of forced dormancy. The OIRU built on the intention to researching and publicising estate heritage and is oriented to the activity of the original organization (1922-1930). It is a non-profit organization, built on the intention to researching and publicising estate heritage.[181] The Society has amongst its ranks specialists in history, history of Russian art, museum workers, archivists and so forth, many of whom regularly report about their works at academic conferences. Valuable research work has been the crowning achievement of the Society.[182] Since 1992, the OIRU has hosted ten conferences, and has also been involved with numerous readings, congresses, and exhibitions.[183] For instance, in October 2003 the exhibition "Russian Estates: Past and Present" was held in the State Duma prepared by the OIRU, the Fund for the Revival of Russian Estate and in collaboration with workers from the State Museum of Architecture. Conferences have been held on various themes, including: the history of the estate, contemporary problems of estate preservation, the culture of the estate, the urban estate, the capital and the estate, and Pushkin and the Russian estate. However, the broad membership of this society is made up of amateurs, not professionals, who often take excursions to various estates and study the history of these monuments. The Society rarely participates in actual attempts to protect of estate heritage, since this, in their opinion, is a function of the specially authorised public bodies. Additionally, their members tend to be against privatization of estates.

---

[180]   Andreas Johannes Wiesand, ed., *Handbook of Cultural Affairs in Europe* (Baden-Baden: Nomos Verlagsgesellschaft, 1995).

[181]   The OIRU's website is at http://oiru.archeologia.ru/index.htm

[182]   *The Russian Estate* (*Russkaia Usad'ba*) is the annual publication of OIRU, *Russkaia usad'ba: sbornik Obshchestva izucheniia russkoi usad'by* (Moscow; Rybinsk: Izdatel'stvo "Rybinskoe podvor'e", 2001), vol. 7(23).

[183]   In each edition of *The Russian Estate* a chronicle of the society's activities is included.

The work of association is accomplished under the management of an elected administration. The chairmanship of the Society was held by the academic Ludmila Ivanovna, until her death in 2000. The current chairman is Yuri Vedenin, a doctor of geographical sciences and is the director of the Russian Scientific Research Institute of Cultural and Natural Heritage.

The "Russian Estate" Fund

A second Russian organization is the "Russian Estate" Fund (*Fond "Russkaia usad'ba"*), which was founded by the Russian Noble Council (*Rossii'skoe dvorianskoe sobranie*), the OIRU and the Institute of Cultural and National Heritage RAN. Like the OIRU, this organization is also involved with publishing and educational activities. The "Russian Estate" Fund published a detailed guide on 582 estates in Moscow's environs and a calendar entitled "The Wreath of Estates" (*Venok Usad'eb*). Like the OIRU, the "Russian Estate" Fund also conducts excursions. Nevertheless the main purpose of the Fund, in the opinion of its leaders Vera Sterlina and (until 2002) Vissarion Aliavdin, is to attempt to revive old estates and organize estate museums and cultural centres.[184] Stirlina has been heavily involved in several projects, including finding owners for specific estates. She has lobbied local and regional officials on behalf of those whom wish to acquire an estate.[185]

The Fund for the Revival of the Russian Estate and the National Fund for the Resurrection of Russian Estates

The Fund for the Revival of the Russian Estate (*Fond Vozrozhdeniia Russkoi Usad'by*) was founded in autumn 2000 and is oriented towards more pragmatic aspects of preservation vis-à-vis the OIRU. The principal activity of the Fund is to draw together public and private initiatives of estate preservation, but they are also involved with fostering tourist programmes.[186] The Fund includes at its "partners" federal, regional and local branches of government, museums, archives and libraries, public academic and cultural organizations

---

[184]   "Fond spaseniia russkoi usad'by," *Rossiiskie vesti* 20/12/2000.
[185]   Interview with Boris Fedorov, op. cit.
[186]   The Fund's web page, www.fovrus.ru, demonstrates its attempt to reach a broader audience. The "Russian Estate" Fund does not have an internet site.

and financial and commercial companies. The Fund and the OIRU often work closely together, and the Fund often collaborates with authors of articles in newspapers and periodicals. The fund has investigated and created a database of almost to 2000 estates. They also published the books *The Serednikovo Estate* and *The Estates of the Moscow Area*. In November 2002, to mark the tenth year anniversary of the OIRU, the Fund for the Resurrection of Russian Estates created photo exhibition 'The Russian Estates: the Past and Present' in the Shchusev Museum of Architecture, followed by an exhibition about Kuz'minki-Liublino in the State Duma and the Moscow City Duma. In 2005 the specialists at the Fund developed a project of support and development for Arkhangel'skoe.

In shifting the onus from the state to private individuals, the Fund for the Revival of the Russian Estate serves as a liaison between the state and private individuals wishing to purchase estates. In practice the Fund fulfils the functions of a specialised realtor agency. As described by the former President of Fund Mikhail Yatkovsky, the organization "works on the system of polygonal agreements, concluded with the local funds on control of property, the committees on culture and state organs on the protection of monuments" and manages information about the lawful status of estates and the surrounding land.[187] In cases of privatization, the Fund aids with legal and practical aspects of the transition: for example, preparing documents, helping reach agreements with the organs of protection of monuments and helping determine the boundaries of the estate's land. In the cases where an estate is leased to individuals or corporations, the Fund also serves as a mediator between the state (the leaser) and the leaseholders.[188] According to the Fund, it is involved with the preparation for proposals on the contemporary use of estate complexes, by taking into account the estates' geographical location, historical and cultural value, and special features of the surrounding landscape.[189]

Vissarion Aliavdin, currently the president of the National Fund for the Resurrection of Russian Estates, left his position as chairman of the admini-

---

[187]   Rudometkina, "Novye russkie bare: Poselit'sia v dvorianskoi usad'be ne tak uzh slozhno."

[188]   Sterlina, from the "Russian Estate" Fund, performs many of the same functions.

[189]   From the Fund's website, http://www.fovrus.ru/, 13/04/2003 Access.

stration of the "Russian Estate" Fund in November 2002 to become vice president (and from October 2003 - the president) of the Fund for the Revival of the Russian Estate. He explained, "Our fund attempts to connect four sides of the picture: the state and society, which are significant to cultural heritage, the monuments themselves and investors. Our fund conducts enlightenment work... We give advice on how to make better use of monuments and how to shift the concern about them from the state to private owners."[190] A central tenet of the Fund for the Revival of the Russian Estate is to attract investors. According to Aliavdin, "A club called 'The Friends of the Russian Estate' has been created and its tasks are obvious. Where there are friends, there are connections. The club will help the Fund find potential owners, investors, sponsors... In two years the Fund was able to draw the attention of wealthy people to the problem of the revival of the Russian estate, published several colourfully designed calendars, and has organized regular excursions to the 'the estate necklace of Russia.'"[191]

In January 2005, he broke from the Fund and created a second organization, adding the word "National" to the original organization's title, the National Fund for the Resurrection of the Russian Estate (*Natsionalny Fond "Vozrozhdenie Russkoi Usad'by"*). According to the current leaders of the original organization, Aliavdin was discharged at the end of 2004. The representatives of new National Fund, in turn, assert that no one dismissed them from the original organization. Dmitriy Oinas, Vice President of new organization, stated, "We wanted to enlarge the activity of fund, its founder was not agreeable. As far as name is concerned, the word combination the 'Resurrection of Russian Estates' is the theme of our work, not only the signboard. We added word 'National' to the name of the fund in order to emphasize our non-commercial essence."[192]

[190]   Ol'gin, "Nasledie: privatizatsiia istorii."
[191]   Olga Nikol'skaia, "Gde druz'ia - tam sviazi," *Vecherniaia Moskva* 19/06/2002.
[192]   Dmitrii Sokolov, "Investory zaputalis' v spasiteliakh russkikh usadeb," *Izvestiia* 18/05/2005.

Figure 13: Dolzhiki - orangerie, S. D. Golitsyn, Kharkov province (G. Lukomskii)

Conclusion

The future of Russia's remaining country estates is uncertain, despite the commitment pledged by governmental authorities.[193] This book has illustrated that the problems facing estates have less to do with residual prejudices stemming from Soviet ideology and more to do with other forms of inheritance of which formal and informal institutional inheritance have been the principle culprits. These Soviet legacies which impede the preservation of culture also include Russia's wavering institutional capacity. Overlapping controls in the sphere of the monument protection amongst ministries and other public organs have fostered the wide gap between policy and practice. These institutional actors continually compete for shifting and scarce resources, resulting in serious conflicts of intra-governmental interests to the detriment of cultural preservation. Institutional effectiveness is directly linked to the state's overall facility to command. The loss of autonomy and capacity in the state's implementation of cultural policy has had injurious results. Much as in the Soviet period, current relations between elites are still largely determined by means of contacts, *blat* and bribery and not through the precedent of the rule of law. Pervasive corruption is both symptomatic and a cause of weak formal institutions in face of ubiquitous informal relations, and this is true of many interactions in the cultural sphere.

For various reasons, the implementation of the rule of law in the Soviet Union was infrequent and post-Soviet Russia has inherited this general disregard for law. This disregard for legality has also stymied institutional capacity. Roosevelt epitomises the relationship between law and culture by drawing attention to those buildings, on which there are these marble plaques that say,

---

[193]   As indicated by Boris Fedorov, very little hope remains for Russia's country estates. The estate-museums which exist today may survive, but for those un-owned and desolate remainders, he believes that change will not occur quickly enough to save them. He contends that Russians, both officials and the public, lack the will or impetus to change the status quo. Interview with Boris Fedorov, op. cit.

'This is a monument of culture, damaging it is punishable by law.' As she noted, "theoretically they are protected, but legally, the long arm of the law is very short in rural areas."[194] In reality, Russia's inability to form a *pravovoe gosudarstvo*, or law governed state, greatly affects not only the protection afforded to monuments, but also the future of their privatization. Privatization of estates could offer tremendous opportunities for retaining and re-using historical buildings through their sale to responsible investors. Unable to afford maintenance costs, the St. Petersburg government recently announced that it is preparing to auction off several estates and palaces to prevent them from becoming derelict. Valentina Matvienko, the city's governor said it was the only way to save the decrepit mansions that were once the homes of pre-revolutionary Russia's most noted families.[195] However, if the state is incapable of creating and regulating "guarding agreements," privatization could also lead to the further destruction or neglect of estates. The prospect of removing the onus for estate preservation from the state has been born of necessity. The achievement of many of the state's professed goals has been greatly hampered by economic crises and general under-funding for preservation of patrimony.

Additionally, Russian civil society still tends to be weak; Soviet civil society was only beginning to emerge before 1991 and afterwards was not provided with strong foundations to expand upon. Historically, Russians have had very little familiarity with public participation in civic undertakings or with organizing public constituencies (groups of people interested in estate preservation did exist, but this was an exception rather than the rule). Efforts to build public support for various interests are today often viewed with suspicion. Nevertheless, despite the opposition, charitable donations are being made. At present, numerous large corporations are donating to culture, but to what degree is unknown. Putin lectured business leaders in November 2003, maintaining that they must "fully recognize their social duties" and develop "a system of new social guarantees for the population."[196] Since Putin's attack on YUKOS, culminating in the arrest of its' chief Mikhail Khodorkovsky in October 2003, it is possible that businesses may now feel new pressure to give

---

[194]   Elizabeth Wolfe, "A Struggle to Save Dying Heritage," *Moscow Times* 11/08/2000.

[195]   "St. Petersburg's palaces to be privatized," *United Press International* 21/04/2004.

[196]   Levitov, "Corporations Flaunt Their Social Conscience."

openly, in a bid to appease the state. Furthermore, despite popular disinclina-
tion to become involved, some amateurs and specialists have become involved with the preservation of country estates. The organizations involved
with estate preservation, the "Russian Estate" Fund, the Fund for the Revival
of the Russian Estate and the National Fund for the Revival of the Russian
Estate, have been formed to counter the dearth of institutions capable of
channelling the growing demand to preserve Russia's patrimony. These organizations look to aggregate group interests and represent the interests of
estates, and differ from the OIRU in that they seek both access to political
channels for expressing their demands and control over the outcome of estate preservation. It is important that these groups exist – in probing deeper
into their *raison d'être*, their ambition is not merely physical preservation, but
a concept of preserving a form of Russian self identity. These groups are
adamant about how estate culture affects Russians and their *Russianness*.
The creation and actions of these organizations could be seen not only as a
preservation movement but as an identity-based movement.

Russians generally attach great importance to the cultural achievements of pre-revolutionary Russia; the historical overview provided in this
book has shown that estates were instrumental in promoting art, music and
literature. Estates, having served as powerful agents of intellectual and artistic culture, are intimately bound with Russian culture and national identity.[197]

---

[197]   In his survey work on Russian self-identity, Timo Piirainen concluded that "a high
level of culture - and a pride in Russian culture - was widely acknowledged as a basic characteristic of the Russian people.... When the interviewees were asked to
mention especially important figures from Russian history, the names of writers and
composers were the ones that were mentioned most often. This reveals the importance of culture as a constituent of Russian national self-identity." Timo Piirainen,
"The Sisyphean Mission: New National Identity in Post-Communist Russia," *Imperial and National Identities in Pre-Revolutionary, Soviet, and Post-Soviet Russia*,
eds. Chris J. Chulos and Johannes Remy (Helsinki: Finnish Literary Society, 2002)
157.

Figure 14: Mikhailovskoe, M. Shcherbatov's estate in Yaroslavl province (Courtesy of the Yaroslavl State Historical Museum)

As with other monuments of cultural heritage, their mere existence contributes directly to this national identity and its orientation. In her work on charting out the "geography" of Russian identity through cognitive mapping, Kathleen Parthé has identified four different spatial schemata by which Russians define themselves: the imperial map of great Russia (*velikaia Rossiia*), the spiritual map marking sacred places, the internal and portable map and the symbolic map of idealised locations. Here, as a symbol exemplifying the "pure, unspoiled, even righteous" aspects of Russia's past, any perceived "harm or neglect" suffered by the actual estates of beloved writers, and even imaginary estates of fictional characters (such as the estate Oblomovka in Ivan Goncharov's novel *Oblomov*), "may threaten the well-being of Russia itself."[198] This reassertion of cultural identities may be even more important for a society contending with its Soviet legacy, which had fallen from a position as a world super-power into the difficult reality of an economy and polity in transition. In this sense, estate preservation as an aspect of policy, is of enormous importance for an inheritance is disappearing, one which future generations may value more highly.

Russian country estates formed the main assets of a social class whose status in Russian history is being re-examined. It is possible that these estates may once again become residences for Russia's new elite classes. Perhaps this tradition of individual charity will become revitalised, particularly as a sense of *noblesse oblige* amongst Russia's *nouveaux riches*, as a result of Russia's improving economic situation. In this context, estate preservation could once more become a defining feature of elite Russian identities. In addition, the question remains as to whether those Russians with financial means, principally the "new Russians" (*novye russkie*) would renovate country estates rather than construct the extravagant and vulgar dachas for which they have become infamous. Several articles in the Russian press have emphasised potential new social "status" involved with the renovation of estates, going as far as to claim that estates can re-enter their original purpose and serve as the seat of a new kind of "aristocratic" Russian. Banking on the fact that renovation is expensive can be used as an outward display of one's wealth. "It is good to create an association of owners of estates, which would

---

[198]   Kathleen Parthé, *Russia's "Unreal Estate": Cognitive Mapping and National Identity* (Washington, D.C.: Woodrow Wilson International Center for Scholars, 1997), 2-7.

become the club of people of moral and business, successful simultaneously", observed Chizhkov, the former vice president of the Fund for the Revival of the Russian Estate.[199] Lermontov, seconded this view, for he considered that the creation and strengthening of material welfare goes hand in hand with new ideas about the style of life, including defining how and where it is necessary to live, as well as the concept of creating a "family seat" for Russia's new "aristocracy."[200]

What Will Happen to the Country Estate? Questions about Preservation

The question remains as to what will happen to Russia's surviving country estates? Several suggestion have been put forth as to how estates can be used in Russia today. The principle suggestion is to reconvert estates into private residences, either as permanent abodes or as dachas.[201] According to the data of the Fund for the Revival of the Russian Estate, a demand for historic estates does exist. They believe that monuments of architecture and significant amounts of agricultural land actually can enter the market for elite real estate.[202] Lermontov thinks that the investors' current interest is only speculative because of uncertainty surrounding the subsequent resale of restored estates. However, Chizhkov deems that the secondary market will be formed in three or four years from now.[203] Closely associated with the private residences, estates could be purchased by corporations, and serve as recreation centres for the directors and guests of the company. Estates can be transformed into hotels, specialized clubs (for such rural pastimes as horse riding, hiking hunting, and so forth) or lodges. This has been the course of development for many of France's preserved chateaux, and could be particularly relevant in the estates located in the regions where horse breeding was tradi-

---

[199]   Iur'eva and Zharkov, "Novye pomeshchiki."

[200]   Bochkarev, "Istoriia ne prodaetsia. No ob usad'be stoit podumat'."

[201]   As the majority of estates are not located within commuting distance from Russia's principle financial centres, Fedorov thinks that the estate could be used as a *dal'nia dacha* or a third, and primarily a vacation, home. Interview with Boris Fedorov, op.cit.

[202]   Anni, "Sud'ba rezidentsii'."

[203]   Iur'eva and Zharkov, "Novye pomeshchiki."

tionally a strong enterprise. "Included in the composition of estates in the Orel, Penza, Kursk, Ryazan provinces, and in the south of the Moscow and Tula regions, mangers, stables and other infrastructure were preserved," reported Chizhkov. "All this can be restored."[204] Estates could also be converted to serve various uses as boarding schools, tourist complexes or rural cultural centres. In all of these cases, the Russian economic elite will play a crucial part in estate preservation.

The conference *The Russian Estate on the Eve of the 21st Century: Problems of Preservation and Survival*, hosted at Khmelita estate in the Smolensk *oblast* in the summer 2000, attracted specialists on estate preservation from throughout the world, and included many Russian experts. The participants at the conference created a list of six conclusions and recommendations as to what should be done for Russia's country estates. The first counsel was that a legislative framework must be developed that will encourage and support estate preservation. Second, an inventory of surviving estates is needed. This list should then be ordered by need, priority given on accordance of the importance and condition of the estate.[205] Third, they stressed that it should be born in mind that the museums are businesses. Historic properties create jobs for the local population, often to a significant level.

For those estates which have been transformed into museums, much of the estate's preservation and survival depend upon the directors themselves. Directors must take an active role in keeping abreast of new opportunities and take advantage of all available resources. Directors must also follow accountability standards, which is critical for attracting forthcoming prospects for international and private investment. Fourth, a clear system of ownership of Russia's cultural heritage is needed. Currently overlapping and conflicting interests amongst state institutions have directly impeded beneficial action. Fifth, although immediate solutions for the problems facing estates are not immediately forthcoming, measures can be taken to minimise the damage

---

[204]   Ibid.

[205]   Important inventories of estates are being undertaken in certain regions. For examples, see *Tverskaia usadba. Dvorianstvo. Gerby. Arkhivnye dokumenty, knigi, stati, fotografii. Putevoditel' XVIII-XX veka* (Tver': Tverskoi gosudarstvennyi' universitet, 2000). and E. N. Podiapol'skaia, *Pamiatniki arkhitektury Moskovskoi oblasti: illiustrirovannyi nauchnyi katalog*, 3 vols. (Moscow: Stroiizdat, 1998/1999).

done to estates without recourse to large amounts of funding. A stabilization programme, in which steps are taken to close up the house to prevent further deterioration, would be a practical measure. Stabilization would at least protect the house until such time that a restoration or adaptive re-use programme could be undertaken. Sixth, estate renovation must at all times serve local social and economic needs.[206] For rural estates in particular, the integration of the preservation of the estate with the requirements of the local populations is needed. Roosevelt used the estate of Khmelita as an exam ple, "...this area was a big dairy area, there are still lots of cows, and there were a lot of cheese factories before the Revolution. If Viktor [Kulakov – the director if Khmelita] succeeds in getting enough investment capital, his plan is to start reviving some of the same agricultural activity that used to go on in the area as a means of employing local people."[207] Mixed usage, by which rural museums sell farm produce or handicrafts, could provide support for museums inhibited by the chronic under-funding by the state.

---

[206]   Roosevelt, *The Russian Estate on the Eve of the 21st Century: Problems of Preservation and Survival.*

[207]   Wolfe, "A Struggle to Save Dying Heritage."

Figure 15: Khmelita, Smolensk oblast, 29 Oct. 1987

International Experience

Learning from other countries' experience in preserving culture is invaluable for the Russian government and people. As seen in Chapter Five, the central government plays only a small role in historic preservation in the United States. Also, the private sector's involvement in preservation is largely aided by tax incentives. Here, action is also fostered by allowing non-profit organizations to enjoy tax-exempt status. In France, on the other hand, the issue of preservation of country estates was achieved through a hybrid of government and private investment initiatives. This system stipulates that there will be greater tax benefits by increasing the availability of a heritage site to the public.

It is the preservation achievements in Great Britain, with the resounding success of the National Trust, which are most notable however. The Trust is a registered charity independent from the government, which protects and opens to the public over two hundred historic houses. Their sources of income are derived through membership fees (2.7 million members), shops (for period reproductions and crafts), hotels, restaurants, working farms, rent from interim use of properties, the production and sale of books and publications and donations.[208] Russia does not host an organization such as the British National Trust. Presently the fledgling organizations involved with the protection of Russia's country estates have not approached the scope or effectiveness of the British National Trust. The creation of a Russian National Trust, based on the applicable experience of other countries' previous efforts, seems to be an optimal, although distant, solution. Reducing governmental interference while boosting public participation would benefit these estates, which are currently wasting away under government tenure. The administration for estates could be delegated from the Ministry of Culture, which is very much under-funded and would hypothetically provide more flexibility than governmental institutions. The Trust would have three principle advantages over government ownership: it would attract donations, as people generally do not donate to the government; it would attract grass roots support, through volunteerism and membership; and as a well-established charity it would be

---

[208]   See the National Trust's website at http://www.nationaltrust.org.uk/main/ for more information.

easier to attract government grants. Careful utilisation of the historic buildings themselves could generate revenue. Cooperation between the Ministry of Culture and Information, lawmakers, the Ministry of Finance and active members of civil society would be a necessary step to establish the mechanisms for the formation of a Trust.[209]

However, there are many impediments to the creation of such an entity. As previously mentioned, there is a lack of background conducive to investment and to non-profit organizations. A national trust calls for the participation of the Russians themselves on a wide scale. Societal reluctance to volunteer hinders the formation of such an organization. The obstacles in face of a healthy tourist industry also directly deter the formation of a trust. Even if a Russian National Trust were to be formed, it would take years to build a membership whose fees could cover the budget.

Tourism

Attracting tourism may offer another solution in face of inadequate levels of state funding for culture. Tourism has continued to be one of the most profitable and intensively developing branches of the world economy. The World Tourism Organization's (WTO) *Tourism 2020 Vision* forecasts that, globally, international arrivals are expected to reach over 1.56 billion by the year 2020. The total tourist arrivals by region show that by 2020 the top receiving region will be Europe, including Russia, with an estimated 717 million tourists.[210] Additionally, according to *Russia in Figures* from 2002, the number of foreign citizens from non-CIS countries entering into Russia for tourist purposes has steadily increased.[211] This increase is tangible; Russia's former deputy minis-

---

[209]   Merlin Waterson, *Engaging the Public: The Experience of the National Trust* (Prague, Olomouc, Banská Štiavnica and Bratislava: World Monuments Fund, 1992).

[210]   *World Tourism Organization*, 2004, Available: http://www.world-tourism.org/index. htm, 08/04/2004 Access.

[211]   State Committee of the Russian Federation on Statistics, *Russia in Figures: Concise Statistical Handbook* (Moscow: Gosudarstvennyi komitet Rossiiskoi Federatsii po statistike, 2002) 135.

ter for economic development and trade, Vladimir Strzhalkovsky, reported that over eight million foreign tourists visited Russia in 2003.[212]

The development of tourism often plays an influential role in social and economic development patterns. In their study of the profitability of protecting British cultural heritage, Marcus Binney and Max Hanna stress that Britain's historic buildings are a major economic resource and an irreplaceable capital asset, which contribute significantly through tourism to earnings of foreign exchange, to local employment and prosperity and to central government taxation. As a result of tourism, small country villages can continue as viable economic units and country crafts are given a better chance of survival. The pair conducted market research in two historic towns dominated by great houses - Arundel and Woodstock. Both towns were heavily dependent on tourism, and several jobs stemmed directly from the opening of these houses, such as guides, cleaners, gardeners and maintenance. Secondary establishments, such as hotels, restaurants, pubs and shops also depended enormously on the local manor house.[213] In addition, strategic planning becomes important as links between the major cities and the provinces need to be fostered. Tourism as a whole represents a branch of the economy, which permits rather small capital investments to aid in the economic use of "local resources" - historic-cultural heritage, traditions and nature.

It is feasible that estates can play their part in Russia's budding tourist industry. In August 2003 the Committee of Tourism of the Moscow Region established a new tour-project named "The Pushkin Ring of the Moscow Area." This tourist network is to link places associated with the famous writer, including several estates. The tourist potential for estates in the Moscow area, in the opinion of specialists, has hardly been realized. This holds especially true for and cognitive and literary tourism, subdivisions of tourism into which estates could be integrated.[214] International efforts to promote Russia's cultural tourist initiatives have been undertaken. For instance, the Colonial Williams-

---

[212]   "Over 8 mln foreign tourists visit Russia in 2003," *Itar-Tass Weekly News* 29/01/04. Vladimir Strzhalkovsky is now the head of the Federal Tourist Agency.

[213]   Marcus Binney and Max Hanna, *Preservation Pays: Tourism and the Economic Benefits of Conserving Historic Buildings* (London: Save Britain's Heritage, 1978) 77.

[214]   Marina Zakharova, "A uchit' budet Pushkin liubit' prekrasnoe, dobroe, vechnoe," *Moskovskii komsomolets* 11/08/2003.

burg Foundation hosted a conference on Cultural Tourism Development in Russia in November 1998. "Russia is in the midst of a defining moment politically as well as culturally, and the fact that they were willing to send such a prominent delegation to the conference demonstrates Russia's commitment to cultural tourism," said Colonial Williamsburg President Robert Wilburn. "Given the crossroads in which they find themselves, we believe it fitting that the Russian officials gathered in this historic town to discuss their vision for future development of this vital industry." The primary focus of the conference concerned the business and infrastructural development necessary to support the growth of Russian cultural tourism.[215] Another initiative is the Russian Heritage Highway, a recent international effort dedicated to economic development and diversity in European Russia.[216] This programme will focus its attention on the 700-kilometre route from Moscow to St. Petersburg, which passes through the historic Tver and Velikiy Novgorod regions. Major funding is expected to be acquired through incentive cultural and infrastructure appropriations from the European Union and United Nations. Additional funding will be provided from the Russian government as well as from the regional and local governments along the route.[217]

In spite of the efforts being made, both in Russia and abroad, to increase tourism, there still exist major inhibitors to creating a viable tourist industry. A flow of the negative information in foreign press about Russia has not aided Russia's tourist industry. Tourism is still inhibited by several barriers: a strict visa system, especially for tourists from countries which have imposed their own entry restrictions of Russians, a poor tourist and travel infrastructure, the fact that most visitors do not have knowledge of the Russian language and the Cyrillic script, and that there is little signposting and infor-

---

[215]   The Colonial Williamsburg Foundation, *Cultural Tourism Development in Russia* (Williamsburg: 1998).

[216]   Mikhail Gorbachev, the former Premier of the Supreme Soviet and President of the Soviet Union, was there to promote the Highway's institutional founding in Las Vegas. The Russian Heritage Highway (RHH) was conceived by Thomas Tait, the former CEO of the Nevada Commission on Tourism and the current Vice President of the multibillion dollar Lake Las Vegas Resort project. Tait is also a consultant on tourism to Eastern Europe, and has been elected President of the RHH Foundation.

[217]   "Mikhail Gorbachev Comes to Nevada This Weekend to Introduce New Tourism Initiative to the World," *PRNewswire* 17/03/2004.

mation in foreign languages. All of these problems are amplified in rural Russia.

Figure 16: Interior Niche of a Russian Estate

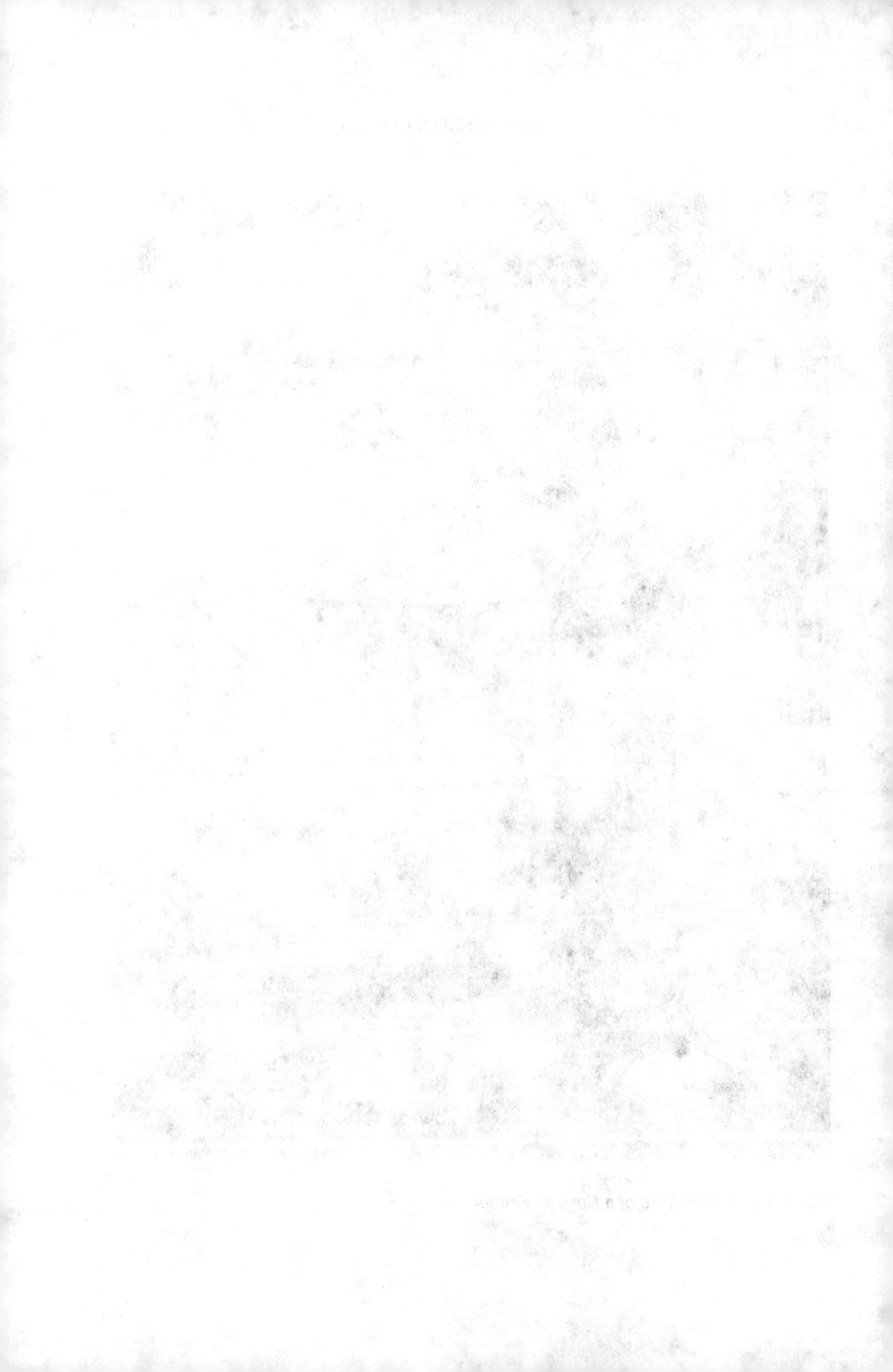

Bibliography

Personal Interviews

Viktor Dlugach, Director of Arkhangel'skoe Estate-Museum, Moscow, 12/08/2003

Boris Fedorov, and former Deputy Prime Minister and Minister of Finance of Russia, London, 19/04/2004

Lia Lepskaya, Theatre Director at Ostankino Estate-Museum, Moscow, 9/08/2003

Prince and Princess Obolensky, Washington D.C., 10/12/2003

Viktor Oudovechenko, UNESCO Chair in Urban and Architectural Conservation, Moscow, 19/8/2003

Priscilla Roosevelt, Author of *Life on the Russian Country Estate : A Social and Cultural History* and director of the organization American Friends of Russian Country Estates, Washington D.C., 12/2003

Valeri Shestakov, National Programme Officer for Culture of the UNESCO Moscow office, Moscow, 12/08/2003

Russian Periodicals

Argumenty i fakty
Biulleten' Schetnoi palaty Rossiiskoi Federatsii
Dom gazeta
Ekho Moskvy
Elit Dom
Ezhenedel'nyi zhurnal
Gazeta
Inter'er+dizai'n
Itar-Tass Weekly News
Itogi
Izvestiia (Rossiia)
Kommersant-Daily
Kommersant-Vlast'
Konservator
Krasnaia zvezda
Kul'tura
Mir i Dom
Moskovskaia pravda
Moskovskii komsomolets
Moscow Times
Nashe nasledie
Nezavisimaia gazeta
Novaia gazeta
Novye Izvestiia
Obshchaia gazeta
Official Kremlin International News Broadcast
Pamiatniki Otechestva
Parlamentskaia gazeta
Rossiia
Rossiiskaia gazeta
Rossiiskie vesti
Russkii' Fokus
Russkii Telegraf

Salon" nedvizhimosti
Slovo
Trud
Vedomosti
Vecherniaia Moskva
Versiia
Vremia MN
Vremia novostei
Zhizn' v usad'be

Other Periodicals

American Benefactor
Business Week
Christian Science Monitor
Milwaukee Journal Sentinel
New York Times
Russian Review
PRNewswire
United Press International
Washington Post

Books in Russian

Mir russkoi usad'by. Moscow: Moskva Nauka, 1995.

Usadebnoe ozherel'e iugo-zapada Moskvy. Moscow: Mosgorarkhiv, 1997.

Turizm v Rossii: Ofitsial'noe izdanie. Moscow: Gosudarstvennyi komitet Rossiiskoi Federatsii po statistike, 2000.

Chalaia, I. P., Vedenin, Iu. A. *Kulturno-landshaftnoe rai'onirovanie tverskoi oblasti.* Moscow: Nauchnoe Izdanie, 1997.

A. B. Chizhkov. *Podmoskovniue Usad'biu Segodnia: Putevoditel' s kartoi'-skhemoi'.* Moscow: AIRO-XX, 2000.

Dal', V. I. *Tolkovyi' slovar' zhivago velikoruskago iazyka.* 2 ed. Vol. 4. 4 vols. St. Petersburg; Moscow, 1882.

Evangulova, O. S. *Khudozhestvennaia "vselennaia" russkoi usad'by.* Moscow: Progress Traditsiia, 2003.

Ivanova, L. V. *Russkaia usad'ba v istorii otechestva. Istochniki po istorii russkoi usadebnoi kul'tury.* Moscow, 1999.

---, ed. *Dvorianskaia i kupecheskaia usad'ba v Rossii XVI-XX vv.: istoricheskie ocherki.* Moscow: URSS, 2001.

Kazhdan, T. P. *Khudozhestvennyi mir russkoi usad'by.* Moscow: Traditsiia, 1997.

Obshchestvo izucheniia russkoi usad'by. "Russkaia usad'ba: sbornik Obshchestva izucheniia russkoi usad'by." Moscow; Rybinsk: Izdatel'stvo "Rybinskoe podvor'e", 1994. Vol. 1(17).

---. *"Russkaia usad'ba: sbornik Obshchestva izucheniia russkoi usad'by."* Moscow; Rybinsk: Izdatel'stvo "Rybinskoe podvor'e", 1997. Vol. 3(19).

---. *"Russkaia usad'ba: sbornik Obshchestva izucheniia russkoi usad'by."* Moscow; Rybinsk: Izdatel'stvo "Rybinskoe podvor'e", 1998. Vol. 4(20).

---. *"Russkaia usad'ba: sbornik Obshchestva izucheniia russkoi usad'by."* Moscow; Rybinsk: Izdatel'stvo "Rybinskoe podvor'e", 1999. Vol. 5(21).

---. *"Russkaia usad'ba: sbornik Obshchestva izucheniia russkoi usad'by."* Moscow; Rybinsk: Izdatel'stvo "Rybinskoe podvor'e", 2000. Vol. 6(22).

---. *"Russkaia usad'ba: sbornik Obshchestva izucheniia russkoi usad'by."* Moscow; Rybinsk: Izdatel'stvo "Rybinskoe podvor'e", 2001. Vol. 7(23).

---. *"Russkaia usad'ba: sbornik Obshchestva izucheniia russkoi usad'by."* Moscow; Rybinsk: Izdatel'stvo "Rybinskoe podvor'e", 2001. Vol. 8(24).

---. *"Russkaia usad'ba: sbornik Obshchestva izucheniia russkoi usad'by."* Moscow; Rybinsk: Izdatel'stvo "Rybinskoe podvor'e", 2001. Vol. 9(25).

Petrikov A., Uzin V. *"Zemel'nii otnosheniia: problemy i reshenia."* APK: Ekonomika, upravlenie 6 (1999).

Podiapol'skaia, E. N. *Pamiatniki arkhitektury Moskovskoi oblasti: illiustrirovannyi nauchnyi katalog.* Vol. 1. 3 vols. Moscow: Stroiizdat, 1998.

---. *Pamiatniki arkhitektury Moskovskoi oblasti: illiustrirovannyi nauchnyi katalog.* Vol. 2. 3 vols. Moscow: Stroiizdat, 1999.

---. *Pamiatniki arkhitektury Moskovskoi oblasti: illiustrirovannyi nauchnyi katalog.* Vol. 3. 3 vols. Moscow: Stroiizdat, 1999.

Prentice,R. *Opyt stanovleniia i razvitiia kul'turnogo turizma: uchebnoe posobie* (Experiential Cultural Tourism). 2nd ed. St. Petersburg: Izdatel'stvo Sankt-Peterburgskogo gosudarstvennogo universiteta ekonomiki i finansov, 2001.

Prokhorov, A. M., ed. *Bol'shaia Sovetskaia Entsiklopediia.* 3rd ed. Vol. 27. Moscow: Sovetskaia Entsiklopediia, 1977.

Shmidt, O. I., ed. *Bol'shaia Sovetskaia Entsiklopediia.* 1st ed. Moscow: Gosudarstvennyi Institut "Sovetskaia Entsiklopediia", 1936.

Sluon'kova, I. N. et al. *Russkaia usad'ba v starinnoi' otkrytke: Al'bom s annotirovannium ukazatelem.* Moscow: Profis, 2003.

Tikhonov, Y. A., Ivanova, L. V. *Mir russkoi usad'by: ocherki.* Moscow: Nauka, 1995.

Tverskoi Gosudarstvennyi Universitet. Tverskaia usadba. Dvorianstvo.
Gerby: Arkhivnye dokumenty, knigi, stati, fotografii. Putevoditel' XVIII-XX veka. Tver: Tverskoi Gosudarstvennyi Universitet, 2000.

Vvedensky, B. A., ed. *Bol'shaia Sovetskaia Entsiklopediia.* 2nd ed. Vol. 44. Moscow: Gosudarstvennoe nauchnoe izdatel'stvo, 1956.

Zlochevskii', G. D. *Russkaia usad'ba: istoriko-bibliograficheskii' obzor literatury, 1787-1992.* Moscow: Institut naslediia, 2003.

Other Sources

AlSayyad, N. *Consuming Tradition, Manufacturing Heritage: Global Norms and Urban Forms in the Age of Tourism.* London: Routledge, 2001.

Ashworth, G. J., Tunbridge, J. E. *The Tourist-Historic City: Retrospect and Prospect of Managing the Heritage City.* Advances in Tourism Research Series. Amsterdam; Oxford: Pergamon, 2000.

Binney, M., Hanna, M. *Preservation Pays: Tourism and the Economic Benefits of Conserving Historic Buildings.* London: Save Britain's Heritage, 1978.

Brown, I., Andersen, V., Gordin, V. E., eds. *Cultural Tourism: The Convergence of Tourism and Culture at the Start of the 21st Century.* St. Petersburg, Edinburgh: St. Petersburg State University of Economics and Finance; Queen Margaret University College, 2000.

Bunce, V. *Subversive Institutions: The Design and the Destruction of Socialism and the State.* Cambridge: Cambridge University Press, 1999.

P. Burns. "Tourism in Russia: Background and Structure." *Tourism Management* 19.6 (1998): 555-65.

Chulos C. J., Remy J., eds. *Imperial and National Identities in Pre-Revolutionary, Soviet, and Post-Soviet Russia.* Helsinki: Finnish Literary Society, 2002.

Cohen J., Arato, A. *Civil Society and Political Theory.* Cambridge, MA: MIT Press, 1992.

Colloquy on Sustainable Tourism Development (1996: Maribor Slovenia). *Sustainable Tourism Development: Conciliation of Economic, Cultural, Social, Scientific and Environmental Interests.* Environmental Encounters. Vol. 34. Strasbourg: Council of Europe, 1997.

Committee for Tourism of the Moscow City Government. "Comprehensive Program of Development of Tourism in the City of Moscow." Moscow, 1998 of *The Attachment to the Order of the Mayor of Moscow.*

Dax, O. D. *On the Estate: Memoirs of Russia before the Revolution.* London: Thames and Hudson, 1986.

Diamond, L. "Rethinking Civil Society: Towards Democratic Consolidation." *Journal of Democracy* 5.3 (1994): 4-17.

European Commission Tourism Unit. *Using Natural and Cultural Heritage to*

Develop Sustainable Tourism in Non-Traditional Tourist Destinations. Luxembourg: Office for Official Publications of the European Communities, 2003.

European Commission. Directorate General for Research. *Endangered Heritage. European Research in Action.* Luxembourg: Office for Official Publications of the European Communities, 2000.

Fish, M. S. *Democracy from Scratch: Opposition and Regime in the New Russian Revolution.* Princeton: Princeton University Press, 1995.

Gitelman, Z. Y., Pravda, A., White, S., eds. *Developments in Russian politics 5.* 5 ed. Basingstoke: Palgrave, 2001.

Graham, B. J., Tunbridge, J. E., Ashworth, G. J. *A Geography of Heritage: Power, Culture and Economy.* London: Arnold, 2000.

Gubenko, N. N. *Conclusion of the Committee on Culture and Tourism on the Draft of the Federal Law "On the Federal Budget for 2002".* Moscow: Committee of Culture and Tourism of the State Duma of the Russian Federation, 2001.

Howard, M. M. *The Weakness of Civil Society in Post-Communist Europe.* Cambridge: Cambridge University Press, 2003.

International Council on Monuments and Sites. *Heritage & Tourism: ICOMOS European Conference, Canterbury, University of Kent, 27th-30th March 1990.* London: International Council on Monuments & Sites, 1990.

Jandl, H. W. "Preservation Tax Incentives in the United States." Trans. SRI International and the Trust for Mutual Understanding Samuel H. Kress Foundation. *Architectural Conservation in the Czech and Slovak Republics.* Prague, Olomouc, Banská Štiavnica and Bratislava: World Monuments Fund, 1992. 37-42.

Kirshenblatt-Gimblett, B. *Destination Culture: Tourism, Museums, and Heritage.* Berkeley; London: University of California Press, 1998.

Ledeneva, A. *Russia's Economy of Favours: Blat, Networking, and Informal Exchange.* Cambridge: Cambridge University Press, 1998.

Linz, J. J., Stepan A. C. *Problems of Democratic Transition and Consolidation: Southern Europe, South America, and Post-Communist Europe.* Baltimore; London: Johns Hopkins University Press, 1996.

Lovell, S. *Summerfolk: A History of the Dacha, 1710-2000.* Ithaca, NY: Cornell University Press, 2003.

Mandler, P. *The Fall and Rise of the Stately Home*. New Haven, CT; London: Yale University Press, 1997.

McFaul, M. "State Power, Institutional Change, and the Politics of Privatization in Russia." *World Politics* 47.2 (1995): 210-43.

Mikhailovsky, S. *Report on a Visit to the Country Estate at Arkhangel'skoe*. Moscow: World Monuments Fund, 2000.

Nabokov, V. V. *Speak, Memory: An Autobiography Revisited*. Everyman's Library. Revised and expanded ed. London: David Campbell, 1999.

O'Brien, D. J., Wegren, S. K. *Rural Reform in Post-Soviet Russia*. Baltimore, MD; London: Woodrow Wilson Center Press, 2002.

Orbasli, A. *Tourists in Historic Towns: Urban Conservation and Heritage Management*. London; New York: E&FN Spon, 2000.

Parrott, B., Dawisha, K., eds. *Democratic Changes and Authoritarian Reactions in Russia, Ukraine, Belarus and Moldova*. Cambridge: Cambridge University Press, 1997.

Parthé, K. *Russia's "Unreal Estate": Cognitive Mapping and National Identity*. Washington, DC: Woodrow Wilson International Center for Scholars, 1997.

Preuss, U. K., Offe, C., Elster, J. *Institutional Design in Post-Communist Societies: Rebuilding the Ship*. Theories of Institutional Design. Cambridge: Cambridge University Press, 1998.

Razologov, K., Fedorova T. *Cultural Policies in Europe: A Compendium of Basic Facts and Trends*. Strasbourg, Bonn: Council of Europe/ERICarts, 2003.

Robinson, M., Andersen, H. C. *Literature and Tourism*. London: Continuum, 2002.

Robinson, N., ed. *Institutions and Political Change in Russia*. Basingstoke: Macmillan, 2000.

Roosevelt, P. R. *Life on the Russian Country Estate: A Social and Cultural History*. New Haven, CT; London: Yale University Press, 1995.

---, ed. "The Russian Estate on the Eve of the 21st Century: Problems of Preservation and Survival." Khmelita Estate, Smolensk Oblast, 2000.

Sakwa, R. *Russian Politics and Society*. 2 ed. London: Routledge, 1996.

Smith, M. K. *Issues in Cultural Tourism Studies*. London: Routledge, 2003.

State Committee of the Russian Federation on Statistics. *Russia in Figures:*

Concise Statistical Handbook. Moscow: Gosudarstvennyi komitet Rossiiskoi Federatsii po statistike, 1999.

---. *Russia in Figures: Concise Statistical Handbook.* Moscow: Gosudarstvennyi komitet Rossiiskoi Federatsii po statistike, 2000.

---. *Russia in Figures: Concise Statistical Handbook.* Moscow: Gosudarstvennyi komitet Rossiiskoi Federatsii po statistike, 2001.

---. *Russia in Figures: Concise Statistical Handbook.* Moscow: Gosudarstvennyi komitet Rossiiskoi Federatsii po statistike, 2002.

---. *Russia in Figures: Concise Statistical Handbook.* Moscow: Gosudarstvennyi komitet Rossiiskoi Federatsii po statistike, 2003.

The Colonial Williamsburg Foundation. "Cultural Tourism Development in
Russia." Williamsburg, 1998.

The World Bank. *Anticorruption in Transition: A Contribution to the Policy Debate.* Washington DC, 2000.

Timothy, D. J., Boyd, S. W. *Heritage Tourism: Themes in Tourism.* Harlow:
Prentice Hall, 2003.

UK Trade & Investment. *Tourism, Heritage and Museums: British Expertise.*
London: UK Trade & Investment, 2003.

UN Economic Commission for Europe. *The Land Administration Review of
the Russian Federation.* Geneva: UN Economic Commission for
Europe, 2004.

Urban, M. E. *The Rebirth of Politics in Russia.* Cambridge: Cambridge University Press, 1997.

Walle, A. H. *Cultural Tourism: A Strategic Focus.* Boulder, CO; Oxford: West-
view Press, 1998.

Waterson, M. "Engaging the Public: The Experience of the National Trust."
Trans. SRI International and the Trust for Mutual Understanding Sam-
uel H. Kress Foundation. *Architectural Conservation in the Czech and
Slovak Republics.* Prague, Olomouc, Banská Štiavnica and Bratislava:
World Monuments Fund, 1992. 83-91.

Wegren, S. K. *Trends in Russian Agrarian Reform*: RFE/RL, 1993.

Wegren, S. K., O'Brien, D. J., eds. *Rural Reform in Post-Soviet Russia.*
Washington, DC: Woodrow Wilson Center Press, 2002.

Weigel, M. A. *Russia's Liberal Project: State-Society Relations in the Transition from Communism.* University Park, PA: Pennsylvania State Univer-

sity Press, 2000.

White, A. "The Memorial Society in the Russian Provinces." *Europe-Asia Studies* 47.8 (1995): 1343-46.

Wiesand, A. J., ed. *Handbook of Cultural Affairs in Europe*. Baden-Baden: Nomos Verlagsgesellschaft, 1995.

Wirtschafter, E. K. "In Search of the People, In Search of Russia." *The Russian Review* 60.October 2001 (2001): 497-504.

Wuthnow, R., ed. *Between States and Markets: The Voluntary Sector in Comparative Perspective*. Princeton, NJ: Princeton University Press, 1991.

Yale, P. *From Tourist Attractions to Heritage Tourism*. 2nd ed. Huntingdon: ELM Publications, 1997.

Appendices

Appendix I: Diagram of the Federal Institutions Involved with Culture, before the 2004 reforms[218]

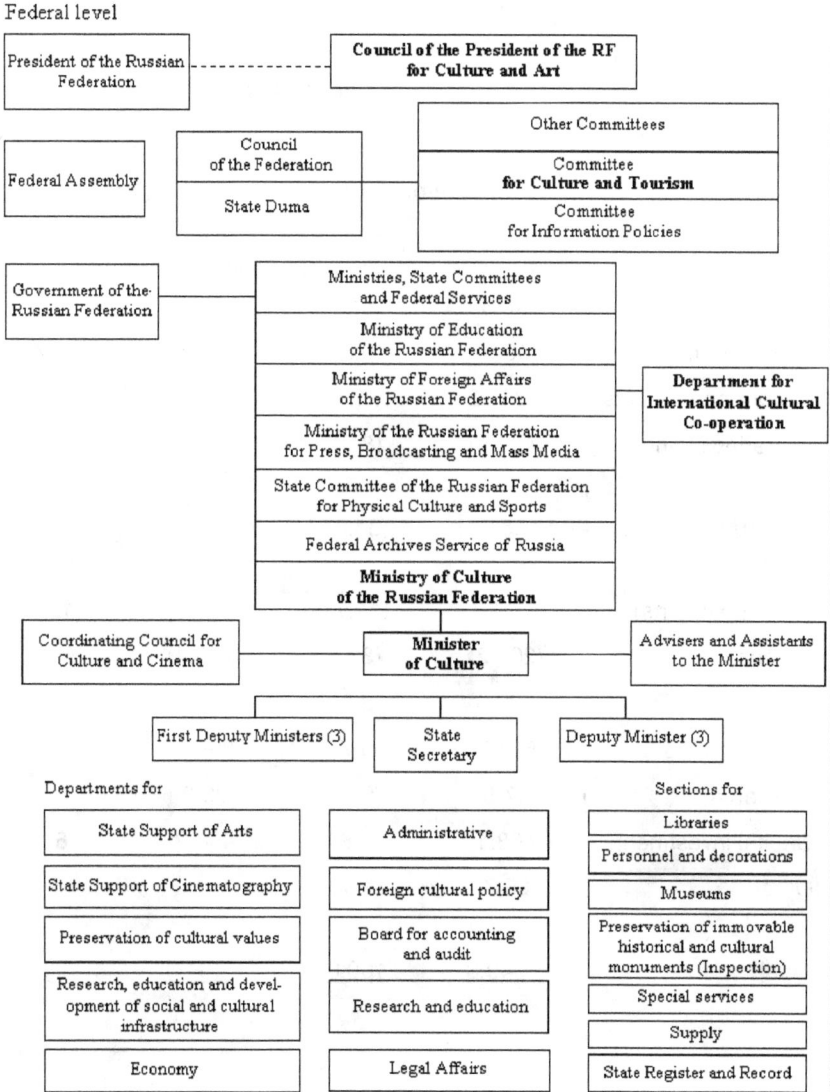

Federal level

| President of the Russian Federation | - - - - - - - - - | Council of the President of the RF for Culture and Art |

| Federal Assembly | Council of the Federation |
| | State Duma |

Other Committees

Committee for Culture and Tourism

Committee for Information Policies

| Government of the Russian Federation | Ministries, State Committees and Federal Services |

Ministry of Education of the Russian Federation

Ministry of Foreign Affairs of the Russian Federation

Ministry of the Russian Federation for Press, Broadcasting and Mass Media

Department for International Cultural Co-operation

State Committee of the Russian Federation for Physical Culture and Sports

Federal Archives Service of Russia

Ministry of Culture of the Russian Federation

| Coordinating Council for Culture and Cinema | **Minister of Culture** | Advisers and Assistants to the Minister |

| First Deputy Ministers (3) | State Secretary | Deputy Minister (3) |

Departments for

Sections for

State Support of Arts	Administrative	Libraries
		Personnel and decorations
State Support of Cinematography	Foreign cultural policy	Museums
Preservation of cultural values	Board for accounting and audit	Preservation of immovable historical and cultural monuments (Inspection)
Research, education and development of social and cultural infrastructure	Research and education	Special services
		Supply
Economy	Legal Affairs	State Register and Record

---

[218]   Chart from Razologov and Fedorova, *Cultural Policies in Europe: A Compendium of Basic Facts and Trends.*

Appendix II: Public cultural expenditure: sector breakdown for the Ministry of Culture, 2000/2001[219]

Field	Federal level			
	2000		2001	
	Total in million RUB	% share of total	Total in million RUB	% share of total
Administration	46.0	0.8	51.2	0.7
Culture and the arts	4 317.2	71.5	5 006.5	69.6
(Libraries maintenance)	(499.5)	(8.3)	(629.9)	(8.8)
(Museums maintenance)	(2 051.1)	(34.0)	(2 263.7)	(31.5)
(Performing arts)	(704.3	(11.7)	(883.6)	(12.3)
(Circus)	(207.2)	(3.4)	(286.4)	(4.0)
Cinema	528.6	8.8	710.0	9.9
Education (arts)	586.7	9.7	899.7	12.5
Research	27.5	0.5	33.2	0.5
Capital investment	468.1	7.8	494.2	6.9
Other	66.7	1.1	-	-
Total	6 040.8	100.0	7 194.8	100.0

---

[219]   Ministry of Culture of the RF, "Funding for the Institutions of Culture, Arts and Cinema by the Ministry of Cultural of the RF," *Cultural Policy Orientations* (Moscow: 2001).

Appendix III: Kuskovo: one of the best preserved estates in Moscow, undergoing upkeep, summer 2004

Dr. Andreas Umland (Ed.)

SOVIET AND POST-SOVIET
POLITICS AND SOCIETY

ISSN 1614-3515

This book series makes available, to the academic community and general public, affordable English-, German- and Russian-language scholarly studies of various *empirical* aspects of the recent history and current affairs of the former Soviet bloc. The series features narrowly focused research on a variety of phenomena in Central and Eastern Europe as well as Central Asia and the Caucasus. It highlights, in particular, so far understudied aspects of late Tsarist, Soviet, and post-Soviet political, social, economic and cultural history from 1905 until today. Topics covered within this focus are, among others, political extremism, the history of ideas, religious affairs, higher education, and human rights protection. In addition, the series covers selected aspects of post-Soviet transitions such as economic crisis, civil society formation, and constitutional reform.

SOVIET AND POST-SOVIET POLITICS AND SOCIETY

Edited by Dr. Andreas Umland

ISSN 1614-3515

29   *Florian Strasser*
      Zivilgesellschaftliche Einflüsse auf die Orange Revolution
      Die gewaltlose Massenbewegung und die ukrainische Wahlkrise 2004
      Mit einem Vorwort von Egbert Jahn
      ISBN 3-89821-648-9

30   *Rebecca S. Katz*
      The Georgian Regime Crisis of 2003-2004
      A Case Study in Post-Soviet Media Representation of Politics, Crime and Corruption
      ISBN 3-89821-413-3

31   *Vladimir Kantor*
      Willkür oder Freiheit
      Beiträge zur russischen Geschichtsphilosophie
      Ediert von Dagmar Herrmann sowie mit einem Vorwort versehen von Leonid Luks
      ISBN 3-89821-589-X

32   *Laura A. Victoir*
      The Russian Land Estate Today
      A Case Study of Cultural Politics in Post-Soviet Russia
      With a foreword by Priscilla Roosevelt
      ISBN 3-89821-426-5

FORTHCOMING (MANUSCRIPT WORKING TITLES)

Nicola Melloni
The Russian 1998 Financial Crisis and Its Aftermath
An Etherodox Perspective
ISBN 3-89821-407-9

Stephanie Solowyda
Biography of Semen Frank
ISBN 3-89821-457-5

Margaret Dikovitskaya
Arguing with the Photographs
Russian Imperial Colonial Attitudes in Visual Culture
ISBN 3-89821-462-1

Stefan Ihrig
Welche Nation in welcher Geschichte?
Eigen- und Fremdbilder der nationalen Diskurse in der Historiographie und den Geschichtsbüchern in der Republik
Moldova, 1991-2003
ISBN 3-89821-466-4

Sergei M. Plekhanov
Russian Nationalism in the Age of Globalization
ISBN 3-89821-484-2

Михаил Лукянов
Российский консерватизм и реформа, 1905-1917
ISBN 3-89821-503-2

Robert Pyrah
Cultural Memory and Identity
Literature, Criticism and the Theatre in Lviv - Lwow - Lemberg, 1918-1939 and in post-Soviet Ukraine
ISBN 3-89821-505-9

Dmitrij Chmelnizki
Die Architektur Stalins
Ideologie und Stil 1929-1960
ISBN 3-89821-515-6

Andrei Rogatchevski
The National-Bolshevik Party
ISBN 3-89821-532-6

Zenon Victor Wasyliw
Soviet Culture in the Ukrainian Village
The Transformation of Everyday Life and Values, 1921-1928
ISBN 3-89821-536-9

Nele Sass
Das gegenkulturelle Milieu im postsowjetischen Russland
ISBN 3-89821-543-1

Josette Baer
Preparing Modernity in Central Europe
Political Thought and the Independent Nation State
ISBN 3-89821-546-6

Ivan Katchanovski
Cleft Countries
Regional Political Divisions and Cultures in Post-Soviet Ukraine and Moldova
ISBN 3-89821-558-X

Julie Elkner
Maternalism versus Militarism
The Russian Soldiers' Mothers Committee
ISBN 3-89821-575-X

Maryna Romanets
Displaced Subjects, Anamorphosic Texts, Reconfigured Visions
Improvised Traditions in Contemporary Ukrainian and Irish Literature
ISBN 3-89821-576-8

Alexandra Kamarowsky
Russia's Post-crisis Growth
ISBN 3-89821-580-6

Martin Friessnegg
Das Problem der Medienfreiheit in Russland seit dem Ende der Sowjetunion
ISBN 3-89821-588-1

Florian Mühlfried
Postsowjetische Feiern
Das Georgische Bankett im Wandel
ISBN 3-89821-601-2

Nikolaj Nikiforowitsch Borobow
Führende Persönlichkeiten in Russland vom 12. bis 20 Jhd.: Ein Lexikon
Aus dem Russischen übersetzt und herausgegeben von Eberhard Schneider
ISBN 3-89821-638-1

Anton Burkov
The Impact of the European Convention for the Protection of Human Rights and Fundamental
Freedoms on Russian Law
ISBN 3-89821-639-X

Katsiaryna Yafimava
The Role of Gas Transit Routes in Belarus' Relations with Russia and the EU
ISBN 3-89821-655-1

Christopher Ford
Borotbism: A Chapter in the History of Ukrainian Communism
ISBN 3-89821-697-7

Series Subscription

Please enter my subscription to the series *Soviet and Post-Soviet Politics and Society*, ISSN 1614-3515, as follows:

❐ complete series   OR   ❐ English-language titles
                                                   ❐ German-language titles
                                                   ❐ Russian-language titles

starting with
❐ volume # 1
❐ volume # ___
      ❐ please also include the following volumes: #___, ___, ___, ___, ___, ___, ___
❐ the next volume being published
      ❐ please also include the following volumes: #___, ___, ___, ___, ___, ___, ___

❐ 1 copy per volume   OR   ❐ ___ copies per volume

Subscription within Germany:

You will receive every volume at 1st publication at the regular bookseller's price – incl. s & h and VAT.
Payment:
❐ Please bill me for every volume.
❐ Lastschriftverfahren: Ich/wir ermächtige(n) Sie hiermit widerruflich, den Rechnungsbetrag je Band von meinem/unserem folgendem Konto einzuziehen.

Kontoinhaber: _____ Kreditinstitut: _____
Kontonummer: _____ Bankleitzahl: _____

International Subscription:

Payment (incl. s & h and VAT) in advance for
❐ 10 volumes/copies (€ 319,80)   ❐ 20 volumes/copies (€ 599,80)
❐ 40 volumes/copies (€ 1.099,80)
Please send my books to:

NAME_____ DEPARTMENT_____
ADDRESS _____
POST/ZIP CODE_____ COUNTRY _____
TELEPHONE _____ EMAIL_____

date/signature_____

A hint for librarians in the former Soviet Union: Your academic library might be eligible to receive free-of-cost scholarly literature from Germany via the German Research Foundation. For Russian-language information on this program, see
      http://www.dfg.de/forschungsfoerderung/formulare/download/12_54.pdf.

Please fax to: **0511 / 262 2201 (+49 511 262 2201)**
or mail to: ***ibidem*-Verlag, Julius-Leber-Weg 11, D-30457 Hannover, Germany**
or send an e-mail: ibidem@ibidem-verlag.de

***ibidem*-Verlag**
Melchiorstr. 15
D-70439 Stuttgart
info@ibidem-verlag.de
www.ibidem-verlag.de
www.edition-noema.de
www.autorenbetreuung.de

CATHOLIC FAMILIES
OF
SOUTHERN MARYLAND

CATHOLIC FAMILIES
OF
SOUTHERN MARYLAND

Records of Catholic Residents of
St. Mary's County in the Eighteenth Century

Compiled by Timothy J. O'Rourke

CLEARFIELD

TABLE OF CONTENTS

FOREWORD

This collection of original documents should prove valuable to all those who engage in genealogical research on Southern Maryland Catholic families of the colonial period. Most of the documents appear in print for the first time; others have been printed only in periodicals of limited circulation and not always accessible in most libraries. All the documents interrelate one to the other so that the researcher will find many of his lines treated herein.

The most significant portion of this work contains the marriages and baptisms from the Jesuit parishes of St. Francis Xavier and St. Inigoes. I first began working on translating the entries from Latin abbreviations about 1971. In the meantime, Tom Jennings of Baltimore, undertook the same task and his version was included in a bicentennial edition of the previously published work, JESUIT MISSIONS OF ST. MARY'S COUNTY. Mr. Jennings was most helpful to me as we compared our versions trying to decipher every jot and squiggle.

Acknowledgement is hereby made to the Archives of the Archdiocese of Baltimore for permission to publish "Marylanders in Missouri Petition for a Priest" and Census, St. Mary's Congregation, Bryantown, Maryland"; to the Maryland Historical Society for permission to publish "Oath of Allegiance, Subscribers in St. Mary's County, 1778"; to the Archives of the Maryland Province of the Society of Jesus for permission to publish "Baptisms, St. Francis Xavier and St. Inigoes Congregations"; "Marriages, St. Francis Xavier and St. Inigoes Congregations"; "Censuses, St. Inigoes Congregations, 1768 and 1769; "Baptisms, St. Joseph's Congregation"; to the Archives of St. Mary's of The Barrens Seminary, Perryville, Missouri, for permission to publish "Census, St. Mary's of The Barrens, Perry County, Missouri"; and to the Hall of Records, Annapolis, Maryland, for permission to publish "Maryland Catholic Subscribers to Boston Relief"; and "Voting Lists, 1789 and 1790".

I am also very grateful to Crolian Edelen who helped me at an early stage of this work by making an alphabetical listing of the baptismal records and to Brother Thomas W. Spalding who has made valuable suggestions and alerted me to the existence of certain documents as well as writing an introduction to this work.

INTRODUCTION

"On the feast of the Annunciation of the Most Holy Virgin in the year 1634," wrote Father Andrew White, the Jesuit superior who accompanied the Maryland Pilgrims, "we celebrated Mass for the first time on this island [St. Clement's Island]. This had never been done before in this part of the world. After we hed completed the sacrifice, we took upon our shoulders a huge cross hewn from a tree, and advancing in order to the place appointed, with the help of the governor and his aides and other Catholics, we raised the trophy to Christ Our Savior, humbly reciting on bended knees the litany of the Holy Cross with great emotion." Though contrary to the instructions of Cecil Calvert, second Lord Baltimore, the Catholic leaders could not forego this public display of the joy and gratitude they felt for the new era that opened before them.

A few days later two Jesuit priests and a lay brother converted a bark hut abandoned by the Indians into a chapel on an estuary the colonists called St. Mary's River. The village that grew around it was named St. Mary's City. This "city" was the capital of Maryland for sixty years. There the first legislative grant of religious toleration in the New World was made in 1649.

St. Mary's County is where it all began, "the cradle of Catholicity." There was established the first Catholic parish, the first Catholic school, the first community of religious men in English-speaking America. In St. Mary's County the initial difficulties of transplanting English Catholicism were met and overcome. In St. Mary's County the vision of George Calvert, first Lord Baltimore, of Catholics and Protestants living in peaceful communion in a small corner of the New World was finally realized. In St. Mary's County the first experiment in separation of church and state in the modern world was attempted.

In terms of numbers, if for no other reason, St. Mary's County remained a vital nucleus in the development of the Catholic Church in English-speaking America. A survey of 1708 revealed that 1,238 of the 2,974 Catholics living in the then twelve counties of Maryland could be found in St. Mary's County. In 1734 the rector of All Faith's Anglican Parish reported: "Papists are supposed now to exceed Protestants at least three to one in this County." In the province as a whole Catholics could claim a ratio of only one in twelve. Proportionally the Catholics of St. Mary's County continued to increase, making it perhaps the most Catholic county in the nation. At the time of the establishment of the Patuxent Naval Air Station within its limits in 1947, the county could boast 11,036 Catholics in a total population of 14,626.

The unsung heroes are the plain people. And so it was with the Catholics of St. Mary's County, mostly farmers whose roots in America reached back to almost the beginning of their state. Such immigrant ancestors as John Cissell, Cuthbert Fenwick, Richard Gardiner, John Greenwell, Francis Hayden, Thomas Howard, John Jarboe, Thomas Jenkins, Thomas Mattingly, John Medley, Peter Mills, Thomas Spalding, and Robert Thompson were all there before the "Glorious Revolution" brought an end to the Catholic phase of the colony. Each of them produced a mighty progeny. A sampling of other Catholic names that would constitute St. Mary's County's legacy to the country at large would include Aud, Bowles, Brewer, Clark, Knott, Moore, Newton, Norris, Payne, Raley, Shercliffe, Wheatley, Wimsatt, and Yates. One might also include those Protestant families who by the time of the American Revolution had sprouted Catholic branches, such as the Abells, Alveys, Lees, and Tarltons.

The most important contribution of St. Mary's County to the newly organized church in a nation that had just won its independence from Great Britain was to spearhead the westward expansion of Catholicism. In 1785 the first of several Catholic families from St. Mary's County crossed the mountains to find land in Kentucky, led by the Haydens and the Lancasters, as Archbishop Martin John Spalding, one of the most noted representatives of the diaspora, tells us. In the 1790s St. Mary's County surrendered 1,538 of its white inhabitants and in the following decade another 520. In the period 1790-1810, in fact, it lost twenty-five percent of its white population. It was largely a Catholic exodus. Charles and Prince Georges, the two counties with the next greatest number of Catholics, suffered comparable losses but in the decade 1800-1810. The Catholic Church in Maryland was deprived of at least a fourth of its membership, mostly farmers compelled by economic necessity to seek more and cheaper land in Kentucky, Missouri, Georgia, Louisiana, and other states. But it was their religion that kept them together in identifiable groupings. So great, in fact, was the number who chose Kentucky as their future home that a diocese was created for these transplanted Marylanders in 1808.

This Catholic migration is an historical episode of which genealogists are perhaps more aware than historians. The compilations found within the covers of this book will constitute an indispensable reference work for the products of this migration who are interested in tracing their ancestry. They will serve also to document -- to pay homage -- to the real heroes of an historically significant venture, the plain people.

Brother Thomas W. Spalding, C.F.X.
Spalding College
Louisville, Kentucky

MARYLAND CATHOLIC SUBSCRIBERS TO BOSTON RELIEF, 1760

On March 20, 1760 Boston, Massachusetts suffered a disastrous fire in which 350 buildings burned. Subscriptions for the relief of its citizens were undertaken in several colonies. In Maryland Governor Horatio Sharpe issued a proclamation on May 6, 1760 calling for aid for the victims. The Hall of Records in Annapolis has preserved original lists of contributors, among which are two from Catholic congregations in St. Mary's County.

#A.D.S. 1 p., 37.9cm x 30.6cm

Return for Ł9 17s. 9d. from [the Chapel of St. Mary's?] to aid the sufferers from the Boston fire; sheriff's receipt for the money collected.

Signature: James Ashby

Subscribers:

James Ashby, John Buchman, William Buchmore, Peter Carberry, John Carburey, Jr., Philip Clark, Henry Cooper, Edward Digges, James Gough, Peter Gough, Clement Haden, William Hemersley, James Herd, John Herd, John Lucky, Clement Mattingley, Elizabeth Miles, Bennet Neale, H. Neale, Jeremiah Neale, Wilford Neale, Leonard Paine, John Peak, Ann Resick, John Baptist Resick, Thomas N. Risick, James Roark, John Roberts, James Sisel, John Sisel of Arther, John Baptist Sisel, William Sisel, Ignatius Sisell, Edward Spink, George Slye, Ann Thompson, Raphael Thompson, Robert Thompson, Thomas Thompson, Thomas Thompson of John, Ignatious Whealer, Jr., James Wheatley, Francis Yates, Thomas Yates.

#D.S. 1p. 38.1cm x 30.5cm

Return for Ł5 11s. 0-1/2d. from [the Roman Catholics] to aid the sufferers from the Boston fire.

Signature: Joseph Mosley

Subscribers:

Frances Boarman, Richard Boarman, Mark Brewer, Ignatius Brown, Henry Bryan, Edward Cole, Robert Cole, Elizabeth Cooper, Benjamin Finwick, Cudbert Finwick, Ignatious Finwick, John Grant, William Howard, Henry Howe, John King, Clement Parsons, John Power, James Price, John Shercliff, Thomas Spalding, Jr., Cornelius Wildman, Richard Wimsatt.

Reproduced by permission of the Hall of Records, Annapolis, Maryland

REGISTER OF BAPTISMS AND MARRIAGES

CONGREGATIONS OF ST. FRANCIS XAVIER AND ST. INIGOES

ST. MARY'S COUNTY, MARYLAND

Illegibility or omission signified by ---.

NC = non-Catholic

Note: Translations from Latin abbreviations
1780-1785 are missing
Entries from St. Inigoes are indicated by †

BAPTISMS

1766	Person baptized and parentage	Godparents
26 Dec	Stephen Williams of Sarah	Dick Joy, John Baptist Drury

1767		
11 Jan	Benedict Jarboe of Joshua and Jane	Joseph Siford, Alethea Abel
2 Feb	John Drury of John and Elizabeth	Robert Wellmore, Elizabeth Drury
3 Feb	Ann Brown of Peter and Frances	Benedict Riley, Susan Jarboe
8 Feb	--- Dyne of Thomas and Mary	Richard Pillekton, Susan Pyke
3 Mar	--- Thompson of Ignatius and Elizabeth	Philip Brewer, Mary Ann Siford
8 Mar	--- Ford of Athanatius and Ann	John Greenwell, Mrs. Slye
25 Mar	Joseph Jarboe of Matthew and Mary	Joseph Jarboe, Ann Ford
25 Mar	Mary Joy of Athanatius and Dyana	Michael and Mary Drury
5 Apr	James Joy of Ignatius and Ann	John and Monica Riley
12 Apr	Matthew Bradburn of Benjamin and Ann	Anthony Brown, Lucy Ford
12 Apr	Raphael Mattingly of Joseph and Ann	Thomas Jones, Mary Ann Brown
† 12 Apr	Eleanor Jarbo of Rodolphus and Elizabeth	William Angel, Henrietta Jarbo
† 12 Apr	George Atwood of Charles and Teresia	Mark Jarbo, Mary Swan
14 Apr	William Jarboe of Peter and Margaret	Joseph (of John, Sr.) Ford, Ann Winsatt
19 Apr	James Knot of Basil and Mary	Fran. and Monica Drury
28 May	Rebecca Brown of Barnard and Henrietta	Peter and Susan Brown
31 May	Cristina Lucas of Henry and Ann	Joseph Millard, Eleanor Campbel
14 Jun	Dorothy Hall of Joseph and Mary	William Stone, Mary Bennet
14 Jun	--- Pyke of William and Henrietta	John Heard, Eleanor Shirkley
14 Jun	--- Reily of John and Ann (NC)	Mary Hall
5 Jul	Elizabeth Brown of Matthew and Statia	Richard Ford, Mary Brown
12 Jul	Joseph Wellmore of Robert and Elizabeth	John Drury and dau. Monica
2 Aug	--- Sewel of Henry and Mary	Joseph (of John, Sr.) Ford, Frances Hopewell
30 Aug	Mildred Dosse of John and Winifred	Ignatius Joy, Jane Low
30 Aug	Elizabeth Dyne of John and Mary	Ignatius Joy

6 Sep	Dorothy Fenwick of Ignatius and Dorothy	Jane Fenwick and son Bennett
13 Sep	--- of Elizabeth Craycraft	her blacks
10 Oct	--- Fenwick of Benjamin and Jane	William Fenwick, Barbara Fenwick
18 Oct	--- Peacock of Paul and Sarah	Ignatius Joy, Susanna Cicil
30 Oct	--- Mattingly of Barton	Joseph and Rachel Nivet, brother and sister of Barton's wife
1 Nov	Ann Coachman of William and Eleanor	Fran. and Susanna Wheatley
1 Nov	--- Pilketon of Richard and Ann	Thomas and Margaret Dyne
6 Nov	Ann --- of John and Rebecca	John Drury, Susanna Heard
7 Nov	Frances Pane of Leonard	
30 Nov	Rebecca Mattingly of Alexius and Winifred	Zachariah Knott, Ann Boarman
Dec	--- Booth of Thomas and Mary	Ignatius Ford, Dorothy ---
20 Dec	Ann Mills of Jesse and Mary	Charles Dant, Ann Greenwell
20 Dec	Michael Riley of Gabriel and Ann	John and Jane Stone
28 Dec	Hanna Henly	Joseph and Ann Price
29 Dec	Henrietta Boarman of Richard and Catherine	Richard Boarman, Ann, his dau.
29 Dec	Elizabeth Cole of John and Mary	Jeremiah and Mary Cole
31 Dec	Aloysius Hazel of John and Ann	Robert Cole, Ann Brown
Dec	--- Hardisty of John and Elizabeth	Richard and Ann Boarman

†	16 Jan	Mary Tawney of Francis and Elizabeth	Henry and Ellen Sewall
†	31 Jan	Ann Allison of of Henry and Mary	Priscilla Tompson
	1 Feb	Belinda More of John and Mary	Bartholomew Greenwell, Eliz. Moor
†	2 Feb	John Lee of Joseph Leigh and Elizabeth	John Wiseman, Barbara Heard
†	16 Feb	George Norris of M. and Mary	---
†	16 Feb	Lewis Leigh of Massey and wife	Richard Fenwick, Mrs. Clark
†	16 Feb	Bennet Vaughan of ---	Thomas Drury
	17 Feb	Barbara Ford of John and Elizabeth	John Mattingly, Dorothy Abel
†	27 Feb*	Mary Ann Taylor of ---	James and Henrietta Atwood
	29 Feb	Thomas McGill of Thomas and Susanna	Samuel Belwood, Ann Jarboe
	29 Feb	Elizabeth Hall of Benjamin and Ann	Thomas and Sarah Newton
	7 Mar	Enoch Byrn of Nicholas and Mary	Brigit Vaughan
	10 Mar	-- Macwilliams of Thomas and ---	Edward and Ann Mattingly
	22 Mar	Richard Mareman of Joseph (NC) and Eliz.	James Taylor, Statia Cecil
	22 Mar	Ann Mattingly of Mary	Anastasia French, William Brewer
	22 Mar	Cornelius Brothers of Cornelius and Eliz.	Walter Davis, Mary Spalden
	25 Mar	Ambrose Spalden of Joseph and Ann	John Millard, Sarah Spaldin
†	27 Mar*	Sarah Fenwick of John and Elizabeth	Richard and Helena Fenwick
	29 Mar	Mary Drury of John Baptist and Mary	Philip Fenwick, John (or James) Drury's dau.
	29 Mar	Peter Greenwell of Ignatius and Elizabeth	Peter Drury, Bibiana Newton
	12 Apr	Mary ---	brother of infant, Ann Boarman
	16 Apr	Mary --- of Ann	Anthony Brown, Eleanor Campbell
	16 Apr	Ann Brown of Peter and Frances	Peter, son of Nicholas Brown, Susan Jarboe
	16 Apr	--- Medcalf of John and Elizabeth	Philip Ford, Elizabeth Thompson
	Apr	Anthony Brown of Anthony and Mary	Thomas Howard, Jane Wilkeson
	17 Apr	Bennet Drury of Nicholas and Monica	Richard Ford, Polly Thompson
	May	Elizabeth Pain of Baptist and Ann	Anthony and Mary Ann Brown
	1 May	Francis Fenwick of Robert and ---	Samuel Belwood, Elizabeth Clarke
	May	Edward Yets of Edward and Mary	Joseph Ford, Sarah Fading
	May	Belinda Gaudard of John and Eleanor	John Drury, Rebecca Ros
†	9 May*	Anna Hagur of Mathews and Eleanor	Anna Smith
	23 May	Ignatius Tawney of Rodulphus and Eleanor	Ignatius and Mary Fenwick
	29 May	Baptist Lucas of Baptist and Ann	Francis Boarman, Eleanor Wimsatt
	5 Jun	Elizabeth Stone of William and Dresden	Henry Stone, Henrietta ---
	5 Jun	Francis Jarboe of Bennett and Monica	Richard Jarboe of Bennett, Dorothy Ford

* date of <u>birth</u>

1769

8 Dec	Henry Wheatley of James and Henrietta	Jeremiah and Monica Maning
8 Dec	George Heard of John and Ann	Ignatius and Eleanor Heard
Dec	Joseph Jarboe of Peter and Margaret	Richard Wimsatt, Mary Ann Bowler
17 Dec	Enoch Joy of Peter and Rachel	Charles and Thecla Joy
17 Dec	Elizabeth Greenwell of Ignatius and Susan	John Greenwell, Sarah Newton
30 Dec	Joseph of John Haret and Margaret Swales	Peter Jarboe
31 Dec	--- Clarke of Abraham and Cloe	Basil Brown, Jane Stone

2 Jan	Augustine Fenwick of Benjamin and Jane	Edward Crecraft, Monica Fenwick
6 Jan	Monica Combs of Ignatius and Mary	John and Monica Fenwick
7 Jan	Mary Low of John Baptist and Elizabeth	Walter Davis, Ann Yets
14 Jan	Joseph Fenwick of Robert and Belinda	John Fenwick, Elizabeth Miles
14 Jan	William Conaly of Joseph and Cloa	Sylvester and Monica Wheatley
14 Jan	Susan Combs of Philip and Mary	John and Monica Combs
21 Jan	Rebecca Greenwell of Ignatius and Eliz.	[Monica?] Davis, Joseph, brother
28 Jan	Susan and Elizabeth More of Ignatius and Mary	---, --- Cole
18 Feb	Robert Harris of Samuel and Elizabeth	Robert or Barton Greenwell, Eleanor Campbell
25 Feb	Eleanor Wheatley of Ignatius and Henrietta	Nicholas and Anastasia Mills
25 Feb	Dorothy Maning of John and Susan	Mark Manning, Ann Fenwick
27 Feb	Elizabeth Semmes of Anthony and Mary	Henry Ford, Ann Semmes
27 Feb	--- Medcalf of John and Elizabeth	Joshua Millard, --- Brown of Nic.
27 Feb	Susan Greenwell of Jesse and Mary	Thomas McGill, Samuel Belwood
4 Mar	Anastasia Howard of Joseph and Mary	George Collins, Monica Howard
11 Mar	Ann Booth of John and Mary	Matthew and Margaret Heard
11 Mar	Aloysia Gough of James and Susan	Stephen and Ann Gough
18 Mar	Jeremiah Parsons of James and Elizabeth	Barton Davis, Ann Lucas
18 Mar	Rebecca Yets of Edward and Mary	John Yets, Eleanor Campbell
8 Apr	Joseph Norris of Bennet and Frances	Mary Norris, Monica Spink
8 Apr	Mary Medley of Clement and Mary	Nicholas Mills, Mary Ann Greenwell
8 Apr	James Wooton of Joseph and Mary	Philip Nottingham, Susan Wheatley
11 Apr	Nicholas Fenwick of Robert and Susan	Ben Greenwell, Jr., Ann Greenwell
16 Apr	Joseph Mattingly of John and Ann	Joseph Ford, Catherine Ford
16 Apr	Jonathan Goldsberry of Jonathan and Monica	Peter and Betty Joy
16 Apr	John Dossey of John and Winifred	John Baptist and Margaret Drury
18 Apr	Sarah Diegs of William (NC) and Mary	Francis Brooke, Henrietta Spalden
20 Apr	Matthew Mattingly of Alexius and Winifred	John Manock, Susan Branson
28 Apr	--- of Dorothy Field	her sister
29 Apr	Bernard Hayden of Francis and Mary Ann	Monica Waitfield, Joseph Mehoney
6 May	John Combs of Bennet and Elizabeth	William Combs, Mildred Greenwell
18 May	Mary Cecil of Ignatius and Mary	Bernard Cecil, Rachel Cecil
19 May	Dorothy Drury of Robert and Mary	Ignatius Yates, Eleanor Drury
20 May	Ignatius Bright of John and Elizabeth	Hatten and Eleanor Stone
20 May	Mary Brothers of Cornelius and Elizabeth	Walter and Sarah Davis
20 May	Gabriel Mattingley of Robert and Frances	Ignatius and Bibiana Ford
20 May	--- Wimsatt of Robert and Dorothy	James Ford, Molly Abel
27 May	Henrietta Greenwell of John Baptist and Susan	John Wiseman Greenwell, Mary Shirley
27 May	Susan McGill of Thomas and Susan	Ignatius Greenwell, Susan Wheatley
27 May	John Norris of John and Dresden	Philip Norris, Monica Greenwell
17 Jun	Thomas Delahay of Rhod. and Elizabeth	Thomas and Ann Delahay
17 Jun	Eleanor Hager of Matthew and Eleanor	James and Susan Gough
30 Jun	Joseph Fenwick of Robert and Rebecca	William Fenwick, Eleanor Heard
30 Jun	Elizabeth Crecraft of Edward and Eleanor	Robert Fenwick, Jr., Eleanor Crecraft
5 Jul	Enoch Greenwell of Thomas and ---	Susan Wheatley

Date	Child	Sponsors
8 Jul	Ann Heard of Matthew and Margaret	Luke and Eleanor Hopewell
0 Jul	Mary Ann Benfield of Sam and Dorothy	Jane Spalden, sister Dorothy
5 Jul	Bernard and Enoch Yates of John and Mary	Ignatius Chamberlain, Jinny Campbell, Ignatius and Eleanor Campbell
2 Jul	John Sanson of John and Mary	Rodulphus Martin, Mary Medley
9 Aug	Ignatius More of John and Mary	Barton Greenwell, Elizabeth Clark
6 Aug	Elizabeth --- of Thomas and Ann Cloe	Justin and his sister
2 Sep	Joseph and Mary Drury of Nicholas and Monica	Michael Drury, Ann Thompson, Michael and Ann Ford
9 Sep	John Semmes of Anthony and Mary	Mark Norris, Jr., Sarah Semmes
9 Sep	William Norris of Philip and Monica	Mark Norris, Ann Gough
6 Sep	Joseph Mills of Jess and Mary	Charles Dant, Ann Greenwell
1 Oct	Ann Neale of Wilford and Elizabeth	John Diggs, Elizabeth Slye
7 Oct	Mary Brown of Peter and Frances	Peter of Nic. Brown, Susan Jarboe
9 Oct	Joseph and Henry Taney of Francis and Elizabeth	James (Taney?), Henrietta Taney, Catherine Smith
4 Oct	Teresa Tarlton of Moses and Eleanor	James Gough, Jr., Mary Joy
4 Oct	Wilford Clark of Richard and Cloe	Robert and Mary Cole
1 Oct	Alley Dean of Thomas and Margaret	Philip Abell, Jane Reily
1 Oct	Dorothy Sewall of Henry and Mary	Billy Fenwick, Dorothy Boarman
4 Nov	Charles Jarboe of Joshua and Jinny	Philip and Mary Abel
8 Nov	--- Spalden of Bennet	Betsy Fenwick and sister
8 Nov	Edward Herbert of John and Anastasia	Barton Smith, Henrietta Spalding
9 Nov	Sarah Murrein of James and Mary	Samuel Queen, Rebecca Swan
7 Nov	Elizabeth Drury of Baptist and Mary	John Mattingley, Mary Drury
8 Dec	Mary Ann Gough of James and Susan	Thomas Norris, Elizabeth Gough
8 Dec	female Newton of Clement and Mary	Gabriel and Mary Newton
8 Dec	Benjamin Mason of Henry and Mildred	Negroes
6 Dec	James Greenwell of James and Eleanor	John Mills, Mary Ann Dant
6 Dec	Mary Reiley of John and Monica	Ignatius and Mary Goddard
6 Dec	Bennet Reiley of Gabriel and Anne	Joseph Stone, Justin Greenwell
3 Dec	Ignatius Combs of William and Mary	Bennet and Molly Combs
8 Dec	Elizabeth Greenwell of George and Elizabeth	Philip and Winifred Greenwell

1771

Date	Child/Parents	Sponsors
3 Jan	--- Greenwell of John and Ann	Nicholas Greenwell, Sarah Joy
13 Jan	Athanatius Greenwell	William Greenwell,
	of John, Jr. and Mildred	Elizabeth Ford
27 Jan	John Norris of Ignatius and Lucy	Rodulphus and Dorothy Norris
2 Feb	Abraham Fenwick of Ignatius and Dorothy	Philip Fenwick, Sarah Thomson
3 Feb	George Stone of William and Dresden	Monica Yets, Peter Brown, Jr.
3 Feb	Eleanor Ford of Ignatius and Dorothy	John and Ann Mattingly
3 Feb	Joseph Millard of Joseph and Rebecca	Philip Fenwick, Ann Ford, Jr.
24 Feb	--- Wheatley of George and Elizabeth	Rodulphus Greenwell, Bibiana Ford
2 Mar	Dorothy Drury of Ignatius and Anastasia	Michael and Eleanor Drury
4 Mar	Mary Hazel of Benedict (NC) and Susan	Ignatius Goddard, [Mlmy ?] Hall
10 Mar	Clara Greenwell of Philip and Winifred	William Greenwell, Frances
		Matt (?), sr. of William
24 Mar	Thomas Thomas of John (NC) and Dorothy	sister Dorothy, Eleanor Hagur
24 Mar	Benedict Joy of John and Sarah	Moses and Eleanor Tarlton
24 Mar	Joseph Downs of Joseph and Ann	Rodulphus Martin, Frances Delahay
24 Mar	Eleanor Greenwell of Clement and Jane	Jos. Greenwell, Dorothy Greenwell
25 Mar	Jane Nottingham of Mary	Stephen Gough, Jane Medley
27 Mar	Susan Saunders of Sinnet and Ann	Jeremiah Cole, Eleanor Stone
3 Apr	Aloysia Drury of Enoch and Tabitha	Philip Drury, Mary Davis
3 Apr	Teresa Ford of Athanatius and Ann	Josua Millard, Mary Ford
5 Apr	Elizabeth Hardesty of John (NC) & Eliz.	Samuel Queen, Catherine Boarman
14 Apr	Susan Mills of Nicholas and Anastasia	Nicholas and Mary Ann Greenwell
21 Apr	Belinda Stone of William, Jr. & Elizabeth	Philip Abel, Ann Stone
28 Apr	Stephen Norris of Baptist and Mary	Stephen Norris, Susan Gough
28 Apr	Mary Ann Delahay of John and Winifred	Leonard Wheatley, Frances Delahay
5 May	Zachariah Lucas of Baptist and Ann	John Dosse, Catherine Drury
19 May	Joseph Greenwell of Edward and Ann	Ignatius and Susan Greenwell
19 May	Philip Joy of Athanatius and Diana	Bennet Thompson, Mildred Drury
16 Jun	Bernard Drury of Philip and ---	Philip's sister, brother's wife
2 Jun	Monica ---	Dorothy Greenwell
2 Jun	Dorothy ---	
21 Jun	Zachariah Cecil of John and Susan	William Russell, Mary Davis
21 Jun	Mary Ann Clark of Abraham and Cloe	Nicholas Brown, Jane Clark
21 Jun	Sylvester Wheatley of Sylvester and Sarah	Matthew and Mary Jarboe
23 Jun	Rose Greenwell of Edward and Catherine	Richard Clark, Sarah Greenwell
1 Jul	Richard Boarman of Richard and Ann	Samuel Queen, Monica (both widowed)
5 Jul	Dorothy Bowes of Timothy (NC) and Mary	Bennet Medley, Mary Abell
7 Jul	John Jarboe of Ben and Monica	Philip Abel, Dorothy Ford, widow
7 Jul	John Thompson of Basil and Sarah	James Thompson, Susan Payn
7 Jul	Eleanor Payn of Baptist and Ann	William Russell, Dorothy Brown
21 Jul	Catherine Russell of John (NC) and Susan	William Russell, Mary Brown
28 Jul	Elizabeth Newton of Bernard and Mary	Gabriel Newton, Ann Payn
18 Aug	Bennet Medley of Ann	Bennett ---
25 Aug	Mary Norris of Rodulphus and Dorothy	John Bowls, Jr., Monica Norris
1 Sep	Bennet Medley of Nancy	Bennet Spalden
8 Sep	Philip Shange of Sylvester and Anastasia	John and Frances Medley (siblings)
15 Sep	Thomas Scot of James and Elizabeth	Peter and Eleanor Drury

22 Sep	Enoch Fenwick of Robert and Belinda	John Greenwell, Jr., Margaret Combs
22 Sep	Raphael Wheatley	John and Winifred Delahay
	of Ignatius and Henrietta	
6 Oct	Joseph Parsons of James and Elizabeth	Barton Davis, Sarah Davis
6 Oct	Winifred Brown of Baptist and Henrietta	Joseph Davis, Mary Brown
6 Oct	Joseph French of Ignatius and Elizabeth	James French, Sarah Newton
12 Oct	Jeremiah Newton of Joseph and Mildred	Richard and Cloe Clark
13 Oct	William Peak of William and Henrietta	Luke Heard, Eleanor Hopewell
1 Nov	James Medcalf of John and Elizabeth	Walter Davis, Ann Wheatley
1 Nov	Joseph Heard of John and Ann	Edmund Plowden, Elizabeth Ford
2 Nov	Elizabeth Mattingley of John and Ann	Anthony Semmes, Elizabeth Spalden
2 Nov	John Peak of Edward and Ann	Peter Brown, Mary Brown, Jr.
3 Nov	Richard Collins of George and Ann	George Booth, Mary Ann Brown
3 Nov	John Leigh of William and Mary	William Fenwick, Winifred Dosse
7 Nov	Peter Drury of Richard and Elizabeth	Michael and Elizabeth Drury
7 Nov	Elizabeth Anderson	Arthur Thompson, Jr., Eliz. Anderson
	of John Baptist and Ann (NC)	
24 Nov	--- of Rodulphus Hacket and Ann Medley	Ignatius Jarboe, Mary Pyke
30 Nov	Eleanor Alvi of Jesse and M'reney*	Jesse Thompson, Eleanor Campbell
30 Nov	Enoch Fenwick of Philip and Rebecca	Joseph and Rebecca Millard
1 Dec	Eleanor Fenwick of Robert and Rebecca	Ignatius Fenwick, Eleanor Heard
1 Dec	Susan Suales of John (NC) and Margaret	Jesse Greenwell, Elizabeth Suales
1 Dec	Elizabeth Hazel of John (NC) and Ann	Ignatius Joy, Jr., Elizabeth Clark
1 Dec	James Drury of James and Sarah	Bennett Thompson, Catherine Drury
Dec	--- Wathan (of St. Joseph's)	
15 Dec	Edward Drury of Michael and Ann	Ignatius Drury, Dorothy Yets
15 Dec	John Peak of John and Susan	James Yets, Mary Brown
26 Dec	Catherine of Dorothy Jones (NC), widow	Thomas Wooten, Ann Wheatley

* Emerentiana ?

1772

1 Jan	Eleanor Saxon of Robert and Elizabeth	John and Ann Mattingley
23 Feb	Clement Norris of Bennet and Frances	Cuthbert Clark, Ann Spink
23 Feb	John Raney of James and Dorothy	Thomas and Elizabeth Wooton
23 Feb	Mary Greenwell of James and Anastasia	Cuthbert Norris, Dorothy Greenwell
13 Mar	Alethia Joy of Ignatius and Ann	Philip Drury, Jane Reiley
Mar	Eleanor Greenwell of Ignatius and Susan	Barton Greenwell, Sarah Newton
1 Mar	--- Thompson of Arnold and Elizabeth	Arthur Thompson, Jr., Henrietta McGui[re?]
8 Mar	Stephen Greenwell of Elizabeth	Stephen Gough, Frances Milburn
13 Mar	John Heyden of Francis and Mary	Ignatius Heyden, Ann Witfield
22 Mar	Joseph Gough of Stephen and Ann	James and Susan Gough
22 Apr	Cloe Combs of Ignatius and Mary	Billy and Nelly Fenwick
5 Apr	Stephen More of Ignatius and Mary	James and Mary More
5 Apr	Ann Wimsatt of Robert and Dorothy	Henry Ford, Mary Abel
5 Apr	Mary Jarboe of Matthew and Mary	Basil Thompson, Ann Jarboe
5 Apr	Ann Drury of Robert and Mary	John Mattingly, Mary Aud
5 Apr	Stephen Bright of John and Elizabeth	William Bright, Mary Ann Brown
12 Apr	Mary Heard of Matthew and Mary	William Heard, Eleanor Hopewell
12 Apr	--- Greenwell of Ignatius and Elizabeth	Robert Drury, Mary Aud
16 Apr	Ann Dresden Norris of John and Dresden	Wm. Bellwood, Emerentiana Greenwell
16 Apr	Elizabeth Cole of Francis and Catherine	James Fisher, Eleanor Cole
16 Apr	Ben. Fisher of James and Elizabeth	Thomas ---, Ann Jarboe
16 Apr	Anastasia Mattingly of Robert and Frances	Anthony and Mary Semmes
16 Apr	William Payn of William and Henrietta	James and Eleanor Payn
16 Apr	Elizabeth Jarboe of Clement and Ann	Henry Belwood, Elizabeth Fisher
10 May	Henrietta Greenwell of Clement and Jane	Joseph and Dorothy Greenwell
18 May	Philip Abel of Philip and Ann Dresden	Philip Ford, Mary Abel
18 May	Elizabeth Medley of Ben. and Elizabeth	James Williams, Belinda Fenwick
28 May	Mary Williams of Joseph and Ann	James and Monica Williams
28 May	Elizabeth Stone of Hatten and Eleanor	John and Mary Hall
28 May	Elizabeth Nugent of Willoughby & Rebecca	Charles Joy, Jr., Mary Ross
28 May	Ignatius --- of Jonathan & wife [slave?]	John Mills, Margaret Suales
14 Jun	Barbara Heard of Basil and Eleanor	Basil and Eleanor Nottingham
Jun	Justinian Greenwell of Thomas and Abelone	Joseph Davis, Mary Greenwell
5 Jul	Stephen Goddard of John and Elizabeth	Peter Drury, Elizabeth Lucas, widow
5 Jul	Mary Jarboe of Alexius and Mary	Thomas Jarboe, Rebecca Howard
12 Jul	Matthew Booth of John and Mary	William Newton, Mary Shirley
19 Jul	Elizabeth Siford, adult	
25 Jul	Matthias Joy of Ann	Moses Tarlton
9 Aug	Ann Gough of James and Susan	Stephen and Ann Gough
16 Aug	Mary Campbell of Ignatius and Mildred	William Brewer, Rebecca Yets
16 Aug	Margaret --- [priest forgot parentage]	William Brewer, Henrietta Payne
17 Aug	Sarah Ford of Athanatius and Ann	Enoch Fenwick, Jr., Sarah Neale
24 Aug	James Combs of Philip and Margaret	Joseph and Mary Jenkins
24 Aug	Barnabas Greenwell of Ben. and Elizabeth	Rodulphus and Dorothy Norris
24 Aug	Susan Pyke of James and Elizabeth	Nicholas and Ann Greenwell
31 Aug	Ignatius Jarboe of Peter and Margaret	Richard Wimsatt, Mary A-- Bowling
6 Sep	Philip Clark of Abraham and Cloe	Joshua Greenwell, Jane Clark
13 Sep	Robert Williams of Mary	Jane Stone

20 Sep	Ann Pilketon of Mary and lawful husband	James Pilketon, Anastasia Brown
4 Oct	Monica Drury of Nicholas and Monica	Raphael and Mary Thompson
5 Oct	Mary Greenwell of Jesse and Mary	Thomas and Susan McGill
5 Oct	Mary Magdalene Reily of Henry and Jane	Jesse Greenwell, Ann Jarboe
13 Oct	Mary Barks of Zachariah and Susan	John and Sarah Thompson
18 Oct	Thomas Ford of Henry and Sarah	Joseph Ford, Elizabeth Spalden
24 Oct	Mary Fenwick of Joseph and Cloe	Thomas James, Catherine Fenwick
25 Oct	Ignatius Medley of Joseph and Ann	William Combs, Mary Abel
25 Oct	Catherine Norris of Ignatius and Lucy	Rodulphus and Dorothy Norris
25 Oct	Mary Duvol of John and Alisia	Thomas Tarlton, Susan Kennan
8 Nov	James Manning of John and Susan	George James, Ann Jarboe
15 Nov	Thomas Hazel of Ben (NC) and Susan	Edward and Jane Campbell
16 Nov	Eleanor Cole of Jeremiah and wife	Jeremiah's unmarried sister
7 Dec	Joseph Greenwell of Philip and Winifred	Stephen Gough, Ann Spink
20 Dec	William Yates of Martin and Ann	Henry Horell, Mary French
20 Dec	Elizabeth Drury of Enoch and Tabitha	Philip Drury, Mary Davis
20 Dec	Thecla Drury of Philip and Bibiana	Gilbert Newton, Mildred Russel
20 Dec	Joseph Wimsatt of Baptist and Elizabeth	Peter and Mary Brown
20 Dec	Jonathan Campbell of Enoch and Elizabeth	Edward and Eleanor Campbell
29 Dec	Sarah Herbert of John and Anastasia	Philip Fenwick, Rebecca Yets

1773

Date	Child and Parents	Sponsors
3 Jan	Winifred Delahay of John and Winifred	Thomas Wooton, Ann Delahay
6 Jan	Aloysius Fenwick of Benjamin and Jane	James Heard, Jr., Elizabeth Combs
24 Jan	Jeremiah Gough of Benjamin and Susan	Charles Gough, Eleanor Nottingham
2 Feb	Ignatius Semmes of Anthony and Mary	Peter Ford, Bibiana Ford
2 Feb	James Stone of Edward and Ann	Peter Joy, Lydy Stone
6 Feb	Edward Ford of John and Henrietta	Joshua Millard, Ann Ford
7 Feb	Mary Spalden of Benedict and Alethia	John Wimsatt, Lucy Briant
8 Feb	Edmund Greenwell of John and Ann	Joseph Millard, Ann Greenwell
14 Feb	Elizabeth Wheatley of James and Henrietta	Mark Norris, Jr., Frances Milborn
14 Feb	Cornelius Greenwell of John Baptist and Susan	Archibald Greenwell, Ann Wheatley
28 Feb	Zachariah Tarlton of Moses and Enora	John and Margaret Cole
21 Mar	Zachariah Peacock of Paul and ---	Ignatius Drury, Ann Jarboe
28 Mar	Sarah Brooke of Roger and Mary	John Smith, Jr., Sarah Brooke
28 Mar	Mary Taney of Rodulphus and Eleanor	James and Mary Fenwick
3 Apr	Elias Redmund of Joshua (NC) & Elizabeth	John and Ann Low
4 Apr	Thomas Joy of Peter and Rachel	Philip Drury, Ann Joy
4 Apr	Henrietta Greenwell of William and Ann	Luke Heard, Eleanor Hopewell
4 Apr	Anastasia More of John and Mary	John Barton and Mary Greenwell
4 Apr	John Baptist Dosse of John and Winifred	William Brewer, Mary More
4 Apr	Peter Parsons of James and Elizabeth	Edward Campbell, Dorothy Stewart
4 Apr	James Harris of Samuel and Elizabeth	Francis and Mary Ann Haden
10 Apr	James Goldsberry of William (NC) and Mary Ann	John Bowls, Elizabeth W[heat?]ley
13 Apr	Sarah Norris of James and Monica	Joshua Clark, Ann Jarboe
14 Apr	Henrietta Fenwick of Robert and Belinda	William Fenwick, Eleanor Miles
14 Apr	Robert Ends of Vincent (NC) and Susan	Henrietta Hacket
17 Apr	Samuel Bowes of Timothy (NC) and Mary	Joseph Ford, Eleanor Abel
20 Apr	William Leach of William (NC) and Mary	Mary's sister
21 Apr	John Murrein of James and Mary	Leonard Johnson, Sarah Janes
2 May	John Thompson of Rodulphus and Abelona	James and Mary Ann Thompson
2 May	Francis Roberts of Francis and Mary	Francis Roberts, Susan Shanks
3 May	Ann Norris of Baptist and Mary	Edmund Jenkins, Mary Hagur
9 May	William Greenwell of John and Mildred	William Greenwell, Elizabeth Ford
9 May	Charles Stuart of Alexander and Mary	James Gough, Cloe Tarlton
9 May	Charles Combs of William and Mary	Robert Fenwick, Anastasia Medley
16 May	Eleanor Thompson of Thomas (NC) and Henrietta	Edmund Greenwell, Susan Abel
16 May	Belinda Abel of Zachariah (NC) and Martha	Joseph Davis, Tabitha Drury
23 May	Ann Norris of Mark and Elizabeth	Matthew and Ann Heard
30 May	Eleanor Cecil of Ignatius and Mildred	Philip and Catherine Drury
6 Jun	James Davis of Joseph and Jemima (NC)	James and Frances Wimsatt
6 Jun	Edward Greenwell of Edmund and Ann	Edward and Sarah Joy
6 Jun	John Yets of John and Mary	Edward and Jane Campbell
18 Jun	Ann Reily of Gabriel and Ann	Jane Stone and Joseph, her son
27 Jun	Thomas Norris of Rodulphus and Dorothy	John Low, Sarah Reily
4 Jul	Charles Jarboe of Joshua and Jane	Bartholomew Greenwell, Mary Abel
4 Jul	Martin Medcalf of Elizabeth	John French, Susan Fardin
4 Jul	Jeremiah Brothers of Cornelius & Eliz.	Walter and Sarah Davis

11 Jul	Cornelius Manning of Robert and Monica	William and Ann Fenwick
11 Jul	Charles Smith of James (NC) and Mary	Nicholas Greenwell, Ann
11 Jul	Elizabeth Williams of Joseph and Ann	James and Monica Williams
18 Jul	John Russel of John and Susan	William Russel, Dorothy Brown
25 Jul	Ann Boarman of Richard and Ann	Jane Taney, Eleanor Miles
30 Jul	John Baptist Delahay of Rodulphus and Elizabeth	Stephen Gough, Ann Delahay
30 Jul	Susan Wherret of Abner (NC) and Eleanor	Moses and Susan Tarlton
8 Aug	Cornelius Clark of Richard and Cloe	Raphael Greenwell, Elizabeth Gough
29 Aug	Louis Thompson of Joseph and Ann	Philip and Elizabeth Brian
Sep	Edward Peak of John and Susan	Enoch Fenwick, Mary Brown
8 Sep	female Clark of Joshua and Eleanor	
12 Sep	Charles Wooton of Joseph and Mary	John and Susan Wooton
Sep	Lydya Cecil of John and Susan	Thomas Brewer, Hentietta Joy
Sep	Ignatius Drury of Ignatius and Anastasia	Benedict French, Thecla Joy
Sep	Elizabeth Dyne of Matthew and Mary	Cornelius Brothers, Eliz. Thompson
Sep	Mary Stone of William and Dresden	Barton Greenwell, Mary Jarboe
26 Sep	Jeremiah Downs of Joseph and Ann	Thomas Wooton, Mary Greenwell
26 Sep	Dorothy Norris of Thomas and Mary Ann	John Baptist Norris, Jane Gough
26 Sep	Monica Nottingham, of Mary, widow	Catherine Nottingham
Sep	--- Pyke of James and Mary Ann	Archibald Greenwell, Elizabeth Mills
3 Oct	Henrietta Stone of William, Jr. and Elizabeth	Anthony Brown, Mary A--- Bright
20 Oct	Edward Fenwick of Robert and Rebecca	William Fenwick, Barbara Fenwick
25 Oct	Henry Forest of Zephaniah and Mary	Michael Spalden, Henrietta Forest
31 Oct	Ann Jarboe of Thomas and Ann	Charles Joy, Jr., Elizabeth Lucas
31 Oct	John Goddard of Ignatius and Ann (NC)	Basil Raily, Eleanor Wimsatt
31 Oct	Ann Anderson of James and Elizabeth	Ignatius French, Elizabeth Anderson
1 Nov	Zachariah Saxton of Robert and Elizabeth	Matthew Jarboe, Eleanor Hopewell
7 Nov	Joseph and Mary Hall of Aquilla (NC) and Mary	Francis Wimsatt, Rebecca Greenwell, Philip Ford, Eleanor Abel, Jr.
14 Nov	Stephen Joy of John and Sarah	Barnabas and Eleanor Cole
14 Nov	Elizabeth Conolay of Joshua and Ann	Monica Wheatley
20 Nov	John Williams of Hugo and Lydia	Francis Xavier Stone, Eliz. Williams
21 Nov	Eleanor Brown of Ignatius and Ann	Joshua Millard, Mary Ross
21 Nov	Ann Millard of Joseph and Rebecca	Philip and Rebecca Fenwick
24 Nov	Ann Dyer of James (NC) and Mary	Bibiana Greenwell
28 Nov	Elizabeth Norris of Philip and Monica	Benedict Norris, Susan Greenwell
8 Dec	Mary Wheatley of George and Elizabeth	Henry Wheatley, Bibiana Ford
19 Dec	Sarah Fenwick of Ignatius and Dorothy	Henry Medley, Sarah Joy
19 Dec	Joseph Stone of Joseph and Dorothy	Raphael Greenwell, Mary Spink
27 Dec	John Medley of Ignatius and Mary	John and Frances Medley

1774

3 Jan	Henrietta Joy of Enoch and Rebecca	Robert and Ann Greenwell
2 Feb	Joshua Drury of Michael and Ann	Bartholomew and Monica Yets
6 Feb	Ann Bright of John and Elizabeth	William Bright, Dorothy Brown
6 Feb	Eleanor Drury of Enoch and Tabitha	John and Eleanor Wimsatt
27 Feb	Mary Ann Thomas of John (NC) and Dorothy	Thomas Tarlton, Eleanor Hagur
27 Feb	Elizabeth Chrismond of Lucy (NC)	John and Monica Horell
27 Feb	Joseph Heard of Matthew and Margaret	John Heard, Eleanor Hopewell
27 Feb	Ignatius Laton of John and Jane	John and Henrietta Low
27 Feb	Joseph Peak of William and Henrietta	Matthew Heard, Frances Hopewell
Mar	Robert Cole of Francis and Catherine	John and Margaret Cole
Mar	John Baptist Greenwell of James and Anastasia	Mark Norris, Monica Peak
Mar	Ursula Greenwell of Edward and Catherine	Richard and Cloe Clark
Mar	--- Fenwick of Cuthbert and Eleanor	Richard Fenwick, Eleanor Hopewell
4 Apr	Joseph Haden of Francis and Mary	Peter Drury, Rachel Joy
4 Apr	Elizabeth Greenwell of James and Eleanor	Francis Haden, Mary Peak
10 Apr	James Fenwick of Robert and Susan	Matthew Heard, Eleanor Hopewell
10 Apr	Stephen Tarlton of Enoch and Susan	Moses Tarlton, Eleanor Wherret
17 Apr	William Joy of Ignatius and Ann	John and Henrietta Raily
May	Elizabeth of John Baptist Goddard and --- Hazel (NC)	John Raily, Jr., Rebecca Yets
12 May	--- Joy of Athanatius and Dresden	Francis Thompson, Jane Joy
12 May	Ann Suales of John (NC) and Margaret	Justinian Greenwell, Eliz., siste
22 May	Agatha Newton of Alban and Mary Ann	Henry Pike, Mary Ann Pike
2 Jun	--- Walker of Richard and Ann	George Haden, Mary ---
4 Jun	Aloysius Gerard, adult	Joshua Millard, Mary Ford
5 Jun	Zachariah Hazel of John (NC) and Ann	Peter Joy, Mary Ann More
12 Jun	Dorothy Haney of James and Elizabeth	Henry Pyke, Ann Wheatley
Jun	John Allan of Susan	Thomas Wooton, Elizabeth Rollin
19 Jun	Ignatius Carroll of Ignatius and Winifred	---
10 Jul	James Henry of Martin and Mary	Vincent Payn, Elizabeth Taylor
17 Jul	Eleanor Brown of Peter and Frances	Baptist Payn, Susan Jarboe
17 Jul	Stephen Davis of Stephen and Ann	Walter and Sarah Davis
17 Jul	Thomas Drury of James and Sarah	Benjamin Thompson, Alethar Drury
7 Aug	James Mills of Justinian and Mary	Charles Dant, Ann Greenwell
14 Aug	Ann Wheatley of Sylvester and Elizabeth	Ignatius Cecil
9 Oct	Margaret Norris of Ignatius and Lucy	Rodulphus and Dorothy Norris
15 Oct	Ann Brewer of Thomas and Ann Minta	Joseph and Ann Dosse
16 Oct	John Brown of Peter and Susan	Rodulphus and Abelony Thompson
23 Oct	John Stone of Enoch and Monica	Walter Davis, Elizabeth Suales
23 Oct	Henry Low of Baptist and Elizabeth	Bartholomew Yets, Dorothy ---
1 Nov	George Moore of Ignatius and Mary	Benedict and Eleanor More
6 Nov	--- Cullens of James and Susan	Justinian Floyd, Henrietta Fenwic
6 Nov	--- Rigby of Anastasia	--- Ford, Dorothy Stuart
18 Dec	Philip French of John and Jane	Walter Davis, Mary Rogers
18 Dec	Joseph Ford of Robert and Sarah	Robert Mattingly, Jane Ford
18 Dec	Ignatius Jarboe of Matthew and Mary	William Bradburn, Susan Stone

6 Jan	Andrew Greenwell of Ignatius and Elizabeth	Mary More
2 Feb	Joseph Greenwell of Joshua and Jane	Bartholomew Greenwell, Mary Abel
2 Feb	Samuel Drury of Philip and Bibiana	Delbert Newton, Catherine Drury
2 Feb	Susan Dyne of Thomas and Susan	Richard Pilketon, Anastasia Brown
5 Feb	Bernard Campbell of Ignatius and Mildred	Rebecca Yets
5 Feb	Andrew Greenwell of Ignatius and Mary	Delbert Newton
5 Feb	Ignatius Yets of Martin and Ann	Bartholomew Yets, Sarah Joy
18 Feb	Richard Harpar of John and Anastasia	Henry Medley, Elizabeth Clark
19 Feb	Anthony Semmes of Anthony and Mary	Henry and Bibiana Ford
19 Feb	Barbara More of James and Mary	John Brewer, Jr., Ann Moore
19 Feb	Elizabeth Davis of Joseph and Jemima	James and Frances Wimsatt
19 Feb	Mary Fenwick of Philip and Rebecca	Joseph Millard, Rebecca ---
19 Feb	Jane Campbell of Enoch and Elizabeth	Edward and Ann Campbell
26 Feb	Thomas Nugent of Willoughby (NC) and wife	Basil Raily
6 Mar	--- Brown of Nicholas and Eleanor	Joshua Millard, Mary Brown
2 Apr	Ann Greenwell of Edmund and Ann	Matthew and Mary Jarboe
9 Apr	Bernard Brown of Anthony and wife	Peter Brown, Jr., Ann Stuart
15 Apr	Frances Wimsatt of Stephen and Mary	Elizabeth Taylor
17 Apr	--- Brown of Leonard and Ann	Peter and Mary Brown
15 Jun	Elizabeth Spalden of Benedict and Aloysia	John Wimsatt, Elizabeth Spalden
17 Jun	Aloysius Jarboe of Peter and Margaret	Edmund and Margaret Plowden
25 Jun	--- Mattingly of Henry and Ann	Philip Ford, Bibiana Ford
Jul	--- Tomkins of John and Mary	George Howard, ---
11 Sep	Ann Smith of John and Elizabeth	Athanatius Ford, (grandfather), Catherine Ford (friend)
23 Sep	--- Joy of Peter and Rachel	James Russell, Catherine Drury
1 Oct	Jane Clark of Cuthbert and Mary Ann	Francis Thompson, Jane Clark
15 Oct	--- Austin of George and Eleanor	Sarah Joy
22 Oct	Elizabeth Forest of Jesse and Mary	Ralph Greenwell, Elizabeth Reily
22 Oct	Mimy Clark of Abraham and Cloe	Francis Thompson
24 Oct	Monica Fenwick of Thomas and Elizabeth	Benedict Fenwick, Eleanor Abel
26 Nov	Martin Brown of Peter, Jr. and Susan	Nicholas and Mary Brown
Dec	--- Floyd of Jesse	Peter Ford, Elizabeth Joy

Date	Child	Sponsors
14 Jan	Jesse Howard of Peter and Elizabeth	Thomas Howard, Susan Payn
21 Jan	Charles Stone of Hatten and Eleanor	Enoch and Monica Stone
21 Jan	John Greenwell of John and Ann	Edward Joy, Dorothy Greenwell
11 Feb	Elizabeth Bradburn of Benjamin and Mary Ann	Thomas Thompson, Mary Ann Bowling
11 Feb	Charles Drury of Ignatius and wife	Bernard French, Elizabeth French, children of John French
18 Feb	Henry Thompson of Ignatius and Dorothy	Philip Ford, Jr., Jane, dau of Weaver Ford
18 Feb	Sarah Jarboe of Susan	John and Mary Ann Thompson
10 Mar	--- Cecil of John and Mary	Eleanor Cecil, Thomas ---
3 Mar	Susan Sewall of Henry and Mary	John Baptist Peak, Elizabeth Joy
3 Mar	John Baptist Russell of William and Dresden	Ignatius Russell, Eleanor Abel
3 Mar	Ann Williams of Hugo and Lydia	Francis and Jane Stone
3 Mar	Ann Davis of Joseph and Jemima	James and Frances Wimsatt
3 Mar	William Joy of Ignatius and Ann	John and Henrietta Raily
17 Mar	Eleanor Greenwell of William and Ann	Matthew and Mary Jarboe
17 Mar *	Mary Canning of Andrew and Winifred	Andrew Mulanny, Sarah Shirden
17 Mar	James Dorsy of John and Winifred	William Russell, Mary Clark
24 Mar	Elizabeth Greenwell of Ignatius and Susan	Walter Davis, Sarah Newton
24 Mar	Elias --- [priest forgot parents' names]	Bartholomew Greenwell, Mary Newto
9 Apr	James Drury of Enoch and Tabitha	Baptist and Catherine Drury
12 Apr	John Hatten More of John and Mary	Thomas Fenwick, Cavey Aud
14 Apr	Zachariah Aud of Thomas and Priscilla	John Brewer, Sarah Greenwell
28 Apr	Elizabeth Bowls of William and Mary	Ignatius Bowls, Anastasia Cecil
5 May	Ann Thompson of Rodulphus and Abelona	John and Ann Thompson
5 May	Uriah Pilketon of Richard and Ann	Francis Thompson, Monica Dugent
26 May	--- French of James and Susan	
2 Jun	George Dyne of John and Mary	James and Ann More
2 Jun	Sarah Goddard of Ignatius and Ann	Edward Campbell, Rebecca Yets
16 Jun	--- French of John and Jane	Ignatius Drury, Mary Rogers, sr. of Jane
23 Jun	--- Culins of James and Susan	James and Ann More
12 Jul	white infant	Benedict Thompson, Eleanor Daft
14 Jul	Henrietta Thompson of Baptist and Mary	Joseph Carbery, Ann Thompson
28 Jul	Ignatius Ford of Robert and Sarah	Charles Joy, --- Gough
28 Jul	Elisha Abel of Ignatius and Mary	Anthony Semmes, Eleanor Abel
28 Jul	Joseph Russell of Susan widow,	Jesse Ford, Ann Mattingly
9 Aug	Sarah McWilliams of Kelly and wife	Clement and Ann Mattingly
11 Aug	Eleanor Cecil of Ignatius and wife	Susan Cecil
11 Aug	Jane Taylor of Ignatius and Mary	Vincent and Mary Ann Payn
15 Aug	Jane Cecil of Baptist and Mary	Vincent and Elizabeth Payn
15 Aug	John Riswyck of Thomas and Mary	John and Elizabeth Nottingham
25 Aug	--- Jarboe of Matthew and Mary	Susan Jarboe
1 Sep	Peter Mills of Jesse and Mary	his brother, her sister
15 Sep	Catherine Peak of John and wife	Joshua Millard, Anastasia Brown, widow

* see 1778

-16-

22 Sep	Jesse Drury of Peter and Eleanor	Michael Drury, Ann Stuart
22 Sep	Aloysia Joy of Athanatius and Mary Ann	Francis Thompson, Catherine Drury
22 Sep	Mary Goddard of John and Jane	Peter Drury, Monica Raily
22 Sep	John Yets of John and Mary	Edward and Ann Campbell
6 Oct	Mary Brown of Ignatius and Ann	Joshua Millard, Susan Peak
27 Oct	Catherine Ford of Philip and Elizabeth	Joshua Millard, Catherine Ford
27 Oct	Edward Brewer of Thomas and Minta	John Brewer, Dorothy Dosse
24 Nov	John Mattingly of William and Mary	Basil and Margaret Payn
1 Dec	Sarah Stone of Ann	Francis Fenwick, Margaret Medley
1 Dec	Catherine Yets of Martin and Ann	Robert Greenwell, Eleanor French
15 Dec	Rebecca Hall of Aquilla and Mary	Thomas Greenwell, Eleanor Wimsatt
29 Dec	Dorothy Drury of Michael and Ann	Peter Drury, Dorothy Yates
30 Dec	George Jarboe of Benedict and Monica	Henry Reily, Catherine Jarboe
31 Dec	Edward Stone of Enoch and Monica	

1777

Date	Child	Sponsors
19 Jan	Sarah Brown of Nicholas and Eleanor	Enoch and Ann Drury
2 Feb	William Brewer of George and wife	Thomas Brewer, Susan Cecil
9 Feb	Jane Newton of Bernard and Mary Ann	Negro, Ann Greenwell
9 Feb	John Leaton of John and Jane	Thomas and Elizabeth Wooton
16 Feb	Joseph Harris of Samuel and Elizabeth	James and Mary Horell
16 Feb	Wilfred Greenwell of Rodulphus and Cloa	Joseph and Dorothy Stone
9 Mar	Ann --- of George and wife	William and Ann Spink
23 Mar	Joshua Millard of Joseph and Rebecca	Joshua Millard, Margaret Medley
26 Mar	Sarah of James Thompson and Susan Jarboe	Ignatius Russels, Eleanor Stone
31 Mar	Thomas Mattingly of Bartholomew and Mildred	Joseph and Mary Nevitt
31 Mar	Jane Cecil of John Baptist and Eleanor	Leonard Payn, Rachel Cecil
1 Apr	Ann Clark of Abraham and Cloe	William Russel, Mary Clark
5 Apr	Eleanor Morgan of Benedict (NC) and Winifred	Bernard Medley, Eleanor Abell
6 Apr	Lydia Hazel of John and Ann	Edward Campbell, Mary Drury
6 Apr	Dorothy Dyne of Thomas and Margaret	James and Eleanor Dyne
6 Apr	John Jarboe of Joshua and Jane	Edmund and Dorothy Greenwell
20 Apr	Catherine Herpard of John and Anastasia	Ignatius Chamberlain, Monica Drury
20 Apr	Richard Spalden of Benedict and Aloysia	Peter Ford, Eliz., wife of Phil Fo
4 May	--- Kibby of Thomas and Elizabeth	John Ford, Susan Thompson
17 May	Henrietta Peacock of Paul and Sarah	Edmund Greenwell, Rebecca Yets
20 May	Elizabeth Raily of Kiley and Mary	Basil and Jane Nottingham
29 May	Henrietta Anderson of Thomas and Cloe	Joseph Carbery, Susan Clark
1 Jun	Richard More of James and Ann	Ignatius Russell, Ann Minta Brewer
20 Jul	Barbara Taylor of Anastasia	Basil Bright, Mary Ann More
20 Jul	Sarah Reily of Henrietta	Ignatius Joy, Sr., Athanatius Joy, Jr., Elizabeth, his daughter
21 Sep	Francis Xavier Carr of Ambrose and Eleanor	Edward Campbell, Aloysia Yets
21 Sep	Henry Nugent of Willoughby (NC) and Rebecca	Ignatius Joy, Lydia Reily
13 Oct	Ann Greenwell of Ignatius and Ann	Ann Brown
19 Oct	Ann Abell of Ignatius and Mary	Robert and Eleanor Abell
19 Oct	--- Campbell of Ignatius and Mildred	Edward and Ann Campbell
26 Oct	Rose Brown of Peter, Sr., and Frances	William Raper, Mary Brown
9 Nov	--- Cecil of John Baptist and wife	Leonard Payn, Priscilla Vowls
16 Nov	Ann Ford of Henry and Sarah	Anthony Semmes, Elizabeth, his da
7 Dec	Wilfrid Brown of Anthony and Ann	Bennet Thompson, Ann Stuart
7 Dec	Charles Abell of Zachariah and Mary	Ignatius Joy, Jr., Mary Ann More
7 Dec	Mary Leich of William and Mary	Bartholomew Smith, Mary Spalden
14 Dec	Richard Fenwick of Thomas and Elizabeth	Eleanor Abell
14 Dec	Aloysia Payn of William and Henrietta	Mary Newton
14 Dec	Mary Howard of Peter and Elizabeth	Sarah Peacock
21 Dec	Charles Ford of Robert and Dorothy	Benedict Thompson, Jane Ford
21 Dec	Mary Cecil of John and Mary	Edward Spink, Mary Cecil
27 Dec	Emerentiana Drury of Philip and Ena	John Baptist Drury, Thecla Joy

1778

Date		
25 Jan	Thomas Clark of Jane	Henry Horell, Eleanor Wimsatt
Feb	--- French of Ignatius and Elizabeth	---, Elizabeth Anderson
Feb	--- Payn of Rodulphus and Tabitha	James Taylor and wife
16 Mar	James Brown of Basil and Ann	John and Elizabeth Ford
22 Mar	--- Russell of Ignatius and Mildred	Enoch Drury, Jr., Catherine Drury
22 Mar	--- Blake of Ann	Margaret Shanks
19 Apr	Eleanor Davis of Joseph and Mima	Jeremiah Drury, Eleanor Wimsatt
20 Apr	Elizabeth Cunningham of Andrew and Winifred	John Ford, Jr., Elizabeth ---
27 Apr	Mary Ann Dyne of John and Mary	James More, Barbara Fenwick
27 Apr	Sarah Dyne of James and Eleanor	James and Ann More
10 May	Rebecca Mareman of Joseph and Elizabeth	William Bowls, Rachel Cecil
7 Jun	Elias Smith of Elias and Benedicta	Joshua Millard, Clara Stone
9 Jun	Robert Ford of Robert and Sarah	Charles Joy, Jane Ford
14 Jun	Jonathan Reily of John Michael and Mary	Lydia Williams
14 Jun	Susan Reily of John and Susan	Philip Nottingham, Mary Gough
18 Jun	Martha Carbery of Thomas and Martha	Ann Carbery
18 Jun	Mary Ann Bowls of William and Mary	Ignatius Bowls, Anastasia Cecil
18 Jun	Ann Nevit of Joseph and Ann	John Payn, Susan Gough
5 Jul	Francis Davis of Stephen and Ann	Walter and Sarah Davis
5 Jul	Ignatius Joy of Ignatius and Ann	John and Henrietta Raily
19 Jul	George Greenwell of John and Ann	Ignatius and Eleanor Joy
19 Jul	Juliana Jarboe of Peter and Margaret	Joshua Abell, Mary Ann Bowling
26 Jul	male Norris of Bartholomew and Ann	James and Mary Williams
Jul	male Fenwick of Robert and Belinda	Catherine Fenwick
31 Jul	female Cecil of Ignatius and wife	Basil Howard, Rachel Cecil
6 Aug	John Shercliff of Thomas and Elizabeth	Zachariah Mattingly, Eleanor Duggans
6 Sep	William Stone of William and Elizabeth	John Baptist Maraman, --- Bright
6 Sep	Aloysius Pilketon of Richard and Ann	James More, Ann Dunn
20 Sep	Winifred Morgan of John and Winifred	John Courts, Birgitta Roberts
20 Sep	Jane Joy of Enoch and Rebecca	Bartholomew and Dorothy Greenwell
16 Oct	John Baptist Clark of Thomas and Elizabeth	Philip Norris, Eleanor Daft
25 Oct	Henrietta Norris of Thomas and Mary	Vincent Norris, Monica Horell
25 Oct	Margaret Heard of Basil and Eleanor	Ignatius Mills, Eleanor Nottingham
25 Oct	Sarah Clark of William and Mary	William Heard, Mary Ann ---
14 Nov	--- Payn of Baptist and wife	
15 Nov	Edward Goddard of Baptist and Ann	Ignatius Goddard, Ann Hazel
Nov	Edward Adams of Solomon and Dorothy	Stephen Gough, Ann Herpard
Nov	Susan Newton of Ignatius and Elizabeth	William Newton, Jane Booth

1779

Jan	Thomas Spalden of Benedict and Aloysia	Gerard Ford, Eleanor Abell
24 Jan	Wilfred Drury of Peter and Eleanor	Michael and Ann Drury
24 Jan	Aloysius Joy of Athanatius and Ann	Peter and Catherine Drury
Jan	James More of James and Ann	Athanatius Joy, Jr., Ann ---
3 Feb	Ann Floyd of Jesse and Mary	Peter Jarboe, Elizabeth Joy
7 Feb	Ignatius Smith of John and Elizabeth	Athanatius and Mary Ford
Feb	Aloysius ---	Zachariah and Aloysia Yates
Feb	Samuel ---	Joshua Abell, Mary Bowes
Feb	James ---	Thomas Aud, Dorothy Dorsy
28 Feb	Ignatius Jarboe of Matthew and Mary	Charles Jarboe, Susan Stone
14 Mar	--- Bowls of William and Catherine	Thomas and Ann Howard
28 Mar	George Carpenter of William and Lydia	Leonard Booth, Elizabeth Mattingly
3 Apr	Ignatius Ford of Philip and Elizabeth	Henry Ford, sister [whose?]
5 Apr	Ignatius Greenwell of Ignatius and Susan	Henry and Mary Greenwell
Apr	--- Williams of Hugo and Lydia	---
18 Apr	Jesse Dyne of James and Eleanor	James Russell, Ann Dunn
24 Apr	Joseph Brown of Nicholas and Eleanor	Peter and Mary Brown
1 May	John Drury of Philip and Emerentiana	Ignatius and Sarah Drury
8 May	Bibiana Clark of Abraham and Cloa	Abner Abell, Ann Brown
May	Jane Baddock of John and Eleanor	James Payn, Sara Anderson's dau
6 Jun	Ann Herpard of John and Anastasia	Edmund Norris, --- Clark

	--- Jenkins of John and Mary	--- Griggs
	--- Asquith of Robert and Cecilia	
	--- Smith of John and wife [NC]	
Apr	--- Herbert of William	
2 Apr	James --- of --- and Mary	
3 Apr	--- Baily of --- and Ann	
	--- of William and ---	
Apr	[?]	Elizabeth Byrne
	Jane --- of John and ---	--- Brooke
May	Sarah Meekins of Matthew and Priscilla	
	Mary --- of Dennis and Mary	--- and Mary Phillips
	--- Brooke of Roger and wife	
27 May	Priscilla Yets of James and wife	George Brewer, Mary Griggs
2 Jul	John Lee of Samuel and Elizabeth	John and Susan Cecil
2 Jul	Richard Rhodes of Bernard and Belinda	John and Elizabeth Rhodes
	--- Fenwick of Richard and Elizabeth	--- Fenwick, Ann ---
	Mary Langley of [John and Jane?]	Richard and Dorothy Ford
6 Jul	Ann Bean of John and Ann	Thomas and Mildred Hilton
	Ann Fish of Joseph and Lydia	Joseph and Elizabeth Rhodes
9 Jul	Eleanor Jordan of John and Susan	Jeremiah Jordan, Elizabeth Bullock
27 Jul	Joseph Smith of William and Ann	James Richard, Susan Cecil
30 Jul	John Lee of Elizabeth	George Brewer, Mary Herbert
30 Jul	Sarah [Diggs?] of Charles and Sarah	Charles Lee, Elizabeth Lucas
6 Aug	Elizabeth Manley of John and Elizabeth	James Michaels, Elizabeth Gough
	Ann Brian of John (NC)	Stephen Wimsatt, Ann Bullock
6 Aug	Bernard Ford of Robert and Sarah	Joseph Cullison and wife
6 Aug	Winifred Thompson of Basil and wife	John Drury, Anastasia Leigh
6 Sep	Ann B--- of John and ---	
11 Sep	John Baley of Edmund and Elizabeth	Catherine Adams
22 Oct	Stephen Meekins of Henry and Elizabeth	Henry Meekins, Sr., Dorothy Meekins
26 Oct	Richard Tubman of Richard and Ann	Richard Tubman, Jr., Dorothy Taylor
27 Dec	Ann Smith of William and wife	Susan Cecil
27 Dec	Benedict Raily of Benedict and Susan	John Drury, Anastasia Manley
31 Dec	Mary Clark of William and Monica	Henry Goodrum, Ann Mills

1787

3 Jan	Jeremiah Cullison of Joseph and wife	---
14 Jan	Rodulphus Manley of Anastasia	Matthew Gough, Mary Herbert
1 Feb	James Cullison of Joseph, Sr. and Mary	Ann Doran
2 Feb	John Laurence of William and Sarah	Thomas Brewer, Barbara Carpenter
	[Henrietta?] Drury of Joseph and Eliz.	Matthew Manley
27 Feb	John Lucas of Henry and Elizabeth	Samuel and Susan Smith
	Catherine Fenwick of John and Jane	Benedict Fenwick, Catherine James
	--- Shinton of J---, Sr. and Rebecca	
	Ann Peak of Ignatius and Frances	Robert Jarboe, Elizabeth Carpenter
	Gabriel Duvol of Miles and Harpi	Moses and Eleanor Tarlton
	Walter --- of Robert and Elizabeth	James Richie, Mary Herbert
Sep	--- Holton of William and Mary	
	Anastasia [or Elexius] Price of Joseph	John Baptist Price, Mrs. John Tear
	and Sarah	
	--- Higman of Daniel and ---	John Baptist Price, Sara ---d
9 Sep	Elizabeth Cole of widow	Enoch and Ann Campbell
23 Oct	Elizabeth Jarboe of John and Ann	Elizabeth Attwood
Nov	Nicholas Leigh of Richard and Mary	Joseph and Elizabeth Mattingly
1 Nov	Mary Sullivan of Jeremiah and Winifred	Benedict Reily, Elizabeth Byrne

Feb	Richard Vowles of Thomas and wife	Richard and Susan Peek
Feb	Juliana Greenwell of Joshua and wife	Priscilla Attwood
Feb	Ignatius Byrne of Nicholas [or Michael] and Priscilla	James Richie, Mary Herbert
17 Mar	Elizabeth Jenkins of Jeremiah and wife	Adam Jenkins, widow Jarbo, sister
18 Mar	Ann Campbell of Enoch and Elizabeth	Thomas and Sarah Newton
21 Mar	male Combs of Enoch and Ann	--- Combs, Jr., Mary Combs
23 Mar	Eleanor Vessels of Charles and Anastasia	John --- Drury, Margaret Williams
	--- Cullison of Joseph and Margaret	
	Ann Cecil of John and Susan	--- Thompson
20 Jul	Mary Jarboe of Henry and Sarah	Henry ---, Elizabeth Taylor
31 Jul	Thomas Carbery of Thomas and Sarah	John Carbery, Barbara Fenwick
24 Sep	Pius Brewer of George and Mary	Benedict More, Mildred More

1789

Date	Child of Parents	Sponsors
1 Feb	Monica Underwood of Charles and wife	--- Herbert
3 Feb	Jane Fenwick of John and Jane	Richard Fenwick, Belinda ---
22 Feb	--- Schafer of Thomas and wife	Thomas Goodrum
22 Feb	Aloysius Greenwell of Joshua and wife	
5 Apr	Joseph Drury of Joseph and Elizabeth	Francis Xavier Drury, Susan Reily
Apr	Thomas Smith of William and Susan	Samuel Smith, Sarah French
9 Apr	Charles Jeffery of widow (NC)	Sarah Vaughan
10 Apr	Sarah Wilkison of James and Elizabeth	John Goodrum, Ann Bright
19 Apr	Charles Clark of Charles and Linda	Ignatius and Ann Clark
19 Apr	Elizabeth Cullison of [Joseph?] and Sarah	Benedict Wheatley
19 Apr	Mary Greenwell of Joseph and Rebecca	Henry Belwood, Ann Leigh
19 Apr	Elizabeth Carter of Henry (NC) and Eliz.	Raphael Howard and wife
20 Apr	Barbara Manley of John and Elizabeth	James Richie, --- Manley
31 May	male Bright of Baptist and wife	Basil Bright, Mary Peak
3 Jun	Samuel Rouarck of Henry (NC) and Rose	Agnes Meekins, sister of Rose
4 Jun	--- of Sarah --- (NC)	Joseph Bennet, Sarah Led---
5 Jun	Mary Harper of Rachel	Bartholomew and Agnes Hale
6 Jun	Henrietta Harpar of Richard and Ann	Henry Meekins, Sr., Elizabeth Ha
7 Jun	Sarah Meekins of Joshua and Rachel (NC)	Joseph Harper, Agnes Hale
7 Jun	Ann --- of Richard and Monica	William Brooke, Rebecca Byrne
7 Jun	Elizabeth Bowes (NC) of Elizabeth (NC)	William Brooke, Mary Prichard
7 Jun	Jeremiah Prichard of Thomas and Mary	Eleanor Prichard, Rachel Prichard
14 Jun	Abram Sullivan of Jeremiah	
17 Jun	Monica [Lee(?) see 1786] of Samuel and Elizabeth	John and Susan Cecil
21 Jun	John Asquith of Robert and Cecilia	Aloysius Leigh, Letitia Sewell
21 Jun	female Dyal of Joshua and Elva	Joseph and Lydia Fish
5 Jul	Dorothy Fenwick of Richard and Elizabeth	John Gough, Priscilla Fenwick
12 Jul	Ann Laurence of William and Sarah	Lydia Gregs, Elizabeth Carpenter
19 Jul	Aloysia Fenwick of Robert and Sarah	Basil Booth, Elizabeth Tanner
19 Jul	female More of William and Elizabeth	John Chrysostom Drury, Margaret Williams
26 Jul	female Asquith of Robert and Cecilia	Edward Bellwood, Letitia Sewall
19 Aug	Joseph McKinny of Ruben and Priscilla	Eleanor Carpenter
11 Oct	Dorothy Staplefoot of Charles and Dorothy	Richard and Mary Tubman
Oct	John Phillips of Elliott and Margaret	Richard Tubman, Hilary Harper
25 Oct	Rebecca Jarboe of Robert and Elizabeth	William Holton, Ann Belwood
Nov	Ann Reily of Benedict and Susan	Francis Drury, Margaret Williams
14 Dec	--- Fairbrothers of Sullivan and Mary	Priscilla Fairbrothers
Dec	John Drury of John Chrysostom and wife	James Richie, Mary Williams

1790

Jan	Teresa Milburne of Joseph and Mary	Charles Clark
20 Feb	Teresa Smith of Moses and Arminta	Adam Lyons, Mary Thomas
Feb	James Fish of Joseph and Lydia	John Goodrum, Jr., Priscilla Aud
Mar	Mary Vessels of Charles and Anastasia	Benedict and Susan Riley
Mar	Jane Cecil of John and Susan	Ignatius Thompson, Frances Clark alias Leigh
20 Mar	Elizabeth Greenwell of Joshua and Eleanor	Jeremiah Jenkins, Eliz. Wilkinson
20 Mar	Elizabeth Wilkinson of James (NC) and Elizabeth	John Goodrum, Sr., Anna Bright
20 Mar	Rachel Jarboe of Robert and Elizabeth	Negroes
29 Mar	Elizabeth Richardson of Willoughby and Mary	Henry Goodrum, Jane Hendley
5 Apr	Elizabeth Jarboe of John and Ann	Henry Belwood, Elizabeth Jarboe
9 Apr	Susan Mc--- of John and Susan	Belinda Rhodes
13 Apr	James Taylor of Eleanor	Ann Doran
20 Apr	Charles Tubman of Richard and Ann	Ellen Phillips, Catherine, dau of William Phillips
21 Apr	Susan Meekins of Henry and Elizabeth	Richard Tubman, Mary Meekins
23 Apr	Matthew Johnson of Robert and Elizabeth (NC)	Rosa Rouark
25 Apr	Anastasia Shinton of William and Rachel	Richard and Sarah Tubman
25 Apr	Sarah Harpar of Richard and Ann	Richard Harpar, Rachel Shinton
16 May	Robert Price of John and Ann	James Richie, Henrietta Coad
6 Jun	Eleanor Price of Joseph and Sarah	John Pain, Elizabeth Gough
Aug	--- Hager of Matthias and ---	Belinda Rhodes
5 Sep	John Jordan of John and Susan	Jeremiah and Ann Jordan
5 Sep	Mary Belwood of Henry and Elizabeth	Jeremiah Heard
19 Sep	Samuel Smith of Samuel and Elizabeth	Basil Booth, Mary Smith
26 Sep	Elizabeth McLean of Arthur and wife	Thomas and Priscilla Aud
26 Sep	Anastasia Shirley of Benedict and Mary	William Holton, Susan Peak
29 Nov	Bennet Greenwell of Benedict and Susan	Joseph and Frances Heard

Jan	Vitus Herbert of William	John Leigh, Mary Fenwick
13 Mar	--- Cecil of Benedict and wife	
20 Mar	Elizabeth Booth of Basil and Elizabeth	Benedict Greenwell, Elizabeth Smith
25 Mar	James Evans of Ignatius and Elizabeth	Henry Bellwood, Elizabeth Gough
27 Mar	James Attwood of Priscilla, widow	[female] Cole
3 Apr	Mary Rhodes of Bernard and Belinda	Ann Clark
17 Apr	Mary Wooton of Joseph and Eleanor	Richard and Elizabeth Wooton
24 Apr	Mary Redmond of Joshua and Elizabeth	Thomas Goodrum, Catherine ---
24 Apr	Ann Cole of Ann	Thomas Wooton, Jr., Winifred Cole
26 Apr	El--- Bullock of Ann	Susan Bullock
5 May	Ann Cullison of Joseph and Margaret	M. Leigh, Mary Thomas
5 May	Sarah Clark of Charles and Synda	William Herbert, Sr., Ann Bellwood
5 May	Mary Higman of Daniel and wife	Baptist ---, Benedict Wheatley
9 Aug	James Laurence of William and Sarah	Eleanor Carpenter
14 Sep	--- Morris of John and Ann	Moses Tarlton and wife
20 Sep	Elizabeth Fenwick of Richard and Belinda	James Richie, Mary Herbert
1 Nov	Ignatius Fenwick of Richard and Elizabeth	Benedict and Sarah Fenwick

15 Jan	James Wheatley of Benedict and Sarah	William and Ann Herbert
29 Jan	Joseph Leigh of Joseph and Frances	James Richie, Mary Heard
15 Feb	Benedict Joseph Heard of Richard and wife	John Heard, Eleanor Wheeler
26 Feb	Sarah Thompson of James and Ann	Ignatius Coad, Mary [bro., sister]
1 Mar	Mary Gill of Dirinda	Susan Bullock
4 Mar	Joseph Raily of Benedict and Susan	Joseph Drury, Ann Dresden Clark
4 Mar	William Rice of George and Susan	Benedict Greenwell, Mary Underwood
21 Mar	Margaret Fish of Joseph and Lydia	Thomas Aud, Jane Cullins
26 Mar	William Cocks of Luke and Susan	Synda Clark
1 Apr	Eleanor Greenwell of Joshua and Eleanor	Joseph Fish, Elizabeth Watts
1 Apr	Ann Wilkinson of --- (NC) and wife	John Goodrum, Ann Bright
5 Apr	Robert Drury of John Chrysostom and wife	Ignatius and Elizabeth Drury
5 Apr	Ann Belwood of Henry and Elizabeth	William and Ann Herbert
9 May	Sarah Lee of Elizabeth, widow	Susan Bullock
13 May	Joseph Price of Joseph and Sarah	Samuel Smith, Mrs. John B. Howard
13 May	John Corbin of James and wife	son and dau of John B. Howard
28 May	Elizabeth Jarboe of Robert and Elizabeth	William Holton, Rebecca Belwood
29 May	--- Leigh of Christopher and Mary	John Goodrum, Eleanor Jarboe
17 Jun	Charles Lee of Richard and Mary	Matthew Manley, Mildred Moore
1 Jul	Lucy Moore of William and Elizabeth	Benedict Moore, oldest dau of Ignatius Moore
22 Jul	--- McLean of Richard and wife	---
15 Aug	Dorothy Cissell of John and Susan	Augustine Cissell, Ann Thompson
9 Sep	Benedict Cooper of Frances, widow	Basil Booth, Mary Ann Edgerton
29 Sep	William Dennis of widow	female slave of William Richardson
7 Oct	Aloysius Pool of Richard and Susan	Joseph and Anastasia Medley
21 Oct	Sarah Vaughan of Elizabeth	Joseph Cullison, Jr., Mary Lee
23 Oct	Mary Herbert of William and Ann	Edward Bellwood, M. Herbert
25 Oct	Elizabeth Bright of Basil and Henrietta	Belinda Spalding
25 Oct	--- Wooton of Thomas	John Denyk, --- Wooton
2 Dec	John Smith of Samuel and Elizabeth	Basil Booth, Dorothy Manley

1793

Epiphany	William and Thomas Herbert of William and Elizabeth	James Richie, slaves
7 Jan	Thomas Smith of Ann	Mary Kilson
13 Jan	Robert Gibbons of Thomas	Benedict Moor, Dorothy Tarlton
27 Jan	Eleanor Manley of Matthew and Mary Ann	John Chrysostom and Monica Drury
4 Feb	Richard Jenkins of William and Elizabeth	Ann Jenkins, Elizabeth's sister
20 Feb	Mary Swan of William and Henrietta	Ignatius Coad, Ann Fletcher
3 Mar	Anastasia Vessels of Charles and Anastasia	Margaret Greggs, oldest brother c young Anastasia
17 Mar	Robert Clark of Matthew and Elizabeth	William Herbert, Helena Fenwick
24 Mar	Mary Catherine Holton of William and Mary	Robert and Elizabeth Jarboe
31 Mar	Thomas Price of John and Elizabeth	Joseph Arthurs, Elizabeth Herbert
31 Mar	Eleanor Fenwick of Richard and Belinda	William Herbert, Juliana Price
7 Apr	Sarah Ford of Robert and Sarah	Charles and Sarah Howard
14 Apr	Elizabeth Cecil of Francis and Susan	Basil Booth, Mary Fenwick
19 May	Anastasia Coad of Joseph and Eleanor	John Gough, Dorothy Cecil
19 May	Solomon McKinny of Ruben and Priscilla	Charles Lee, Ann Duke
26 May	--- Wilkson of John (NC) and wife	John Goodrum, Jr., Ann Bright
2 Jun	Charles Cullison of Joseph and Margaret	Charles Clark, Mary Underwood
2 Jun	Joseph Heard of Benedict and Mary	J. and Frances Heard
9 Jun	Ignatius Greenwell of Benedict and Eleanor	Joseph and Margaret Coad
19 Aug	Elizabeth Dafihan of James (NC)	Richard Pool, slave
13 Oct	Joseph Fenwick of John and Jane	Joseph Herbert, Margaret Fenwick
21 Oct	Elizabeth Hagar of Matthew and wife	Belinda Rhodes
10 Nov	Zachariah Tarlton of Zachariah and Mary	bro. and sister of Zachariah
24 Nov	Ann McLean of Richard and Elizabeth	Rebecca Belwood, Allison Field
8 Dec	James Thompson of James and Ann	William and Ann Herbert
8 Dec	Susan Wooten of Joseph and Eleanor	Thomas and Ann Wooten
17 Dec	Benedict Biscoe of Bennett and Mary	Jane Brian
30 Dec	Francis Fish of Joseph and Lydia	Basil and Elizabeth Booth

1794

2 Mar	Richard Fenwick of Richard and Elizabeth	Richard Fenwick, Jr., Ann Gough
16 Mar	Jeremiah Cissell of Jeremiah and Dorothy	Nicholas Sewall, Jr., Grace Fenwick
29 Mar	Eliza Thomas of Philip and Eleanor (NC)	Susan Moore
30 Mar	El--- Tarlton of Richard and Dorothy	Stephen Moore, Catherine ---
13 May	William Williamson of Mark and Mary	Ann Bright
20 May	Mary Leigh of Joseph and Frances	Thomas Clark, Eleanor Coad
20 May	Ignatius Price of Joseph and Sarah	Ann Price
20 May	Ann Underwood of Charles and Mary	Jeremiah Underwood, Margaret Cullison
25 May	Elizabeth Booth of Basil and Elizabeth	John Goodrum
26 May	Philip Cooper of widow	Elizabeth Gough
28 May	Mar. Vaugan of Elizabeth	Elizabeth Sherley
28 May	Mary Drury of John Chrysostom and ---	Ignatius and Monica Drury
28 May	Walter Jarboe of Rodulphus and Elizabeth	Henry and Elizabeth Bellwood
3 Jun	William Hall of Joseph	Mary Lee
20 Jun	--- Goldsbury of widow	Susan [slave]
7 Jul	Thomas Lee of James	Mary Lee
13 Jul	Joseph Cissell of Joseph and Eleanor	J. Gough, Dorothy Cissell
13 Jul	Mary Williams of Benjamin and Mary	Nicholas and Mary Sewall
19 Jul	--- Laurence of --- and Sarah	Eleanor Carpenter
30 Aug	James and Eleanor Smith of John M. and Anastasia	Ann Smith

In the year 1767, received into ye Roman Church (the following): -----, Bennet
Abell, Eleanor Wimsatt, Ann Reily, Sarah Williams, Zeph Forest, Susan Hall,
Rebecca Goldsmith, Cloe Tarlton, John Letham, John Dyal (Duval?], Jus. Gold-
smith, Thomas Tarlton, Eleanor Fisher, Elizabeth Siford, Jesse Knott's wife,
John Hardesty, Sarah Wheatley, James Anderson, Mary Hazel married to Baptist
Goddard, Ann Hattel[-r?], Ann Rogers, John Drudge, Thomas Forrest, Philip Reed,
William Leach, Stephen Adams, Mary M[egrs?], Mary Logue, Esther Sher[cl?]if,
Esther Henry, Sarah -----, others illegible.

There were many instances in the parochial register where the priest inscribed
in Latin that on such and such an approximate date he baptized x number of
persons whose names he had forgotten. Apparently some of the preceding baptisms
were entered from memory, instances where he remembered the names of the parents
and not the children.

Some of the abbreviations and/or substitutes used for certain names in the preceding baptisms appear below.

Abelona, Abelony - [Apolonia ?]
Alethar, Alethea - Althea
Alisia, Alley - Aloysia
An., Anna - Ann, Anastasia
Barnard - Bernard
Bart. - Barton, Bartholomew
Ben. - Benedict, Bennet, Bennett
Cavey -
Cloa, Cloe - Chloe
Drayden, Dresden -
Ena - Bibiana, Emerentiana
Fran. - Frances, Francis
Harpi - Arpy
Jess, Jesse - Justinian
Joa. - Jane, Joan, Johanna, John
Jos. - Joseph, Josiah
Luc. (female) - Lucy
Luc. (male) - Luke
Lydy, Lydya - Lydia
Mar. (female) - Mary
Mar. (male) - Mark
Minta - Arminta
Rhod. - Rodulphus, Rhodias
Statia - Anastasia
Teresia - Theresa

Surnames have been uniformly transcribed as they were recorded although in some cases the spelling differed from current usage. You will find below a list of alternate spellings of surnames. Odd-looking spellings may stand alone when the correct spelling is doubtful. Some names were never spelled correctly; current usage is given in brackets.

Abel, Abell
Alvi [Alvey]
Bellwood, Belwood
Bowes, Bowls (are they the same)
Bowlen, Bowling
Byrn, Byrne
Cecil, Cicil, Cissell, Sissall
Clark, Clarke
Conaly, Conolay
Craycraft, Crecraft
Cullen, Cullens
Culins [Collins?]
Culleson, Cullison
Dean, Dyne
Diegs, Diggs
Dorsey, Dorsy, Dosse
Duvol [Duvall]
Forest, Forrest
Gaudard, Goddard
Guido, Guither
Harel, Horell, Horrell
Haret
Haden, Hayden, Heyden
Hagar, Hager, Hagur
Harpar, Harper
Heard, Herd
Herbert, Herpard
Hodgkins, Hoskins [Hutchins?]
Jarber,Jarbo, Jarboe
Knot, Knott
Laton, Leaton [Layton]
Lee, Leigh
Low, Lowe
Macwilliams, MacWilliams, McWilliams
Maning, Manning
Manley (sometimes confused with Mattingly?)
Maramen, Mareman
Mattingley, Mattingly
Mehoney
Milborn, Milburn, Milburne
Moor, Moore, More
Nevit, Nevitt, Nivet
Pain, Payn, Payne
Peak, Peek, Pyke

Raily, Raley, Reiley, Reily, Riley
Raper, Rapier
Ros, Ross
Rouarck, Rouark
Russel, Russell, Russels
Scot
Sewall, Sewel, Sewell, Suales, Swales
Shange, Shanks
Shirkley (some entries mean Shirley?)
Shirkley (some entries mean Shircliff?)
Spalden, Spaldin, Spalding
Taney, Tawney
Thompson, Tompson
Vaugan, Vaughan
Vowles, Vowls
Vessels [Vessells]
Wathan, Wathen
Whitfield, Witfield
Wilkeson, Wilkinson, Wilkison
Wimsatt, Winsatt
Wooten, Wooton
Yates, Yets

MARRIAGES

ST. FRANCIS XAVIER AND ST. INIGOES

(St. Inigoes indicated by †)

1767

	23 Jul	John B. Spalden and Ann Jackson
	8 Oct	William Heard and Susan Ford
		Thomas Anderson and Ann Egl---
	23 Oct	Bennet Abell and Mary Greenwell
		Peter Howard and Eleanor Gough

1768

†	10 Jan	William Herbert and Anne Milbourne
	16 Jan	James Parsons and Elizabeth Drury
†	19 Jan	James Atwood and Henrietta Jarboe
†	19 Jan	John Guido and Jane Brooke
†	21 Jan	John Tomkins and Mary Brewer
	30 Jan	John Mattingly and Ann Ford
	9 Feb	James Cullen and Susan Hall (NC)
†	16 Feb	Charles Underwood and Ann Farthing
†	16 Feb	John Baptist Peek and Grace Craghill
	21 Mar	Sylvester Wheatley and Sarah Medcalf, widow

1769

4 Dec	James Murrein and Mary Johnson
11 Dec	John Peak and Susan Yets
11 Dec	Ignatius Drury and Anastasia French
11 Dec	John Payn and Biner Stewart
11 Dec	Bernard Newton and Mary Payn

1770

22 Jan	Zachariah Barnes and Susan Thompson
28 Jan	John Sanson and Mary Jarboe
27 Feb	Edward Stone and Ann Joy
22 Mar	Ignatius Norris and Lucy [Pike?]
18 Aug	John Baptist Norris and Mary Woodward
25 Aug	Stephen Winsatt and Mary ---
3 Sep	Philip Fenwick and Rebecca Greenwell
4 Sep	Philip Drury and Ann Newton
6 Sep	John Russel and Susan French
30 Sep	John and Ann Diggs (exactly as it reads)
Oct	Peter Mattingly and Catherine Spalden
3 Nov	Michael Drury and Ann Yets
3 Dec	Roger and Maria Brook, related in 3rd degree
4 Dec	John Dean and Jane Stone
21 Dec	George Collins and Ann Lucas, widow

1771

29 Jan	Raphael Ford and Ann Spalden
5 Feb	Joseph Williams and Ann Heard, dau of James Heard's widow
7 Feb	Richard Poily [Raily?] and Susan Newton
20 Apr	Bennet Hodgkins and Susan Gatten
21 Apr	James Malohone and Mary Langley
17 Jun	Francis Wheatley and Anastasia Cecil
25 Jun	Michael Taney and Monica Brooke
22 Jul	Ben. Cusack and Ann Jones
5 Aug	Ignatius Carroll, widower, and Winifred Coats, widow
19 Sep	James Vowles and Priscilla Payn
23 Sep	Francis Roberts and Mary Pilbrough
30 Dec	Enoch Campbell and Elizabeth Hall

1772

11 Feb	Luke Mattingly and Eleanor Thompson, related in the second degree
18 Feb	Joseph Shanks and Susanna Goldsmith
23 Feb	Thomas Thompson and Henrietta Abel
29 May	Thomas Curbey and Monica Reily
18 Jul	Richard Pilketon and Elizabeth Siford
11 Oct	Josua Clark and Mary Bowles
15 Oct	Joseph Davis and Jemima Wimsatt
18 Oct	Zachariah Abell (NC) and Mary Strong
19 Oct	Charles Jarboe and Elizabeth Stone
10 Nov	Joshua Melton and Sarah Molohorn
10 Nov	John Fenwick and Mary Thompson
17 Nov	Rodulphus Jarboe and Monica Williams
28 Nov	Thomas Jarboe and Ann Lucust
22 Dec	Aquilla Hall (NC) and Mary Davis
22 Dec	John Horrell and Monica Brown
23 Dec	Ignatius Goddard and Ann Pyke (NC)
29 Dec	Joseph Stone and Dorothy Spink
31 Dec	Ignatius Wimsatt and Mary Medley

1773

14 Feb	Jeremiah Gatten and Elizabeth Drury
6 Mar	James Norris and Monica Greenwell
21 Mar	Hugo Williams and Lydia Stone
30 Mar	Alban Newton and Mary Ann Pike
25 May	James French and Susan Melton
26 May	Edmund Jenkins and Elizabeth Milborn
9 Jul	Patrick Hogan and Eleanor Engleton
27 Jul	Thomas Riswick and Mary Nottingham
7 Sep	Sylvester Wheatley and Elizabeth Fraiser (NC)

1773

27 Sep		Thomas Brewer and Minta Dawsey
28 Sep		Richard Wathan, widower, and Eleanor Mattingly
8 Nov		Ignatius Abell and Mary Abell
11 Nov		Enoch Stone and Monica Goldsberry
18 Nov		John Smith, Sr. and Jane Manning
21 Dec		Peter Brown and Susan Low

1774

11 Jan		Leonard Johnson and Mary Molohorn
31 Jan	*	Anthony Brown, widower, and Ann Brewer
10 Apr		Raphael Greenwell and Cloa Tarlton
27 May		William Russell, Jr., and Ann Draden Abell
Jun		Joshua Greenwell and Elizabeth Newton
19 Jun		Cuthbert Clark and Mary Ann Brown
3 Jul	*	Thomas Fenwick and Elizabeth Thomas, widow
12 Jul		John Drudge and Ann Howard
12 Sep	*	John Dean, widower, and Mary Moore
1 Oct		John Smith and Elizabeth Ford
11 Oct		Wilford Thompson and Ann Shircliff
5 Nov		Jesse Floyd and Elizabeth Suales
31 Dec		Basil Nottingham and Jane Stone, widow

1775

8 Feb		Bernard Newton and Mary Pike
16 Feb		Thomas Joy and Sarah Fields
28 Feb		Richard Pilketon and Ann Hutchings, both widowed
25 Jul		John Hardesty and Catherine Thompson
10 Jul		John Reed and Rebecca Letham
8 Aug		Daniel Friend and Cloe Payn
30 Sep		Philip Ford and Elizabeth Spalden
24 Oct		Gabriel Newton and Henrietta Wheatley, widow
Nov		Ignatius Shirly and Mary Norris
14 Dec	*	Benedict More and Susan Peacock (NC), both widowed
19 Dec		Francis Wheeler and Ann Birchmore

1776

11 Jan		John Bowls and Elizabeth Payn
19 Feb		William Fowler and Mary Mattingly
4 Mar		James More and Ann Dorsy
1 Jun	*	Thomas Forrest and Catherine Mattingly, widow
12 Jun	*	James Fenwick and Henrietta Howard
11 Jul		William Howard and Eleanor Thompson
16 Jul		Philip Reed and Ann Smith
27 Nov		William Heard and Susan Abell
1 Dec		Thomas Leach and Elizabeth Spalden

1777

21 Jan	Ignatius Bowles and Catherine Gough
18 Mar	Jesse Floyd, widower, and Mary Cavey (?) Reed
16 Mar	James Dyne and Eleanor More
20 Jun	Basil Brown and Ann Mattingly
22 Aug	James Fish and Ann Wheatly
3 Nov	Robert Abell and Margaret Mills
20 Nov	Ignatius Low and Priscilla Norris
1 Dec	Thomas Bryan Harris and Mary Mattingly, widow

1778

19 Jan	John Reynolds and Ann French
26 Jan	Zachariah Brewer and Dorothy Cecil
23 Mar	John Wimsatt and Sarah Howard
19 Apr	William Clark and Mary Hopewell
19 Apr *	Samuel Denike (NC) and Ann Witfield
12 Oct	Arthur McGill and Ann Stone
29 Nov	Stephen Adams and Henrietta Low
29 Nov	Joseph Ford and Henrietta Spink
29 Nov	James Fenwick and Catherine Ford
22 Dec	William Bradburn and Elizabeth Edley

1779

7 Feb	Henry Medley and Margaret Ford
21 Feb	Joseph Stone and Elizabeth More
Oct ?	Peter Ford and Mary Sewall
Oct	James Yets and Ann Thompson
Nov	John Daft and Ann Spalden
21 Dec	Benedict Spalden and Ann Stone, both widowed

1780

| 5 Mar | Basil Thompson and Cloe Brown |
| 9 Mar | Basil Booth and Elizabeth Henry |

1784

†	20 Mar	Thomas Fitzgerald and Susan Ellet
†	21 Jun *	Abram Rhodes and Mary Dant
†	4 Jul	Sulavan Fairbrothers and Mary Keech
†	5 Jul	Thomas Baily and Mary Smith
†	6 Jul	Barny Rhodes and Melinda Smith
†	11 Jul	John Manly and Elizabeth Lowry
†	22 Jul *	Charles Lee and Elizabeth Moore
†	1 Aug	James Atwood and Ann Jenkins
†	16 Aug	Bennet Reily and Susanna Drury

* Either they or their descendants eventually settled at The Barrens in Perry County, Missouri.

Census -- St. Inigoes, St. Mary's Co., Md., 1768

Joseph Allison
Mary Angel
William Angel
Ann Atwood
Charles Atwood
Henry Atwood
James Atwood
Teresia Atwood

Tom Baily
Winifred Baily
Ann Brewer
Elizabeth Brewer
George Brewer
John Brewer
John Brewer
Mary Brewer
Mary Brewer
Tom Brewer
Mary Briscoe
Ann Brown
Ignatius Brown

Ellen Carpenter
Elizabeth Carpenter
William Carpenter
Ann Cecil
Elizabeth Cecil
Ignatius Clark
Mary Clark
Thomas Clark
William Clark
Joseph Coad
Sara Coad
Monica Cotterel
Samuel Cotterel

Mary Drury
Matthew Drury
Thomas Drury
Jane Dunbar
John Dunbar

Francisca Egiton
Mary Ann Egiton
Rosmonda Egiton
Thomas Egiton
William Egiton
Ann Ellet
Matthew Ellet

Ann Farthing
Ann Fenwick
Benjamin Fenwick
Cuthbert Fenwick
Dorothea Fenwick
Ellenor Fenwick
Elizabeth Fenwick
Elizabeth Fenwick, Jr.
Henrietta Fenwick
Ignatius Fenwick
Mary Fenwick
Mary Anna Fenwick
Richard Fenwick
Sara Fitzgiffard
Ann Fletcher

Elizabeth Geery
George Gough
Monica Gough
Priscilla Gough
Sara Gough
Elizabeth Greggs
Jane Guida
John Guida
Elizabeth Guleson

Mary Hammon
M. Harper
Barbara Heard
Richard Heard
Abigail Herbert
Bennet Herbert
Francis Herbert
Matthew Herbert
Michael Herbert
Michael Herbert
William Herbert
Ann Hogan
Elizabeth Hogan
Priscilla Holton
Robert Holton
William Holton
Ann Howard
Edward Howard
Henrietta Howard

Elizabeth Jarber
Henrietta Jarber
Nancy Jarber
Assicoa/Andreda? Jarboe

Elizabeth Jarboe
Henrietta Jarboe
Mark Jarboe
Mary Jarboe
Monica Jarboe
Teresia Jarboe
Aaron Jefferys
Richard Joy

Diana Keetch

Joseph Langly
Susan Langly
William Langly
Ann Leigh
Elizabeth Leigh
Jane Leigh
John Leigh
John Leigh, Jr.
Joseph Leigh
Margaret Leigh
Mary Leigh
Mary Leigh
Massey Leigh
Sara Leigh

Mary Mahany
Ann Manly
Bazel Manly
John Manly
Martha Manly
Mary Manly
Matthew Manly
Rhod. Manly
Tom Manly
William Martin
Ann Matthews (dead)
Thomas Matthews
Ann Michael
Elizabeth Milbourne
Ann Moore
Ignatius Moore
Mary Moore
John More
Nicholas More, Sr.
Nicholas More, Jr.
Nelly McCawley
William McCawley

Joseph Noble
Mary Novice

Lydia Sanders
Mary Smith
Elizabeth Spalding
Jane Spalding
Eliz. Stiles
Sen. Stiles
Seth Stiles
Solomon Stiles
Alexander Swan
Ann Swan
Ann Swan
Mary Swan

Edward Tiere
John Tiere
Mary Tiere
Mary Tompson
Rebecca Tompson
Richard Tompson
Joseph Tucker
Mary Tucker

Charles Underwood

Brigit Vaughan
Thomas Vaughan

Elizabeth Wheatly
Joseph Wheatly
Ann Williams, Sr.
Benjamin Williams
William Williams
[J. Adderton] slave owner

Census -- St. Inigoes, St. Mary's Co., Md., 1769

Joseph Allison
Mary Allison
Margaret Angel
William Angel
Ann Atwood
Charles ? Atwood
James Atwood
Teresia Atwood
Thomas Atwood

Mark Baily
Mary Baily
Thomas Baily
Mrs. Bennet
Monica Berden
John Berder
Edward Betty
Arminta Breding
George Brewer
John Brewer
Thomas Brewer
Mary Briscoe
Ann Brown
Michael Burns

Ellen Carpenter
Elizabeth Carpenter
Elizabeth Carpenter
Marian Carpenter
Priscilla Carpenter
William Carpenter
Ellen Cawley
Ann Cecil
Elizabeth Cecil
Cuthbert Clark
Ignatius Clark
Marian Clark
Mary Clark
Tom Clark
William Clark
Joseph Code
Sara Code
Richard Cope
Monica Cotterel
Mr. Cotterel
Mr. Culleson

Elizabeth Dagbon
Ann Drury
Elizabeth Drury
Ellen Drury
Francis Drury
James Drury
John Drury
John Drury, Jr.
Joseph Drury
Joseph Drury
Matthew Drury
Mrs. Drury
Susan Drury
Teresa Drury
Jane Dunbar
John Dunbar

Francisca Egiton
Joseph Egiton
Mary Ann Egiton
Mrs. Egiton
Thomas Egiton
William Egiton
Anna Ellet
Matthew Ellet

Ben Fenwick
Cuthbert Fenwick
Dorothea Fenwick
Ellen Fenwick
Elizabeth Fenwick
Elizabeth Fenwick, Jr.
Ignatius Fenwick
James Fenwick
John Fenwick
John Fenwick
John Fenwick, Jr.
M. Fenwick
Marian Fenwick
Mary Fenwick
Mary Fenwick
Nancy Fenwick
Richard Fenwick
Richard Fenwick
Robert Fenwick

Elizabeth Garry
Elizabeth Gough
Elizabeth Gough
Mary Gough
Priscilla Gough
Stephen Gough
Susan Gough
Sebastian Greggs
Elizabeth Gregs
Jane Guither
John Guither
Jon. Guither

Margaret Harper
Abigail Herbert
Bennet Herbert
Franc. Herbert
Matthew Herbert
Mile Herbert
Michael Herbert
Susan Herbert
William Herbert
Mildred Hilton
Priscilla Holton
Robert Holton
William Holton
Ann Howard
Ed. Howard

Alex Jarber
Elizabeth Jarber
Henry Jarber
Henry Jarber
John Baptist Jarber
Mark Jarber
Mary Jarber
Rhode Jarber
Teresia Jarber
Audreda Jarboe
Mary Jarboe
Nancy Jarboe
Aaron Jefferys
Brigit Jefferys
Elizabeth Jefferys
Ann Jones

Diana Keetch
Mary Kilpatrick
Basil Knot
Mary Knot

Josia Langley
Mary Langley
Susanna Langley
William Langly, Sr.
Jane Lee
Ann Leigh
Ann Leigh
Elizabeth Leigh
Jane Leigh
John Leigh
Joseph Leigh
Margaret Leigh
Mary Leigh
Mary Leigh
Mary Leigh
Massey Leigh
Massey Leigh, Jr.
Molly Leigh
William Leigh

Ann Manly
John Manly
John Manly
Matthew Manly
Rhode Manly
Thomas Manly
Elizabeth Milbourn
Joseph Milburn
Ben Moore
Elizabeth Moore
Diana More
John More
Mary More

Joseph Noble
Lydia Noble

Bernard Oneile

Elizabeth Purtle
Susan Purtle

Elizabeth Redmon
Martha Rogers

Elizabeth Sanders
Ignatius Sanders
Ann Smith
Mary Smith
Basil Spalding
Elizabeth Spalding
Jane Spalding
William Spalding
Eliz. Stiles
John Stiles
Seth Stiles
Solomon Stiles
Stephen Stiles
Lydia Stubbings
Alex Swan
Ann Swan
Mary Swan

Monica Taylor
William Taylor
John Tear
John Tear, Jr.
Mary Tear
Monica Tear
William Tear
Mrs. Tompson
Rebecca Tompson
Richard Tompson
Susan Tompson
Joseph Tucker
Mary Tucker

Ann Underwood
Charles Underwood

Thomas Vaughan
Winifred Vaughan

Mrs. Waugher
Joseph Wheatley
Cate Whoote
Mrs. Williams
Ben. Williams, Jr.
William Williams

BAPTISMS

ST. JOSEPH'S CONGREGATION

ST. MARY'S COUNTY, MARYLAND

Performed by Rev. Joseph Mosley, S.J.

(Parentage was not listed)

Person Baptized	Godparents
14 Aug 1760 Mary Magdalene Wathing	Peter Mills, Monica Mills
7 Sep 1760 Dorothy Barber	Josuah Mills, Mary Anne Mills
7 Sep 1760 Albin Mattingly	Joseph Mosley, Hellen Bryan
7 Sep 1760 Anne Drury	Hellen Grinwell, Joseph Compton
21 Sep 1760 Mary Clare Jackson	Josuah Mills, Mary Anne Mills
12 Oct 1760 Margaret MacKibby	Barton Smith, Dorethey Fenwick
30 Oct 1760 Richard Edlen	James Edlen, Susanna Edlen
1 Nov 1760 James Tompson	Mary Dart, John Booth
1 Nov 1760 Joseph Wright	John Knot
1 Nov 1760 Stiphan Commont	Agnes Commont, Ignatius Babin
2 Nov 1760 Raphael Combs	Thomas Taney, Mary Taney
2 Nov 1760 Enoch Spalding	John Power, Mary Spalding, dau of Tom Coor, Jr.
3 Nov 1760 Aloysia Warren	Josuah Mills, Mary Ann Mills
10 Nov 1760 Teresa Mekins	Raymond Shinton, Mary Shinton
10 Nov 1760 Clara Andrews	John Wingatt, Mary Mekins
11 Nov 1760 Sarah Griffin	John Shinton, Frances Sleakam
11 Nov 1760 William Gouty	John Griffin, Mary Caen
11 Nov 1760 Arena Rolender	Joseph Gouty, Elizabeth Daen
16 Nov 1760 Mary Cole	Henry Bryan, Monica Bryan
14 Dec 1760 Ignatius Drury	James Hamilton, Sarah Hamilton
10 Jan 1761 John Harpor	Mr. Sanbar, Mrs. Howard
17 Jan 1761 Catherine Field	Walter Burn, Elizabeth Clarke
1 Feb 1761 Sylvester Gatten	John Bap. Dent, Anne Dant
1 Feb 1761 Mary Power	Alexius Spalding, Mary Spalding
1 Feb 1761 Mary Anne Drury	William Drury, Mary Scherly
1 Feb 1761 Anne Jinkins	Jesse Joseph, Mary Clarke
2 Feb 1761 Henry Noble	Eliz. Thompson, Richard Scherclift
15 Feb 1761 James Knot	James Brewer, Margaret Brewer
15 Feb 1761 Margaret Mattingly	John Melton, Mary Price
21 Feb 1761 Francis Xaverius Scherclift	Richard Scherclift, Eliz. Scherclift
22 Feb 1761 Jane Boarman	Joseph Mosley, Anne Boarman, sister
1 Mar 1761 Philip Mattingly	Peter Mattingly, Marget Mattingly
7 Mar 1761 Eleonora Spalding	Joseph Mosley, Priscilla Spalding
10 Mar 1761 Charles Taney	Francis Taney, Mrs. Neale
29 Mar 1761 Henry Makins	Joseph Shenton, Helen Shehawn

29 Mar 1761	Mary Shehawn	Joseph Shenton, Mary Shenton
29 Mar 1761	Agnes Thompson	Henry Makins, Jr., Elizabeth Haye
5 Mar 1761	Susanna Thompson	Patrick Machaty, Mary Johnson
22 Mar 1761	Athanasius Langly	Joseph Dant, Anne Langly
22 Mar 1761	Elizabeth Alvy	Elenor Alvy, Leonard Johnson
19 Apr 1761	James Bainey	Joseph Clarke, Mary Clarke
19 Apr 1761	Bernard Drury	John Wotten, Elizabeth Drury
19 Apr 1761	Athanasius Windder	Clement Parsons, Mary Parsons -
19 Apr 1761	William Hatton	Alexius Spalding, Belinda Miles
19 Apr 1761	John Burn	John ---, Anne Wathing
30 Apr 1761	Catharine Spalding	Thomas Spalding, Jr. (son of Thomas Spalding, E.H.), Mary Spalding
3 May 1761	John Baptist King	John Brian and his wife
11 May 1761	Mary Power	Edward Spalding, son of C., Susanna, his sister
17 May 1761	Thomas Haddester	John Knott, Susanna Knott
14 May 1761	John Baptist Mahony	Joseph Mahony, Mary Mahony
24 May 1761	Dorothy Millard	Michael Brooke, Mary Brooke
7 Jun 1761	Ignatius Compton	Robert Cole, Tibitha Miles
7 Jun 1761	Anne Mattingly	Edward Spalding, Jr., Margaret Mattingly
6 Jun 1762	Elisabeth Middleton	Jesse Sanders, Mrs. Middleton
19 Jul 1762	Catherine Boarman	Henrietta Semmes, Thomas James Boarman, Jr.
21 Nov 1762	Guthlack Middleton	
8 Dec 1762	William Curry	Mr. Wheeler, Elizabeth Thompson
23 Jan 1763	--- Brent	Jacky Pyle, Jane Parnham
13 May 1763	Clement Hoxton	Mrs. Hoxton, Sr., Joseph Mosley
17 Sep 1763	Nicholas Boarman	Thomas James Boarman, Sr., Jean Boarman, Jr.
10 Nov 1763	Samuel Middleton	Edward Jinkins, Martha Middleton
11 Nov 1763	Ignatius Middleton	Ignatius Middleton, Charity Middleton
27 Nov 1763	Benedict Boarman	Joseph Mosley, Jean Boarman, dau of B.
27 Dec 1763	Leonard Benedict Boarman	Robert Brent, Jean Boarman, dau of Thomas, Jr.
15 Jan 1764	Gutherick Middleton	Edward Boarman, Widow Hanson

[NOTATION: "18th August 1764, I came to Bohemia, to tend ye Eastern Shore]

A few subsequent entries pertained to families mentioned above.

13 Apr 1766	--- Griffin, child of John Griffin
7 Dec 1766	Elizabeth Mekins, child of Thomas Mekins
7 Dec 1766	Nathan Daen, child of Thomas Daen
19 Nov 1766	Mary Mekins, dau of Abraham Mekins
10 Dec 1766	Anne Tubman, dau of Richard Tubman
13 Dec 1766	[reference to Negroes of Mason Shehawn]

"STATE OF HIS LORDSHIP'S MANORS," 1766, 1767, 1768. RENT ROLLS.

All of these lands were either sold by private sale, before the Revolution, or
by the Intendant of the Revenue, as confiscated British property. They were not
sold under their Manor names, but as seated farm lands.

Surname variations within a lease are underscored

Abbreviations adopted to conserve space

[1],[2], etc.--"No. of Lot or Plat."
(A)--"Date of Lease."
(B)--"To Whom Leased."
(C)--"No. of Acres."
(D)--"Tenant in Possession."
(E)--"Annual Rent."
(F)--"Alienation Fine," "Fines Due."
(G)--"Quality of the Land."
(H)--"Improvements."
(K)--"Price per Acre."
(L)--"On What Livés or Term of Years," "now held."
(M)--"Ages of the Persions mentioned in the Lease and other remarks."

STATE OF HIS LORDSHIP'S MANOR OF BEAVERDAM IN ST. MARY'S COUNTY, MARCH, 1768.

1. (A) Dec. 25, 1741; (B) John Raley; (C) 84-1/2; (D) George Plater; (E)
0-10-0; (F) 2-0-0; (L) Jane Raley, Gabriel Raley, John Mitchel Raley; (M) Jane
34, Gabriel 31, John 28.

2. (A) Dec. 25, 1741; (B) Jonathan Seale; (C) 113-1/2; (D) George Plater;
(E) 0-12-0; (F) 2-8-0; (L) Ann Seall; (M) Ann 33.

3. (A) Dec. 25, 1743; (B) Robert Goldsberry; (C) 161-3/4; (D) Jane Goldsberry;
(E) 0-16-8; (F) 3-6-8; (L) Margaret Goldsberry, John Baptist Goldsberry; (M)
Margaret 32, John 24, gone away. Quere his age if living.

4. (A) May 30, 1761; (B) Henry Goldsberry; (C) 14; (D) Jane Goldsberry; (E)
0-4-0; (L) 14 yrs.

5. (A) Dec. 25, 1741; (B) William Stone; (C) 46; (D) Ignatius Stone; (E) 0-4-9;
(F) 1-0-0; (L) Ignatius Stone; (M) Ignatius 27.

6. (A) July 10, 1741; (B) William Stone; (C) 110; (D) Ignatius Stone; (E)
0-10-10; (F) 2-4-0; (L) Ignatius Stone; (M) Ignatius 27.

7. (A) Dec. 25, 1719; (B) William Stone; (C) 58-3/4; (D) Ignatius Stone;
(E) ---; (F) 2-8-10; (L) William Stone, Jr.; (M) William 53.

8. (A) Dec. 11, 1751; (B) William Stone, Jr.; (C) 50-3/4; (D) William Stone,
Jr.; (E) 0-5-10; (F) 1-3-4; (L) William Stone, Jr., Inonia Stone, Mary Stone;
(M) William 53, Inonia 24, Mary 22.

9. (A) Apr. 9, 1729; (B) Francis Harbert; (C) 100-1/4; (D) Ignatius Fenwick; (E) 0-10-3; (F) 4-4-4; (L) Elizabeth Herbert; (M) Elizabeth 39.

10. (A) Sep. 10, 1742; (B) Francis Harbert; (C) 63; (D) Ignatius Fenwick; (E) 0-6-8; (F) 1-6-0; (L) Francis Herbert, Michael Herbert; (M) Francis 29, Michael 31.

11. (A) Dec. 25, 1746; (B) Jonathan Seale; (C) 90-1/2; (D) Ignatius Fenwick; (E) 0-9-10; (F) 2-0-0; (L) Elizabeth Seall, John Baptist Goldsberry; (M) Elizabeth 22, John 24.

12. (A) June 27, 1761; (B) John Dorsey; (C) 6; (D) John Dorsey; (E) 0-1-6; (F) 0-1-6; (L) 14-1/4 years.

13. (A) June 10, 1743; (B) Thomas Blackman; (C) 211; (D) John Dorsey; (E) 1-4-4; (F) 4-17-4; (L) Tabitha Dent; (M) Tabitha 25.

14. (A) Dec. 25, 1741; (B) John Lucas; (C) 119; (D) Enoch Fenwick; (E) 0-14-4; (F) 2-17-4; (L) John Lucas, Ignatius and Thomas Lucas; (M) John 50, Ignatius 27, Thomas 29.

15. (A) May 1, 1737; (B) Enoch Fenwick; (C) 268; (D) Enoch Fenwick; (E) 1-6-2; (F) 5-5-0; (L) Enoch Fenwick, Ignatius Fenwick, John Miles; (M) Enoch 54; Ignatius 37, John 31.

16. (A) Dec. 25, 1741; (B) William and Charles King; (C) 133; (D) Enoch Fenwick; (E) 0-13-3; (F) 2-13-0; (L) Charles King, James King; (M) Charles 48, very sickly, James 31.

17. (A) May 29, 1760; (B) Enoch Fenwick; (C) 29; (D) Enoch Fenwick; (E) 0-4-8; (L) 13 years.

18. (A) Dec. 25, 1741; (B) John Miles; (C) 165; (D) Levin Cracraft; (E) 0-16-0; (F) 3-4-0; (L) Josias Miles; (M) Josias 28.

19. (A) Mar. 29, 1762; (B) Henry Jewell; (C) 12; (D) Levin Cracraft; (E) 0-1-8; (F) 0-1-8; (L) 15 years.

20. (A) June 30, 1760; (B) Lazarus Ross; (C) 82; (D) Lazarus Ross; (E) 0-16-6; (F) 0-16-6; (L) 13-1/4 years.

21. (A) June 30, 1760; (B) John Raley; (C) 79; (D) John Raley; (E) 0-18-9; (F) 0-16-6; (L) 13-1/4 years.

22. (A) Mar. 28, 1726; (B) Paul Peacock, Jr.; (C) 45-3/4; (D) Lessee; (E) 0-4-8; (F) Samuel Abell, Jr., John Abell; (M) Samuel 49, John 47.

23. (A) June 28, 1760; (B) Paul Peacock; (C) 7; (D) Lessee; (E) 0-1-4; (F) 0-1-4; (L) 13-1/4 years.

24. (A) Mar. 26, 1726; (B) Samuel Abell, Sr.; (C) 134; (D) Samuel Abell, Jr.; (E) 0-13-6; (F) 5-8-8; (L) Sam Abell, Jr., John Abell; (M) Sam 49, John 47.

25. (A) Apr. 2, 1741; (B) Samuel Abell; (C) 62; (D) Samuel Abell, Jr.; (E) 0-6-5; (F) 1-5-0; (L) Lidia Abell, Philip Abell; (M) Lidia 32, Philip 27.

26. (A) Mar. 25, 1762; (B) Samuel Abell; (C) 68-1/2; (D) Samuel Abell, Jr.; (E) 0-18-6; (F) 0-18-6; (L) 15 years.

27. (A) May 29, 1762; (B) Samuel Abell; (C) 34; (D) Samuel Abell, Jr.; (E) 0-8-9; (F) 0-8-9; (L) 15 years.

28. (A) Mar. 25, 1762; (B) Samuel Abell; (C) 7-3/4; (D) Samuel Abell, Jr.; (E) 0-1-10; (F) 0-1-10; (L) 15 years.

29. (A) Dec. 21, 1762; (B) Samuel Abell; (C) 7-1/2; (D) Samuel Abell, Jr.; (E) 0-2-0; (L) 74 years. Condemned for a Mill.

30. (A) Aug. 20, 1745; (B) Ignatius Joy, Sr.; (C) 135; (D) Ignatius Joy, Jr.; (E) 0-13-9; (F) 2-14-0; (L) John Raley, Enoch Joy, and Athanatius Joy; (M) John 33, Enoch 26, Athanatius 23.

31. (A) Dec. 11, 1751; (B) Abell Magill; (C) 54-1/4; (D) Ignatius Joy, Jr.; (E) 0-10-0; (F) 2-0-0; (L) Ann Magill; (M) Ann 26.

32. (A) May 2, 1743; (B) John Goddard; (C) 82; (D) Mary Goddard; (E) 0-8-8; (F) 1-14-0; (L) Ignatius Goddard, Monaca Goddard and John Goddard; (M) Ignatius 26, Monaca 35, John 32.

33. (A) Aug. 21, 1745; (B) Enoch Joy; (C) 75-1/4; (D) Teakler Joy; (E) 0-8-0; (F) 1-12-0; (L) Enoch Joy and Ann Joy; (M) Enoch 26, Ann 33; Enoch gone away.

34. (A) Dec. 17, 1714; (B) Mary Chamberlain; (C) 28; (D) James Drury; (E) 0-3-0; (F) 1-4-0; (L) Eleanor Chamberlain and Mary Chamberlain; (M) Eleanor 62, Mary 54.

35. (A) June 20, 1746; (B) John Mackintach; (C) 143; (D) John Mugg; (E) 0-14-3; (F) 3-0-0; (L) Walter Mugg, John and James Mackintosh; (M) Walter 29. John and James both old and gone away.

36. (A) Dec. 25, 1743; (B) Martin Yates; (C) 122; (D) Martin Yates; (E) 1-2-8; (F) 2-10-0; (L) Martin Yeates, Edward Yates and Martin Yates, Jr.; (M) Martin 68, Edward 39, Martin, Jr. 33.

37. (A) Sep. 1, 1742; (B) John Campbell; (C) 103-1/2; (D) Martin Yates; (E) 0-11-1; (F) 2-4-4; (L) Eleanor Campbell; (M) Eleanor 26.

38. (A) Oct. 20, 1747; (B) Peter Mugg; (C) 38-3/4; (D) John Mugg; (E) 0-4-1; (F) 0-16-4; (L) John Mugg, Thomas Mugg and Peter Mugg, Jr.; (M) John 31, Thomas 27, Peter, Jr. 25.

39. (A) Apr. 26, 1727; (B) Henry Greenwell; (C) 131; (D) Ignatius Greenwell; (E) 0-7-8; (F) 3-2-4; (L) Eleanor Greenwell and Edmond Greenwell; (M) Eleanor 41, Edmond 42.

40. (A) Mar. 25, 1744; (B) Sarah Cecell; (C) 95-1/2; (D) Sarah Secill; (E) 0-10-0; (F) 2-0-0; (L) John Cessell, Thomas Cesell and Ann Cesell; (M) John 29, Thomas 30, Ann 27.

41. (A) Dec. 25, 1741; (B) Peter Drury; (C) 111; (D) Peter Drury; (E) 0-10-9; (F) 2-0-0; (L) Nicholas Drury, Peter Drury and William Drury; (M) Nicholas 30, Peter 28, William 31.

42. (A) Dec. 4, 1743; (B) John Ford; (C) 63; (D) Athanatius Ford; (E) 0-6-4; (F) 1-5-0; (L) Athanatius Ford and John Ford, Jr.; (M) Athanatius 40, John 26.

43. (A) Dec. 25, 1741; (B) William Lucas; (C) 201; (D) Athanatius Ford; (E) 0-19-11; (F) 4-0-0; (L) Charles Lucas; (M) Charles 35.

44. (A) Apr. 3, 1762; (B) Athanatius Ford; (C) 18-1/4; (D) Athanatius Ford; (E) 0-5-8; (F) 0-5-8; (L) 15 years.

45. (A) Dec. 25, 1741; (B) Thomas Howard; (C) 80-1/4; (D) Athanatius Ford; (E) 0-8-9; (F) 1-14-0; (L) William Howard, Thomas Howard, Nicholas Howard; (M) William 40, Thomas 28, Nicholas 30.

46. (A) Mar. 25, 1726; (B) William Bryan; (C) 59; (D) James Greenwell; (E) 0-7-2; (F) 2-17-8; (L) John Abell, Jr., Ignatius Bryan; (M) John 57, Ignatius 40.

47. (A) April 15, 1714; (B) John Miles; (C) 38-1/2; (D) James Greenwell; (E) 0-4-0; (F) 1-12-0; (L) Expired.

48. (A) Dec. 25, 1741; (B) Thomas Spalding; (C) 225-1/4; (D) Thomas Spalding; (E) 1-3-3; (F) 4-13-0; (L) Thomas Spalding, Elictious Spalding and Clem-Joseph; (M) Thomas, 62, Electious 30, Clement 62, Dead.

49. (A) Dec. 25, 1743; (B) Elizabeth Spalding; (C) 124; (D) Theodorita Key; (E) 0-13-3; (F) 2-15-8; (L) Edmund Spalding, James Spalding and Bennitt Spalding; (M) Edmund 40, James 42, Bennitt 25.

50. (A) Dec. 20, 1743; (B) Henry Bryan; (C) 119; (D) Elenor Bryan; (E) 0-13-5; (F) 2-14-0; (L) Edmund Greenwell, Ignatius Abell and Elizabeth Abell; (M) Edmund 42, Ignatius 27, Elizabeth 25.

51. (A) Feb. 20, 1742; (B) John Raley; (C) 88; (D) Joseph Stone; (E) 0-10-2; (F) 2-0-0; (L) Henry Raley, Zachariah Forrest, Ann Raley; (M) Henry 40, Zachariah 25, Ann 30.

52. (A) May 2, 1737; (B) Cuthbert Fenwick; (C) 231; (D) Bennitt Fenwick; (E) 0-12-7; (F) 4-15-0; (L) Bennitt Fenwick; (M) Bennitt 40. Expired.

53. (A) Dec. 25, 1741; (B) Henry Spalding; (C) 107-1/4; (D) Henry Spalding; (E) 0-12-7; (F) 2-11-0; (L) Henry Spalding, Electious Spalding and Edmund Spalding; (M) Henry 43, Electious 30, Edmund 34. The last gone away.

54. (A) Dec. 25, 1742; (B) William Spalding; (C) 156-1/2; (D) Thomas Forrest; (E) 0-17-9; (F) 3-11-0; (L) Basil Spalding; (M) Basil 5[torn].

55. (A) Dec. 25, 1768[?]; (B) William More; (C) 129; (D) Nicholas More; (E) 0-12-6; (F) 5-0-0; (L) Nicholas More and James More; (M) Nicholas 56, James 42. Expired.

56. (A) June 10, 1743; (B) John Brewer; (C) 147-3/4; (D) John Brewer; (E) 0-14-5; (F) 2-17-8; (L) George Brewer, Ann Brewer and Susannah Brewer; (M) George 23, Ann 29, Susannah 25.

57. (A) Dec. 25, 1743; (B) James Wilkinson; (C) 57; (D) James Wilkinson; (E) 0-5-6; (F) 1-1-9; (L) William Wilkinson, David Wilkinson and Aquilla Wilkinson; (M) William 32, David 25, Aquilla 27.

58. (A) Dec. 25, 1741; (B) Charles Joy; (C) 357-1/2; (D) Charles Joy; (E) 1-16-8; (F) 7-6-8; (L) [Vacant; (M) Vacant].

59. (A) June 10, 1743; (B) George Bowles; (C) 79-1/2; (D) Edward Stone; (E) 0-8-3; (F) 1-13-0; (L) Mary Seale, --- Seale and Lydia Seale. Quere their age and if alive.

60. (A) Dec. 25, 1742; (B) Abram Clarke; (C) 129-1/2; (D) Abram Clarke; (E) 0-13-8; (F) 2-14-8; (L) Abram Clarke, Robert Clarke; (M) Abram 50, Robert 40.

61. (A) Dec. 25, 1719; (B) Richard Hazle; (C) 77; (D) Sam Abell, Jr.; (E) 0-7-6; (F) 3-0--0; (L) Richard Hazle, Jr., John Hazle; (M) Richard 37, John 56.

62. (A) Dec. 25, 1741; (B) William Wimsatt; (C) 115-3/4; (D) Joshua Jarbeo; (E) 0-12-6; (F) 0-12-6; (L) James Wimsatt and Tenison Wimsatt; (M) James 45, Tenison 43.

63. (A) Dec. 25, 1742; (B) Richard Wimsatt; (C) 200; (D) Robert Wimsatt; (E) 1-4-1; (F) 4-16-4; (L) Henry Wimsatt, Ignatius Wimsatt; (M) Henry 30, Ignatius 27.

64. (A) Mar. 25, 1742; (B) John Raley; (C) 171; (D) James Brown; (E) 0-16-8; (F) 3-6-8; (L) John Raley and Gabriel Raley; (M) John 59, Gabriel 31.

65. (A) Feb. 1, 1742; (B) James Brown; (C) 125; (D) James Brown; (E) 0-13-7; (F) 2-14-0; (L) John Baptist Brown and Leonard Brown; (M) John 35, Leonard 30.

66. (A) Mar. 24, 1762; (B) John Abell; (C) 151; (D) John Abell; (E) 1-11-4; (F) 1-11-4; (L) 15 years.

67. (A) Dec. 25, 1745; (B) John Nevett; (C) 59-1/2; (D) Ignatius Joy, Sr.; (E) 0-6-10; (F) 1-7-6; (L) John Nevit, John Baptist Nevit and Mary Nevit; (M) John 55, John Baptist 25, Mary 23.

68. (A) Sep. 10, 1742; (B) Bennitt Fenwick; (C) 80; (D) Bennitt Fenwick; (E) 0-8-0; (F) 1-10-0; (L) Bennitt Fenwick and Francis Harbert; (M) Bennitt 44, Francis 28.

69. (A) Dec. 25, 1719; (B) John More, Sr.; (C) 71; (D) John More, Jr.; (E) 0-7-6; (F) 3-0-0; (L) Eleanor More; (M) Eleanor More 62.

70. (A) Dec. 25, 1742; (B) Edward Spalding; (C) 120-1/2; (D) Michael Spalding; (E) 0-17-6; (F) 3-12-4; (L) Edward Spalding and Edward Barton Smith; (M) Edward 77, Edward Barton 28, gone away.

71. (A) June 25, 1761; (B) Ignatius Fenwick; (C) 55; (D) Edward Spalding; (E) 0-26-2; (F) 0-16-2; (L) 14-1/4 years.

72. (A) July 4, 1740; (B) Elizabeth Spalding; (C) 120-1/2; (D) Michael Spalding; (E) 0-17-6; (F) 3-10-0; (L) James Spalding, Michael Spalding and Edmund Spalding; (M) James 42, Michael 41, Edmund 40.

73. (A) Aug. 8, 1739; (B) Henry Greenwell; (C) 84; (D) Edmond Greenwell; (E) 0-9-8; (F) 1-8-9; (L) Edmond Greenwell, Ignatius Greenwell, John Ross; (M) Edmond 40, Ignatius 31, John 22.

74. (A) Apr. 26, 1728; (B) Thomas Spalding; (C) 53; (D) Thomas Spalding; (E) 1-1-2; (F) 2-2-4; (L) Thomas Spalding, Peter Spalding and James Spalding; (M) Thomas 53, Peter 48, James 45.

75. (A) Dec. 10, 1714; (B) Vacant; (C) 461; (D) William Spalding; (L) Patent Land.

76. (A) Dec. 25, 1741; (B) William Spalding; (C) 189-1/2; (D) William Spalding; (E) 1-1-0; (F) 4-8-8; (L) ---; (M) ---.

77. (A) June 12, 1761; (B) James Wimsatt; (C) 89-1/2; (D) James Wimsatt; (E) 0-17-0; (F) 0-17-0; (L) 14-1/4 years.

78. (A) Oct. 23, 1747; (B) Henry Spalding; (C) 92; (D) William and Thomas Spalding; (E) 0-11-8; (F) 1-16-8; (L) Henry Spalding, Electious Spalding, Henry Spalding, Jr.; (M) Henry 43, Electious 30, Henry, Jr., 22.

79. (A) June 25, 1761; (B) Edward Cole; (C) 97; (D) Ignatius Fenwick; (E) 0-17-6; (F) 0-17-6; (L) 14-1/4 years.

80. (C) 44; (D) Joshua Jarbeo; (E) 0-4-8.

81. (A) Oct. 1, 1740; (B) Thomas Taney; (C) 141-1/4 and 35; (D) Raphael Taney; (E) 1-2-0; (F) 4-8-0; (L) Raphael Taney; (L) Patented.

82. (A) Mar. 10, 1694; (B) Henry Lowe; (C) 90; (D) Raphael Taney; (L) Patented.

---. (C) 917-1/2 Sundry Vacancies of which, 'tis said, lies in Delabrook and Fenwick Manors. Total, (C) 9,578-1/4.

STATE OF HIS LORDSHIP'S MANOR OF CHAPTICO, IN ST. MARY'S COUNTY, JANUARY, 1768.

8. (A) Sep. 29, 1742; (B) Leonard Clarke; (C) 266; (D) John Higgs; (E) 1-10-6; (F) 6-2-0; (L) Charles Sothoron Clark and Leonard Clark, son of the Lessee; (M) Charles 26, Leonard 28.

12. (A) June 16, 1752; (B) Zachary Bond; (C) 243-1/2; (D) Lessee; (E) 1-7-0; (F) 5-16-0; (L) Samuel Bond and Samuel Edilin; (M) Sam Bond 20, Samuel Edilin 17.

17. (A) Aug. 20, 1745; (B) Anthony Sims; (C) 203-1/4; (D) Lessee; (E) 1-4-6; (F) 5-1-0; (L) Bennett Sims, Dead, and Jane Sims; (M) Bennett 25, Jane 27.

20. (A) Jan. 10, 1742; (B) Francis Clarke; (C) 132-1/4; (D) Samuel Higgs; (E) 1-8-6; (F) 5-14-0; (L) Susanah Clarke, Francis Clark, son of Lessee; (M) Susanah 50, Francis 28.

35. (A) Jan. 20, 1742; (B) James Swan; (C) 121-1/2; (D) 0-13-7; (E) 2-14-0; (L) John Swan and James Swan; (M) John 46, James 42.

51. (A) Dec. 25, 1746; (B) John Slye; (C) 52; (D) Lessee; (E) 0-4-9; (F) 0-19-0; (L) Mary Slye and Robert Slye; (M) Mary 32, Robert 21.

STATE OF HIS LORDSHIP'S MANOR OF MILL, IN ST. MARY'S COUNTY, JANUARY, 1768.

3. (A) Mar. 5, 1742; (B) John Warren; (C) 102; (D) Mathew Hagar; (E) 0-10-3; (F) 2-1-0; (L) Thomas Warren, Ann Warren and Mary Warren; (M) Thomas 40, Ann 38, Mary 35.

5. (A) Sep. 29, 1742; (B) Martha Wheatley; (C) 109-1/2; (D) William Coombs; (E) 0-10-10; (F) 2-3-0; (L) Martha Wheatley, Joseph Wheatley and Winifred Wheatley; (M) Martha 50, Joseph 30, Winifred 26.

10. (A) Jul. 4, 1714; (B) Francis Cole; (C) 110; (D) Susannah Cole; (E) 0-7-4; (F) 2-19-2; (L) Ann Cole; (M) Ann 60.

11. (A) Apr. 10, 1738; (B) Francis Cole; (C) 29; (D) Susannah Cole; (E) 0-3-0; (F) 0-12-0; (L) Francis Cole, Jr., Judith Cole, Jr. and James Wheatley; (M) Francis 32, Judith 28, James 34.

12. (A) Mar. 10, 1743; (B) Jonathan Seale; (C) 326-1/2; (D) Thomas Key; (E) 1-22-4; (F) 6-9-4; (L) Monaca Seale and Lidia Seale; (M) Monaca 30, Lidia 28.

17. (A) Aug. 6, 1739; (B) John Edwards; (C) 44; (D) Zachariah Forrest; (E) 0-4-9; (F) 0-19-2.

18. (A) Dec. 25, 1743; (B) Joseph Cullison; (C) 30; (D) James Tailton*; (E) 0-7-7; (F) 1-10-4; (L) Joseph Cullison, William Cullison and Ignatius Cullison; (M) Joseph 45, William 42, Ignatius 28.

* presumably this name should be Tarlton

19. (A) Dec. 25, 1750; (B) Joseph Cullison; (C) 30; (D) James Tailton*; (E) 0-3-0; (F) 0-12-6; (L) Joseph Cullison, James Cullison and Joseph Cullison, Jr.; (M) Joseph 45, James 20, Joseph, Jr. 18.

20. (A) Aug. 20, 1761; (B) Joseph Cullison; (C) 53; (D) James Tailton*; (E) 0-10-6; (F) 0-10-6; (L) 14-1/2 years.

21. and 22. (A) Apr. 25, 1729; (B) John Tailton*; (C) 50 and 22-3/4; (D) Michael Beverley; (E for both tracts) 0-7-6; (F) 3-0-0; (L) John Tailton 80, Dead.

23. (A) Apr. 10, 1738; (B) James Tailton*; (C) 35; (D) John Tailton; (E) 0-3-6; (F) 0-14-0; (L) John Tailton, Jr. 30.

* presumably this name should be Tarlton

STATE OF HIS LORDSHIP'S MANOR OF WOOLSEY, ST. MARY'S COUNTY, DECEMBER, 1767.

4. (A) Apr. 9, 1763; (B) Thomas Cecil; (C) 52; (D) Lessee; (E) 0-11-9; (F) 0-11-9; (L) 21 years.

5. (A) May 1, 1761; (B) Clement Jarbo; (C) 59-3/8; (D) Thomas Cecil; (E) 0-12-4; (F) 0-21-4; (L) 21 years.

6. (A) Dec. 25, 1746; (B) Thomas Dogin; (C) 67-5/8; (D) Lessee; (E) 0-8-0; (F) 1-12-0; (L) Thomas Dogin and John Michael Raley; (M) Thomas 48, John 26, but gone away.

7. (A) Nov. 10, 1739; (B) Thomas Watt; (C) 40-1/2; (D) Jeremiah Rhoades; (E) 0-4-0; (F) 0-16-0; (L) Mary Watt; (M) Mary Watt 70.

8. (A) Dec. 25, 1719; (B) Joseph Milbourn; (C) 61; (D) Henry King; (E) 0-6-0; (F) 2-8-0; (L) Stephen Milburn, Jr., Peter Milburn; (M) Stephen 42, gone away, Peter 39. Vide Date of Lease.

14. (A) Dec. 25, 1758; (B) Ephraim Adams; (C) 87-1/4; (D) William Hilton; (E) 0-17-0; (F) 1-12-0; (L) Ephraim Adams, Rebecca Adams and Robert Adams; (M) Ephraim 40, Rebecca 36, Robert 16, all gone away.

15. (A) Dec. 25, 1720; (B) John Milbourn; (C) 34-3/8; (D) Henry Jenkins; (E) 0-3-3-1/2; (F) 1-4-6-1/2; (L) John Milburn, dead, and Ann Milburn, dead; (M) John 47, Ann, expired.

16. (A) Dec. 25, 1740; (B) Robert Clarke; (C) 100-7/8; (D) Robert Clarke; (E) 0-13-2; (F) 2-12-8; (L) Robert Clarke and Ann Clarke; (M) Robert 45, Ann 40.

18. (A) Sep. 15, 1742; (B) John Milburn; (C) 40-1/8; (D) Sarah Breeden; (E) 0-3-10; (F) 0-15-0; (L) Mary Milburn and Ann Milburn; (M) Mary 40, Ann 26.

19. (A) Feb. 29, 1742; (B) Francis Kirby; (C) 53-5/8; (D) Ignatius Bryan; (E) 0-5-6; (F) 1-5-0; (L) Francis Kirby, Mary Kirby and William Kirby; (M) Francis 45, Mary 41, William their son, 22. Vide date of lease.

20. (A) Sep. 7, 1763; (B) Ignatius Bryan; (C) 49-1/4; (D) Ignatius Bryan; (M) held by certificate.

21. (A) Dec. 25, 1719; (B) Stephen Milburn; (C) 48-3/8; (D) Mathew Wise; (E) 0-4-8; (F) 1-17-6; (L) Stephen Milburn, dead, Stephen Milburn, Jr. and Peter Milburn; (M) Stephen 70, Stephen, Jr. 49, but gone away, Peter 47. Vide No. 8. Same lives but different ages.

22. (A) Dec. 25, 1720; (B) Stephen Milburn; (C) 75-5/8; (D) Matthew Wise; (E) 0-7-9; (F) 3-2-7; (L) Stephen Milburn and Rebecca Milburn; (M) Stephen 70, Rebecca 46.

25. (A) Dec. 25, 1741; (B) John Milbourn; (C) 81; (D) Richard Wise; (E) 0-8-2; (F) 1-12-9; (L) Ann Milburn and William Milburn, son of Stephen; (M) Ann 49, William 30, gone away.

28. (A) Mar. 5, 1739; (B) John Hammott; (C) 84-3/4; (D) John Hammott; (E) 0-8-5; (F) 1-14-0; (L) John Hammot, John Hammot, son of Robert and John Norris; (M) John 50, John, son of Robert, 28, John Norris 30.

29. (A) Nov. 13, 1743; (B) James Adams; (C) 52-1/2; (D) James Adams; (E) 0-5-5; (F) 1-0-0; (L) James Adams, Mary Adams, Ephraim Adams; (M) James 51, Mary 51, Ephraim 40, the last gone away.

30. (A) June 24, 1740; (B) James Farthing; (C) 91-1/2; (D) John Tarlton; (E) 0-9-8; (F) 1-19-0; (L) Mary Farthing and Robert Hurtle; (M) Mary 40, Robert 30.

These abstracts are taken from Brumbaugh's collection of colonial Maryland records which was never copyrighted. The original manorial leases are at the Maryland Historical Society.

BIRTHS RECORDED AT ST. ANDREW'S EPISCOPAL CHURCH
LEONARDTOWN, MARYLAND

Extracts of families
presumed to have been Roman Catholic

The complete parish records were published
by the St. Mary's County Historical Society
in their bulletin "Chronicles"

Handwritten transcripts of the original
register may be found on microfilm at the
Mormon Library in Salt Lake City, Utah

ABELL, Caleb and Mary

Issue:

Jeremiah	b. 2 Apr 1766
Elizabeth	b. 12 Nov 1767
Mary	b. 20 Oct 1769
Rachel	b. 29 Sep 1772

ABELL, Edmond and Elizabeth

Issue:

Janet   bpt. 4 May 1783

ABELL, Edward and Statia (Taylor)

Issue:

Barbara	b. 10 Jul 1777
Phannel	b. 8 Jun 1780
Eleanor	b. 10 Mar 1782

ABELL, Edward and Susanna

Issue:

Jane	b. 6 Nov 1760
Benjamin	b. 7 Apr 1764
Catharine	b. 22 Apr 1766
Samuel	b. 23 Jan 1769
John	b. 23 Dec 1769
Mary	b. 7 Nov 1771

ABELL, George and Elizabeth

Issue:

Elizabeth	b. 24 Jan 1766
George	b. 27 Jul 1768
Francis	b. 20 Jun 1774
Pollard	b. 20 Sep 1777

ABELL, John and Ann

Issue:

James	b. 26 Jun 1766
John Standsill	b. 16 Jan 1768

ABELL, John and Elizabeth

Issue:

Jean	bpt. 23 Sep 1781
Jonathan	bpt. 4 May 1783

ABELL, Matthew and Elizabeth

Issue:

James Crane   b. 27 Nov 1813

ABELL, Peter and Lucy

Issue:

Sarah   b. 25 Oct 1769

ABELL, Richard and Ann

Issue:

Alathea   b. 22 Apr 1764

ABELL, Samuel and Eleanor*

Issue:

Samuel	b. 13 Jan 1755
Robert	b. 8 May 1757
Abner	b. 29 Jul 1759

ABELL, Samuel and Sarah

Issue:

Elizabeth   b. 29 Nov 1799

*her maiden name is uniformly given as
O'Bryan. See, Centenary of Catholicity
in Kentucky by Ben Webb; and family
notes by Mary Jane (Lancaster) Spalding,
Filson Club, Louisville, Kentucky.

ADAMS, Abraham and Elizabeth

Issue:

Ann   b. 19 Oct 1812

ADAMS, Abraham and Ann

Issue:

Enoch   b. 18 Sep 1757
Austin   b. 23 Apr 1759
Elizabeth   b. 13 Jan 1762
Abraham   b. 13 Oct 1764

ADAMS, George and Sarah

Issue:

John   b. 28 Jul 1812
Dorothy   b. 10 Jan 1814
Susan   b. 15 Sep 1815

ADAMS, James and Mary

Issue:

Hatton George   b. 11 Apr 1775

ADAMS, Nathan and Sarah

Issue:

Theophilus   b. 2 Oct 1776

ANDERSON, John Baptist and Tabitha

Issue:

James   b. 6 Jan 1758
John   b. 16 Jun 1761

ANDERSON, Thomas and Chloe

Issue:

John   b. 18 Sep 1768

ANDERSON, Thomas and Henrietta

Issue:

Ann   b. 15 Apr 1764
Mary   b. 2 Jan 1766

ANDERSON, William and Elizabeth

Issue:

Margaret   b. 27 Apr 1775

AUSTIN, George and Eleanor

Issue:

Elizabeth   b. 24 Feb 1774
Priscilla   b. 11 Sep 1775

BEAN, George and Anne (Dillion)

Issue:

Barton   bpt. 7 May 1780

BEAN, Robert and Margaret

Issue:

Bennett   b. 4 Aug 1771

BIRCHMORE, William and Margaret

Issue:

Rebecca   b. 8 Dec 1746

BISCOE, Richard and Eleanor

Issue:

James Lewis   b. 7 Oct 1811
Ann Clarke   b. 8 Dec 1813

BOARMAN, Francis and Batris

Issue:

John	b.	8 Oct 1758
Francis Ignatius	b.	14 Mar 1762
Sarah	b.	1 Mar 1764

BOOTH, John and Mary

Issue:

Elizabeth	b.	14 Mar 1762
Jane	b.	14 Aug 1763
Rodolph	b.	30 Nov 1765
John Baptist	b.	10 Mar 1768
Ann	b.	10 Feb 1770

BOOTH, Thomas and Mary

Issue:

Ignatius	b.	4 Nov 1754
Rebecca	b.	4 Jun 1756
Leonard	b.	3 Mar 1758
Mary	b.	7 Sep 1760
Eleanor	b.	17 Jun 1761
Sarah	b.	20 Jun 1763
George	b.	11 Jul 1765
Justinian	b.	12 Nov 1767

BOULD, John and Monica

Issue:

William	b.	7 Jan 1752
Susanna	b.	1 Oct 1753
Jane	b.	25 Mar 1757
Henrietta	b.	15 Sep 1760
John Baptist	b.	15 Nov 1762
Mary	b.	30 Jun 1767
Catharine	b.	20 Oct 1769

BOULD, WILLIAM and Mary
(son of John and Monica)

Issue:

Elizabeth	b.	9 Mar 1776
Mary Ann	b.	1 Jun 1778

BOWES, Timothy and Mary

Issue:

Mary	b.	3 Mar 1763
Eleanor	b.	9 Jun 1766
Joseph	b.	23 Feb 1769

BRADBURN, Benjamin and Ann

Issue:

Mary	b.	4 Jun 1765
Matthew	b.	10 Feb 1767
Anastasia	b.	16 Oct 1768
Sarah	b.	25 May 1772

BRADBURN, James and Mary

Issue:

Mary Ann	b.	15 May 1772

BRADBURN, Mark and Susanna

Issue:

John Baptist	b.	27 Sep 1757
Elizabeth	b.	27 Oct 1759

BRADBURN, Notley and Eleanor

Issue:

Catharine	b.	14 Mar 1772

BROWN, Anthony and Mary

Issue:

Dorothy	b.	27 Mar 1755
Benedict	b.	7 Jun 1758
Susanna	b.	12 Sep 1761
Frances	b.	6 Mar 1764
Anthony	b.	7 Apr 1768
Monica	b.	22 May 1771

BROWN, John Baptist and Henrietta

Issue:

Raphael	b. 4 Oct 1761
Rebecca	b. 4 Apr 1767
Winifred	b. 16 Sep 1772

BROWN, Nicholas and Eleanor

Issue:

| John Barton | b. 6 Mar 1775 |

BROWN, Peter and Frances

Issue:

Mary	b. 30 Sep 1770
Jereboam	b. 16 Nov 1764
Anna	b. 9 Apr 1768
Eleanor	b. 4 Jul 1774
Peter	b. 25 Sep 1779

BROWN, Richard and Anastasia

Issue:

Ann	b. 7 Jul 1756
Richard	b. 8 Aug 1764
Elizabeth	b. 30 Jun 1767

BROWNE, Leonard and Ann

Issue:

Dryden	b. 25 May 1760
Chloe	b. 20 Feb 1762
Leander	b. 27 May 1765
Allusia	b. 13 Aug 1769
Lucy	b. 11 Apr 1775

BROWNE, Peter and Susanna

Issue:

| Martin | b. 16 Nov 1775 |

CHRISMAN, Luke and Elizabeth

Issue:

| John | b. 13 Apr 1766 |

CISSELL, Ignatius and Elizabeth

Issue:

Edmund Barton	b. 25 Jun 1760
James Rodolph	b. 8 Apr 1762
Ignatius	b. 12 Mar 1764
Joseph	b. 28 Jun 1766
James	b. 22 May 1768
Mary	b. 10 Mar 1770
Wilford	b. 10 Jul 1772
Eleanor	b. 22 Jun 1776

CISSELL, James and Elizabeth

Issue:

Bernard	b. 12 Feb 1759
Susanna	b. 28 Jan 1760
Peter	b. 29 Jun 1764

CISSELL, John and Henrietta

Issue:

Anastasia	b. 11 Feb 1745
Mary	b. 4 Jan 1750
James	b. 24 Jan 1753
John	b. 15 Oct 1757
Delbert	b. 30 Jul 1763

CISSELL, John and Margaret

Issue:

| Shedrick | b. 18 Oct 1754 |
| Dorothy | b. 17 Apr 1756 |

CISSELL, John and Mary

Issue:

| Joseph | b. 27 Dec 1772 |

CISSELL, John Baptist and Ann

Issue:

Matthew   b. 20 Feb 1775

CISSELL, John Baptist and Rebecca

Issue:

Thomas   b. 14 Apr 1762
Ann   b. 2 Feb 1766
William   b. 10 Aug 1767
Jeremiah   b. 26 Sep 1773

CISSELL, William and Catherine

Issue:

Mary   b. 8 Mar 1800

CLARKE, John and Eleanor

Issue:

Richard Langhorn b. 19 Jan 1753

CLARKE, Joshua and Mary

Issue:

Eleanor   b. 12 Aug 1773
Susanna   b. 19 Sep 1775

CLARKE, Robert and Ann

Issue:

John   b. 15 Oct 1751
Mary   b. 29 Oct 1755
Robert   b. 17 Nov 1757
Ann   b. 17 Aug 1760
Eleanor   b. 22 May 1764

CLARKE, Thomas and Elizabeth

Issue:

Mary   b. 21 Jan 1771
Ann   b. 2 Mar 1773
Thomas   b. 3 Mar 1775

COLE, Francis and Ann

Issue:

Susanna   b. 27 Feb 1757
Mary Ann   b. 2 Feb 1760
Winifred   b. 3 Sep 1766

COMBS, Bennett and Elizabeth

Issue:

Mary   b. 28 Jun 1765
Barbara   b. 9 Feb 1767

COMBS, William and Eleanor

Issue:

Raphael   b. 6 Oct 1760
Eleanor   b. 29 Aug 1762
Margaret   b. 13 Apr 1764
William   b. 12 Apr 1766
Mary Ann   b. 18 Dec 1768

CONNELLY, Rodolph and Ann Chloe

Issue:

Rodolph   b. 29 Mar 1767

DAFT, William and Elizabeth

Issue:

John Baptist   b. 15 Mar 1759
Mary   b. 6 Apr 1762

DALEY, Daniel and -----

Issue:

| Susanna | b. 29 Jul 1752 |
| Charles | b. 20 Jul 1753 |

DILLEHAY, John and Winifred

Issue:

| Stephen | b. 19 Nov 1766 |
| Joseph | b. 22 Feb 1768 |

DOGAN, John and Ann

Issue:

Eleanor	b. 13 Apr 1761
William	b. 10 May 1763
James	b. 5 Nov 1765
John	b. 15 Apr 1768

DOGAN, Thomas and Monica

Issue:

| Jeremiah | b. 2 Feb 1763 |

DOWNES, Joseph and Ann

Issue:

Ignatius	b. 18 Nov 1759
John	b. 25 May 1762
Mary	b. 26 Mar 1764
Elizabeth	b. 23 Jun 1766
Ann	b. 24 Oct 1768

FENWICK, John and Monica

Issue:

William	b. 30 Dec 1759
Eleanor	b. 17 Oct 1761
Catharine	b. 27 Feb 1763

FORD, Peter and Anastasia

Issue:

| Ignatius | b. 26 Sep 1755 |
| John Francis | b. 8 Mar 1758 |

FORD, Philip and Eleanor

Issue:

| Clara | b. 5 Jul 1771 |
| Charles | b. 2 Jan 1773 |

FORREST, Zachariah and Ann

Issue:

| Richard | b. 15 Nov 1767 |
| Uriah | b. 14 May 1780 |

FRENCH, Ignatius and Elizabeth

Issue:

Mary	b. 28 Oct 1769
Joseph	b. 27 Sep 1771
Ignatius	b. 14 Oct 1773
Elizabeth	b. 27 Nov 1775

FRENCH, John and Jane

Issue:

| Philip | b. 27 Nov 1774 |
| Peter | b. 12 May 1776 |

FRENCH, John, Jr. and Monica

Issue:

Anastasia	b. 29 Jul 1750
Bennett	b. 27 Jun 1757
Ann	b. 16 Sep 1759
Bernadine (m)	b. 20 Dec 1761
Elizabeth	b. 3 May 1764

FRENCH, William and Rinah

Issue:

Rodolph	b.	1 Aug 1755
Jeremiah	b.	13 Oct 1761
Susanna	b.	14 Oct 1766

GOLDSBURY, Athanatius and Mary

Issue:

Athanatius	b.	27 Dec 1815

GOLDSBURY, Jonathan and Christian

Issue:

Charles	b.	4 Mar 1765

GOUGH, Benjamin and Susanna

Issue:

Charles	b.	25 May 1755
Mary	b.	24 Jun 1762
Rebecca	b.	5 Jun 1766
Britannia	b.	19 Dec 1768

GOUGH, James and Susanna

Issue:

Jane	b.	9 Oct 1755
Elizabeth	b.	18 May 1757
Anastatia	b.	9 Apr 1760
John Baptist	b.	18 Feb 1764
Matthew	b.	30 Jun 1766
Ann	b.	3 Feb 1768

GREENWELL, Charles and Eleanor

Issue:

John	b.	2 Oct 1760
Jane	b.	20 Mar 1763
Richard	b.	7 Oct 1765
Edward	b.	30 Jan 1768

GREENWELL, George and Elizabaeth

Issue:

Joseph	b.	2 Aug 1755
Justinian	b.	15 Oct 1757
Bennett	b.	7 Dec 1761
Austin	b.	14 Mar 1765

GREENWELL, Henry and Frances

Emerentiana*	b.	10 Jan 1754
Richard	b.	9 Jan 1760
Joseph	b.	17 Apr 1764

GREENWELL, Ignatius and Jane

Issue:

William	b.	26 Nov 1752
Ignatius	b.	23 Dec 1754

GREENWELL, James and Hannah

Issue:

Bennett	b.	28 Aug 1755
William	b.	12 Jul 1757
Joseph	b.	3 Aug 1759
Elizabeth	b.	23 Jul 1763

GREENWELL, John Baptist and Susanna

Issue:

John Basil	b.	17 Aug 1764
Mary Ann	b.	17 Mar 1767

GREENWELL, John Basil and Eleanor

Issue:

Joshua Leonard	b.	5 Nov 1756
James	b.	15 Jan 1761

*one account gave Eunie (?)
  Ranseau Anna

GREENWELL, Justinian and Mary

Issue:

Noah	b. 10 Nov 1760
Benedict	b. 3 Feb 1763
Elizabeth	b. 1 Sep 1765
Jeremiah	b. 17 Jul 1767

GREENWELL, Philip and Winifred

Issue:

Thomas	b. 4 Sep 1754
Mary	b. 17 Oct 1762
Ann	b. 6 Jun 1767
Elizabeth	b. 23 Feb 1769

HARPER, James and Mary

Elizabeth	b. 15 May 1760
Henrietta	b. 4 Mar 1763
Mary Ann	b. 27 May 1766
Rebecca	b. 25 Jul 1769

HARRIS, Joseph and Susanna

Issue:

| Martha | b. 4 Oct 1811 |
| Jane | b. 21 Jan 1813 |

HARRIS, Samuel and Elizabeth

Issue:

| Zachariah | b. 5 Nov 1763 |
| Austin | b. 13 Oct 1766 |

HEARD, John and Ann

Issue:

Mary	b. 9 Jul 1764
Ann	b. 5 Apr 1766
Helen	b. 29 Sep 1767

HENRY, Martin and Mary

Issue:

| James | b. 17 Jun 1774 |
| Philip | b. 7 Feb 1776 |

HOPEWELL, Bennett and Teresa

| Richard | b. 23 May 1759 |

HOPEWELL, Bennett and Mary Ann

Issue:

Jane	b. 22 Dec 1763
Joshua	b. 23 May 1765
Bennett	b. 4 Oct 1766
Francis	b. 20 Feb 1770
Mary Ann	b. 1 May 1772

HOPEWELL, James and Angelica

Issue:

| James Robert | b. 27 Oct 1813 |

HOPEWELL, Joseph and Dorcas

Issue:

Richard	b. 26 Feb 1753
George	b. 28 Jan 1757
John	b. 3 Jun 1763

HOPEWELL, Richard and Eleanor

| Mary | b. 12 Jan 1763 |

HOWARD, George and Anastasia (Spink)

Issue:

Ignatius	b. 2 Mar 1765
Francis	b. 6 Mar 1767
Elizabeth	b. 14 Jun 1772

HOWARD, George and Ann

Issue:

Sarah   b. 19 Jan 1761

HOWARD, Henry and Mary

Issue:

Mary Ann   b. 24 Jul 1758
Charles   b. 24 Nov 1762
Joseph   b. 3 May 1764

HOWARD, Joshua and Mary

Issue:

Henrietta   b. 8 Oct 1753
Austin   b. 8 Oct 1755

HUTCHINS, Francis and Susanna

Issue:

Frances   b. 10 Oct 1763
Alithea   b. 16 Dec 1765

HUTCHENS, John and Rachel

Issue:

John   b. 27 Jan 1777

HUTCHENS, Robert and Ann

Issue:

James   b. 30 May 1763

HUTCHINS, Francis and Susanna

Issue:

Frances   b. 10 Oct 1763
Alithea   b. 16 Dec 1765

JAMES, Thomas and Mary

Issue:

George   b. 14 Jul 1753
Chloe   b. 2 May 1755
Champion   b. 13 Jun 1757

JARBEO, Clement and Ann

Frances   b. 15 Jun 1762
Eleanor   b. 30 Jul 1764
Monica   b. 26 May 1767

JARBO, Joshua and Jean

Issue:

Abner   b. 9 Dec 1763
Bennett   b. 2 Jan 1767
Eleanor   b. 2 Nov 1768
Charles   b. 21 Jun 1773

JARBOE, Mary

Issue:

Stephen   b. 7 Jan 1765

JENKINS, Joseph and Mary

Issue:

John   b. 5 May 1744
Augustine   b. 12 Jan 1746/7
Thomas   b. 20 Jun 1749
Edmund Courtney   b. 1 Oct 1752

JOY, John and Mary

Issue:

Joseph   b. 20 Sep 1755
Mary   b. 20 Sep 1755

JOY, John and Sarah

Issue:

Winifred	b. 20 Feb 1762
Thomas Tarlton	b. 23 May 1765
Elizabeth	b. 17 May 1768

JOY, John, Jr. and Eleanor

Issue:

Henrietta	b. 3 Aug 1769
William	b. 18 Jul 1760
Benedict	b. 10 Apr 1763

KIRBY, Peter and Henrietta

Issue:

Richard	b. 22 Feb 1754
Rebecca	b. 4 Jan 1762

KIRBY, Thomas and Mary

Issue:

Elizabeth	b. 2 Jan 1764
Henrietta	b. 17 Apr 1766

KIRBY, William and Elizabeth

Issue:

Hopewell (f)   b. 22 Apr 1756

KNOTT, Bennet and Eleanor

Issue:

Ignatius	b. 18 Oct 1754
James	b. 6 Oct 1757

LANGLEY, Josias and Susanna

Issue:

John Francis
  Xaverus   b. 22 Jun 1768

LATHAM, John and Rebecca

Issue:

Jeremiah   b. 25 May 1763

LATHAM, Matthew and Susanna

Issue:

Margaret Ann	b. 25 Dec 1761
William	b. 25 Jun 1765
Mary	b. 8 Mar 1767
James	b. 27 Oct 1770

LAYTON, John and Jane

Issue:

Joseph	b. 13 Jun 1762
Zachariah	b. 13 Jan 1765
Susanna	b. 12 Mar 1765
Ignatius	b. 24 Aug 1768

LUCAS, William and Rachel

Issue:

Joshua   b. 9 Feb 1755

MANNING, Cornelius and Jane

Issue:

Monica	b. 26 Oct 1759
Frances	b. 10 Jan 1762

MANNING, James and Margaret

Issue:

William	b. 22 Jun 1762
Mary	b. 17 Sep 1765
John	b. 27 Mar 1767

MANNING, John and Susanna

Issue:

Joseph   b. 2 Oct 1767

MAREMAN, John and Ann

Issue:

Zachariah	b. 16 Dec 1751
Joseph	b. 6 Jul 1748
Joshua	b. 15 Jun 1746

MAREMAN, Joseph and Elizabeth

Issue:

Richard	b. 13 Feb 1768
Ann	b. 18 May 1775

MAREMAN, Joshua and Susanna

Issue:

James	b. 18 May 1767
Mary	b. 29 Oct 1769
John Baptist	b. 27 Mar 1771
Mary Attaway	b. 6 Mar 1773
Joseph	b. 12 Aug 1775

MAREMAN, William and Mary

Issue:

Lydda	b. 23 Jun 1773
Elizabeth	b. 3 Jul 1776

MAREMAN, Zachariah and Ann

Issue:

William	b. 26 Nov 1775

MATTINGLY, Clement and -----

Issue:

Thomas	b. 28 Mar 1738
John Baptist	b. 28 Jan 1745
Elizabeth	b. 7 Jun 1736
Mary Ann	b. 6 Oct 1741
Ann	b. 6 May 1747
Ruth	b. 23 Jun 1749

MATTINGLY, Robert and Mary Ann

Issue:

Catherine	b. 28 Mar 1778

MEDCALF, Ignatius and Sarah

Issue:

John Kenelm	b. 25 Oct 1760

MEDLEY, Clement and Mary

Issue:

Eleanor	b. 27 Feb 1761
	or 1762
Joseph	b. 3 Nov 1764
Matthew	b. 16 Feb 1766
Ann Elizabeth	b. 1 Feb 1768
Mary	b. 9 Mar 1770

MEDLEY, Clement and Mary Ann

Ann	b. 28 Mar 1755
William	b. 20 Apr 1757
Catharine	b. 20 Jan 1760
Sarah	b. 29 Jul 1763
Mary	b. 14 Nov 1768

MEDLEY, George and Ann

Issue:

Augustine	b. 26 Sep 1763

MEDLEY, Joseph and Anastatia

Issue:

Eleanor	b. 14 Dec 1764
Joseph	b. 22 Mar 1766
Bernard	b. 22 Dec 1768

MEKEN, Augustine and Margaret

Issue:

| Susanna | b. 4 May 1761 |
| Margaret | b. 26 Aug 1764 |

MILBURN, Jeremiah and Elizabeth

Issue:

| Eleanor or | |
| Elizabeth | b. 10 Feb 1757 |

MILLS, Justinian and Mary (Dant)

Issue:

John	b. 5 Feb 1753
Elizabeth	b. 9 May 1755
Winifred	b. 30 Oct 1757
Margaret	b. 30 Jan 1760
Joseph	b. 26 Feb 1762
Justinian	b. 7 Oct 1764
Mary	b. 7 Oct 1764
Ann	b. 5 Dec 1767
Charles	b. 24 Aug 1770

MILLS, Nicholas and ---

Issue:

| Justinian | b. 2 Apr 1728 |

MILLS, Nicholas and Anastasia

Issue:

Ignatius	b. 16 Nov 175_
Bernard	b. 27 Sep 176‾
Ethelbert	b. 12 Nov 176‾
Stephen	b. 2 Jan 1767
Nicholas	b. 9 Mar 1769

NEWTON, Bernard and Mary Ann

Issue:

| Elizabeth | b. 24 Jul 1771 |

NEWTON, Joseph and Mildred

Issue:

Rhodolph	b. 13 May 1763
John Shadrach	b. 1 Jan 1767
James	b. 11 Feb 1769

NORRIS, Bennett and Frances

Issue:

| Winifred | b. 3 Apr 1768 |

NORRIS, Clement and Elizabeth

Issue:

| Thomas | b. 1 May 1753 |
| Vincent | b. 5 Apr 1755 |

NORRIS, John and Mary

Issue:

Philip	b. 25 Dec 1754
Henry Elijah	b. 14 Mar 1758
Arnold	b. 26 Jun 1761
Barbara/Bibiana	b. 17 Mar 1766
Susanna	b. 14 Mar 1771

NORRIS, Joseph and Elizabeth

Issue:

Enoch	b. 27 Feb 1765
Luke	b. 3 Jan 1767
Susanna	b. 27 Sep 1769

NORRIS, Mark and Elizabeth

Issue:

Cuthbert	b. 26 Jun 1760
John	b. 6 May 1762
Henrietta	b. 9 Jul 1765
Matthias	b. 1 Sep 1767
Mary	b. 20 Jul 1769

NORRIS, Philip and Monica

Issue:

Susanna	b. 24 Dec 1761
Henrietta	b. 13 Sep 1764
Eleanor	b. 13 Nov 1767

NORRIS, Rhodolph and Dorothy

Issue:

Mary Ann	b. 22 Apr 1768

NORRIS, Thomas and Ann

Issue:

Mary Ann	b. 1 Nov 1756
Philip	b. 1 May 1758
Mary	b. 22 Oct 1759
William	b. 7 Jun 1761
Joseph	b. 29 Jul 1764

NORRIS, Thomas and Mary

Rebecca	b. 18 Sep 1771
Dorothy	b. 24 Aug 1773

NORRIS, Thomas and Mary Ann

Issue:

Elizabeth	b. 26 Oct 1768

NOTTINGHAM, Athanasius and Mary

Issue:

Mary Ann	b. 18 Nov 1762
Ann	b. 3 Sep 1763
Enoch	b. 25 Dec 1766

NOTTINGHAM, Matthias and Mary

Issue:

Raphael Ignatius	b. 9 Jun 1754
Mary Ann	b. 2 Aug 1757
Elizabeth	b. 5 Jan 1761
Ignatius	b. 12 Apr 1763

PAYNE, Charles and Monica

Issue:

Ann	b. 15 Sep 1767

PAYNE, Henry and Jane

Bernard	b. 27 Nov 1762
Allelusia	b. 17 Apr 1765

PAYNE, John Baptist and Ann

Issue:

Winifred	b. 14 Apr 1763
Mary Ann	b. 22 Sep 1765
Elizabeth	b. 17 Apr 1768
Eleanor	b. 30 May 1771
Rosa Ann	b. 12 Sep 1773

PAYNE, Leonard and Monica

Issue:

Priscilla	b. 19 May 1753
Jeremiah	b. 29 Sep 1760
Henry Berryman	b. 12 Mar 1756
Elizabeth	b. 18 Aug 1758
Monica	b. 13 Mar 1763

PAYNE, Leonard and Teresia

Issue:

Frances	b. 12 Sep 1772

PAYNE, Raphael and Tabitha

Issue:

Elizabeth	b.	9 Apr 1772
Sarah	b. 26 Jun 1775	
Anastasia	b. 12 Dec 1777	

PAYNE, Richard and Priscilla

Issue:

John Barton	b.	3 Aug 1754
Francis Xavier*	b. 12 Sep 1756	
James	b. 28 Feb 1759	

PAYNE, Vincent and Mary

Issue:

Joseph	b.	8 Dec 1771

PEACOCK, Ignatius and Ann

Issue:

John Barton	b. 12 Dec 1774	

PEAKE, Edward and Ann

Issue:

Henry Barton	b.	7 Nov 1754
Henrietta	b. 13 Feb 1757	
Kenelm	b. 11 Mar 1760	
Mary	b.	4 Apr 1762
Francis	b.	4 Feb 1764
Charles	b.	8 Oct 1767
John	b.	8 Oct 1771

PEAKE, John and Susanna

Issue:

Augustus	b. 23 Jan 1757	
Robert	b. 23 Nov 1755	
Joseph	b. 11 Dec 1772	

*one published source gives Francis Exhuerus

PEAKE, Peter and Mary

Issue:

Mary	b.	6 Nov 1755

PEAKE, William and Henrietta

Issue:

Ann	b. 19 Nov 1761	
Raphael	b. 20 Feb 1765	
Eleanor	b.	5 Jun 1767
Joshua	b. 28 Sep 1769	

PYKE, James and Ann

Mary Ann	b. 14 May 1753	
Henry	b.	5 Feb 1756
James	b. 18 Apr 1759	

PYKE, John and Kezia

Issue:

Mary Ann	b. 17 May 1757	
John	b.	1 Jun 1759
William	b. 18 Sep 1761	

REDMAN, William and Ann

Issue:

George	b.	7 Oct 1763
John	b. 11 Apr 1765	
William	b.	6 Aug 1767
Britannia	b.	5 Feb 1769
Benjamin	b.	8 Jun 1770

REDMAN, Zachariah and Fanny (Mattingly)

Issue:

Roseanna	b.	1 Jan 1816

RESHWICK*, Thomas and Mary

Issue:

Joseph   b. 18 Sep 1774

RUSSELL, Ignatius and Mildred

Issue:

Eleanor   b. 22 May 1773
Philip   b. 15 Sep 1775
Allusia   b. 24 Dec 1777

RUSSELL, John and Susanna

Issue:

Catherine   b. 27 Jun 1771

RUSSELL, William and Ann

Issue:

William   b. 29 Apr 1747
Ignatius   b. 10 Mar 1748/9
James   b. 6 Dec 1755
Mary Ann   b. 20 Mar 1757
Charles   b/ 12 Oct 1759

SANSON, John and Mary

Issue:

William   b. 5 Jul 1771

SAUNDERS, Sinnott and Ann

Issue:

Elizabeth   b. 24 Jan 1768

*see also Van Reshwick, below, and
 Riswick in St. Inigoes records

SEWELL, Henry and Mary

Issue:

Clement   b. 10 Jun 1757
Mary Smith   b. 7 Jul 1762
Henry   b. 3 Jun 1764
Charles   b. 20 Jul 1767

SIMS, Anthony and Mary

Issue:

Elizabeth   b. 28 Oct 1768

SPINK, Edward and Monica

Issue:

Mary   b. 21 Dec 1755
Joseph   b. 22 Apr 1759
Mary   b. 29 Jul 1762

STONE, Joseph and Dorothy

Issue:

John   b. 13 Nov 1773

STONE, Ignatius and Monica

Issue:

Ignatius   b. 6 Feb 1762
Matthew   b. 8 Sep 1764

STONE, Joseph and Winifred (Hutchens)

Issue:

Francis   bpt 6 Aug 1781

STONE, Joseph and Dorothy

Issue:

John   b. 13 Nov 1773

TANEY, John and Eleanor

Issue:

| Eleanor | b. 10 Mar 1756 |
| Sarah | b. 26 Dec 1764 |

TARLTON, James and Mary Ann

Issue:

Ignatius	b. 16 Jul 1762
Elijah	b. 20 Jan 1765
John	b. 23 Sep 1772

TARLTON, William and Jane

Issue:

| Jeremiah | b. 12 May 1761 |

TAYLOR, Ignatius and Elizabeth (Spink)

Issue:

Mary	b. 1 Oct 1764
Henrietta	b. 5 May 1768
Ann	b. 15 Sep 1770

THOMAS, Abell and Sarah

Issue:

| Luke | b. 24 Nov 1763 |
| Elizabeth | b. 2 Mar 1769 |

THOMAS, James and Elizabeth

Issue:

| Robert | b. 25 Jul 1765 |
| Jamima | b. 4 Mar 1761 |

THOMAS, John and Dorothy

Issue:

| Ann | b. 16 Dec 1764 |
| John | b. 1 Nov 1766 |

THOMAS, Mark and Elizabeth

Issue:

| Samuel | b. 10 Apr 1769 |

THOMAS, Thomas and Jane (Abell)

Issue:

Edward	b. 13 Mar 1782
Mary	b. 31 Mar 1784
James	b. 16 Oct 1786

THOMPSON, James and Elizabeth

Issue:

John	b. 29 Dec 1761
Elizabeth	b. 14 May 1764
James	b. 6 May 1766
Janet	b. 5 Nov 1768
Mary	b. 11 Jun 1771
Elijah	b. 12 Feb 1774

THOMPSON, James and Ann

Issue:

Raphael	b. 23 Aug 1743
Charles	b. 25 Sep 1746
Eleanor	b. 16 Oct 1748

THOMPSON, John and Rebecca

Issue:

| Samuel | b. 28 Mar 1755 |

THOMPSON, John Baptist and Susanna

Issue:

Sarah   b. 18 Feb 1774

THOMPSON, Mark and Margaret

Issue:

John Gerrard   b. 16 Apr 1753
Mary Ann   b. 17 Feb 1757
Ignatius   b. 29 Oct 1761
Mary   b. 12 Aug 1767

THOMPSON, Raphael and Anastasia

Issue:

John Barton   b. 24 Apr 1773

THOMPSON, Raphael and Susanna

Issue:

Joseph   b. 9 Dec 1764
Mary   b. 9 Mar 1767
James Aloysius   b. 27 Jan 1769
Charles   b. 1 Oct 1770
William   b. 24 Sep 1774

THOMPSON, Robert and Ann

Issue:

James   b. 14 Nov 1757
Mary Ann   b. 20 Feb 1760

THOMPSON, Robert and Elizabeth

Issue:

Susanna   b. 7 Jul 1747
Athanasius   b. 6 Sep 1749
Elizabeth   b. 9 Sep 1752
Mary   b. 10 Feb 1755
Eleanor   b. 7 Aug 1757
Charles James   b. 14 Jul 1760
Bennett   b. 3 Jun 1763
Mary   b. 23 Nov 1765
James   b. 13 Dec 1767

THOMPSON, Thomas and Ann

Issue:

Mary   b. 27 Sep 1754
John Barton   b. 12 Jun 1757
Thomas Alexius   b. 3 Nov 1761
Eleanor   b. 26 Mar 1763
Joseph Edward   b. 16 May 1766
Joseph Zachariah   b. 17 Feb 1769
Mary Ann   b. 1 Apr 1773

THOMPSON, William and Susanna

Issue:

George Matthews b. 11 Dec 1767

TOMPKINS, John and Mary

Issue:

Mary Attaway   b. 17 Sep 1771
Alethea   b. 31 May 1775

VAN RESHWICK, John and Appolonia

Issue:

Thomas   b. 15 Oct 1752
Mary   b. 23 Mar 1755
Joseph Aloysius   b. 15 Aug 1757
Francis   b. 4 Nov 1763

VAN RESHWICK, Thomas and Ann

Issue:

Monica   b. 19 Aug 1753
Wilford   b. 12 Jan 1756

VOWLES, Cyrus and Victoria

Issue:

Jane	b.	25 Dec 1754
John	b.	1 Feb 1758
Mathew	b.	27 May 1762
Ann	b.	11 Feb 1765
Thomas	b.	26 Jan 1767
Sarah	b.	3 Feb 1770
Mary	b.	20 Nov 1772
Elizabeth	b.	9 Jun 1777

VOWLES, James and Priscilla

Issue:

Susanna	b.	7 Jun 1772
Richard	b.	6 Mar 1774

VOWLES, Mathew and Ann

Issue:

Henry	b.	6 Jun 1787

VOWLES, Thomas and Susanna (Chunn)

Issue:

Walter	b.	25 Mar 1749
Henry	b.	25 Sep 1752
Ann	b.	10 Oct 1754

WALKER, John and Mary

Issue:

Mary	b. 16 May 1765

WATHEN, Henry Hudson and Ann

Issue:

Francis Hudson	b.	3 Nov 1764
Henry Hudson	b.	11 May 1766

Adult white males were required to take an Oath of Allegiance to the revolutionary government of Maryland according to a law passed by the General Assembly in the February Session, 1777. Inasmuch as the 1776 census for St. Mary's County was destroyed by fire the following list of some eleven hundred adult males serves as an important genealogical aid.

The Oath as follows is taken from the return of Robert Armstrong:

"I do swear, that I do not hold myself bound to yield any allegiance or obedience to the King of Great Britain, his heirs or successors, and that I will be true and faithful to the State of Maryland, and will, to the utmost of my power, support, maintain, and defend the freedom and independence thereof, and the Government as now established, against all open enemies, and secret and traitorous conspiracies, and will use my utmost endeavours to disclose and make known to the Governor, or some one of the Judges or Justices thereof, all treasons and traiterous conspiracies, attempts, or combinations, against this State or the Government thereof, which may come to my knowledge. So help me God."

A few names which did not appear in earlier published versions were found in copies of the original lists kindly provided by the Maryland Historical Society in Baltimore. Two reproductions appear below of names of ancestors of the author. John Leaton [Layton] was incorrectly rendered John Seaton and Joseph Tucker appeared as Joseph Tewkes in earlier published versions. A comparison with other capital L's on the same page, as in Lancaster, suggests that the name is correctly John Leaton. With Joseph Tucker a comparison was made with other capital T's, u's, c's, k's, e's, and terminal r's.

Abbreviations of Justices who administered the Oaths:

RA	Robert Armstrong	HR	Henry Reeder
RB	Richard Barnes	JR	John Reeder
BB	Bennett Biscoe	JS	John Shanks
IF	Ignatius Fenwick	HS	Henry G. Sothoron
VH	Vernon Hebb	JT	Jenifer Taylor
JI	John Ireland	HT	Henry Tubman
JJ	Jeremiah Jordan	RW	Robert Watts

Arthur Abell	RB		John Blundell	BB
Barton Abell	HR		John Boarman	JS
Clarke Abell	RW		Richard Boarman	JR
Cuthbert Abell	RW		Silvester Boarman	JS
Cuthbert Abell	RW		John Bolds	RB
Cuthbert Abell	RW		Jeremiah Bond	JS
Edmund Abell	HR		John Bond	JS
Enoch Abell, Jr.	RB		John Bond, Jr.	JS
George Abell	HR		Thomas Bond	JJ
Henry Abell	RB		William Bond	JS
John Abell of Samuel	JJ		Joseph Booker	HS
John Abell, Youngest	RW		Basil Booth	RB
John Booth Abell	RW		George Booth	JI
John Horne Abell	BB		James Booth	RB
Joshua Abell	JI		John Booth	VH
Philip Abell	RW		John Booth, Sr.	RB
Robert Abell	JJ		Joseph Booth	RB
Samuel Abell	RB		Leonard Booth	RB
Samuel Abell, Youngest	RB		Richard Booth	RB
Thomas Abell	JJ		John Bothick	JI
Zacharias Abell	IF		William Boulds	JI
John Adams	JJ		Thomas Boult	VH
George Aisquith	RW		Mark Bourn	JS
John Aisquith	RW		Ignatius Bowles	HR
John Allison, Jr.	BB		William Bowling	JS
Thomas Allstan	JJ		James Boyd	JJ
Thomas Allstan, Jr.	JS		James Bradburn	RB
James Alvey	JI		John Bradburn	JI
Jesse Alvey	JI		John Bradburn, Jr.	JI
John Armstrong	VH		William Bradburn	HR
Joseph Anderson	VH		Thomas Branson	IR
Joseph Arthurs	BB		Enoch Breeden	RW
Nathaniel Askum	HS		George Brewer	VH
James Atkinson	RW		James Brewer	JR
James Attwood	BB		John Brewer	JI
John Aud	RB		John Baptist Brewer	HR
Joseph Aud	RB		Mark Brewer	HS
William Aud	RB		Thomas Brewer	HR
John Avery	JS		William Brewer	HR
			Zacharias Brewer	HR
James Baccus	HS		Thomas Bridget	JJ
John Bailey	JS		Thomas Bridgett	HS
Thomas Bailey	BB		James Bright	JJ
Samuel Banfield	IF		John Bright	RB
Archibald D. Barber	JR		John B. Bright	RB
Cornelius Barber	HT		John Hooper Brome	JR
Richard Barnhouse	RA		Michael Brook	JI
Rodolph Barnhouse	BB		Francis Brookes	IF
Zachariah Barns	JR		Hooper Broome	JS
Edmund Bassey	BB		Cornelius Brothers	RB
Joseph Baxter	BB		Anthony Brown	RB
William Bayard	JS		Basil Brown	RB

George Thomas Brown	JJ	Kenelm Cheseldine	JS
Ignatius Brown	RB	William Cheseldine	JS
James Brown	RB	John Chesley	HT
John Brown	JR	Senica Chezeldine	RW
Nicholas Brown	HR	George Chilton	VH
Peter Brown	HR	James Chittim	JS
Peter Brown, Jr.	HR	Jessey Chiverill	BB
William Brown, Jr.	JJ	Barton Cissell	JI
Ignatius Bryan	RW	Bennet Cissell	JI
Philip Bryan	JR	Bernard Cissell	RB
William Bryan	HS	John Baptist Cissell	JI
Robert Buckler	JJ	Raphael Cissell	JI
Charles Buckman	JJ	Cuthbert Clark	RB
Ignatius Buckman	JJ	Richard Clark	RB
Joseph Budd	JI	Richard Clark	RB
George Bullock	JS	Thomas Clark	BB
Benjamin Burroughs	HT	Thomas Clark	JS
Benjamin Burroughs, Jr.	HT	Abraham Clarke	HR
George Burroughs	HT	John Clarke	JI
Hezekiah Burroughs	HT	John A. Clarke	VH
James Burroughs	HT	Kenelm Clarke	RW
John Burroughs, Jr.	HT	Matthew Clarke	JR
John Burroughs, Sr.	HT	Philip Clarke	RW
Joseph Burroughs	HT	Robert Clarke	RA
Matthew Burroughs	HT	Robert Clarke	JR
Richard Burroughs	HT	Robert Clarke	HR
Samuel Burroughs, Jr.	HT	Roger Clarke	RW
William Burroughs	HT	William Clarke	IF
Williamson Burroughs	HT	Thomas Clayton	JJ
Nicholas Byrn	RA	Bennet Clocker	BB
Michael Byrne	BB	James Coad	BB
		John Coad	BB
Thomas Cain	BB	Joseph Coad	BB
Archibald Campbell	HR	Edward Cole	HR
Edward Campbell	JI	George Cole	VH
Enoch Campbell	JR	Isaac Cole	BB
Joseph Carberry	HR	John Cole	VH
Patrick Carbery	JI	Robert Cole	HR
Peter Carbery	JI	Volantine Cole	VH
Justinian Card	JJ	William Collins	JJ
William Card	HT	Bennet Combs	HR
George Carpenter	JJ	George Combs	BB
George Carpenter	RB	Philip Combs	HR
John Carpenter	JJ	John Cook, Sr.	JI
John Carpenter, Sr.	JI	Alexander Cooke	HS
William Carpenter	RB	Ignatious Coombs	BB
William Carpenter	BB	Samuel Cottreal	RA
Ambrose Carr	JR	Bennet Cox	JS
James Carter	JJ	Peter Craig	JI
John Cartwright	JR	Rubin Craige	JI
Ignatius Chamberlain	HR	James Armstrong Crain	VH
Gerard Cheseldine	JS	William Crain	BB

Fielder Crampfoot	IF	Enoch Drury, Sr.	JI
Thomas Crane	VH	Ignatius Drury	JI
James Crawley	BB	James Drury	IF
Edward Craycroft	IF	John Drury, Sr.	JJ
Ignatius Craycroft	HR	John B. Drury	IF
John Crocker	BB	Michael Drury	IF
James Curtis	JJ	Philip Drury	IF
Joseph Curtis	JJ	John Dunbar	BB
		Joseph Dunbar	JI
James Daffin	RW	John Duncaster	RB
Robert Daffin	RW	John Dunnard	IF
William Daffin	RW	Senet Duvall	JJ
Matthew Dafft	RB		
Ignatius Daft	JI	William Eadie	JJ
John Daft	JI	John Edley	HR
William Daft	JI	Benjamin Edwards	HT
Charles Dant	RW	Hezekiah Edwards	HT
John Baptist Dant	BB	Ignatius Edwards	HT
John Dart	JR	Jeremiah Edwards	RB
James Davis	JI	Jesse Edwards	HT
John Davis	HS	John Edwards of John	HT
Joseph Davis	RB	John Edwards of Robert	HT
Moses Davis	BB	Stourton Edwards	HS
Stephen Davis	JI	John Egerton	BB
Walter Davis	JI	Thomas Egerton	BB
James Dean	IF	Matthew Ellet	BB
John Dean	IF	Richard Elliot	IF
Thomas Dean	IF	James Ellis	JJ
William Dean	IF	John Ellis	JJ
Thomas Dennison	RA	Thomas Ellis	JJ
Charles Dent	RW	William Ellis	JJ
George Dent	HT	Joshua Estep	HT
John Dent	HT	Philamon Estep	HT
John Miles Devaul	BB	Philip Evans	IF
Francis Diddle	HS	Philip Evans	BB
John Dillahay	HS	Richard Evans	RW
Road Dillahay	HS	William Evans	BB
Thomas Dillehay	JI	William Evans	JI
Thomas Dillen	RW*		
Henry Dixon	BB	Benjamin Fenwick	IF
Peter Dixon	HS	Bennett Fenwick	RW
William Rooke Dixon	BB	Cuthbert Fenwick	IF
John Dossey	RB	Edward Fenwick	BB
Joseph Downs	BB	Enoch Fenwick	HR
Austin S. Doxey	RA	Enoch Fenwick, Jr.	IF
James Doxey	BB	Francis Fenwick of Ben.	IF
John Doxey	BB	Francis Fenwick of I.	IF
William Doxey	BB	George Fenwick	IF
Robert Drewry	JR	Ignatius Fenwick	VH
Thomas Drewry	JR	Ignatius Fenwick of E.	IF
John Drudge	JI	James Fenwick	JI
Enoch Drury	JI	James Fenwick	VH

* Took oath at Baltimore
as per certificate from
Isaac Van Bibber

-74-

John Fenwick	JI	Edward Gadden	JR
John Fenwick	IF	Jeremiah Gadden	JR
John Fenwick	RA	Richard Ellis Gadden	JR
John Fenwick, Jr.	RA	Clement Gardiner	JS
Joseph Fenwick	HR	John Gardiner	JS
P. Fenwick of Enoch	RB	Caleb Gibbins	VH
Philip Fenwick of P.	IF	Francis Gibbins	VH
Richard Fenwick	BB	John Gibbons	JS
Robert Fenwick of John	RB	Jeremiah Gibson	JS
Thomas Fenwick	HR	John Gibson	JJ
William Fenwick	IF	John Gibson of William	JI
William Fenwick	RB	Joshua Gibson	JJ
Thomas Ferrill	JJ	Roswell Gibson	JJ
William Ferrill, Jr.	JJ	William Gibson	JJ
William Ferrill, Sr.	JJ	Henry Gill	BB
Leonard Fields	JR	Barton Goddart	JR
Nicholas Fielder	RW	Ignatius Goddart	JR
William Fields	JI	Ignatius Goddart, Jr.	IF
Christopher Fisher	RW	John Goddart	IF
William Fitzgo	RW	John Baptist Goddart	JR
Charles Fitzjeffery	BB	Jonathan Goldsbury	IF
Joseph Fitzjeffery	RA	John Goldsmith	JJ
Richard Fitzjeffery	RA	John Goldsmith	JS
Henry Fletcher	BB	John Goldsmith of Ben	JJ
Joseph Flood	JS	Michael Goldsmith	JS
Jeremiah Flower	JJ	Notley Goldsmith	JJ
Thomas Flower	JJ	Thomas Goldsmith	JJ
Jesse Floyd	IF	Thomas Goldsmith	JJ
Raphael Foard	JI	John Goodrum	RW
Henry Ford	RB	Matthew Goodwin	JJ
John Ford	RB	William Goodwin	JJ
John Ford	RW	Bennet Gough	JS
John Ford	HR	George Gough	BB
John Ford, Jr.	RB	Ignatius Gough	HR
John Ford of Peter	HR	Ignatius Gough	JS
Peter Ford	HR	James Gough	RB
Philip Ford	HR	Stephen Gough	RB
Richard Ford	HR	John Gowing	RW
Robert Ford, Sr.	JI	Jeremiah Graves	JI
Robert Ford, C.H.	RB	John Graves	JI
William Ford	JJ	Joshua Graves	JI
Zachariah Forest	HR	John Gray	JR
Thomas Forrest	IF	John B. Greaves	JI
Thomas Forrest	JI	James T. Greenfield	HT
Zepha Forrest	RB	Nathaniel T. Greenfield	HT
Thomas Foyer/Fryer?	HS	Archibald Greenwell	JI
Benedict French	JI	Barnaby Greenwell	HS
Ignatius French	JI	Bennet Greenwell	HR
Raphael French	JI	Clement Greenwell	HR
Daniel Friend	JI	Cuthbert Greenwell	RB
		Edmund B. Greenwell	HR
		Edward Greenwell	RB

Enoch Greenwell	HR		Cartwright Hammett	RW
George Greenwell	HR		Richard Hammett	RW
Henry Greenwell	HR		Robert Hammett	RW
Ignatius Greenwell	HR		William Hammett	VH
Ignatius Greenwell, Jr.	IF		Zachariah Hammett	HS
Ignatius Greenwell of Henry	HR		William Hancock	JR
James Greenwell	RB		James Haney	HR
John Greenwell, Jr.	RB		Ignatious Harbert	BB
John Greenwell, Sr.	RB		William Harbert	BB
John Greenwell of George	RB		John Baptist Hardin	JS
John Greenwell of James	RB		Joseph Hargiss	JI
John E. Greenwell	RB		James Harper	HS
Joseph Greenwell	RB		John Harper	HR
Joseph Greenwell	HR		Josias Harris	HR
Joshua Greenwell	RB		Samuel Harris	RB
Justinian Greenwell	JJ		Benjamin Haskins	JI
Leonard Greenwell	HR		John Haskins	JI
Nicholas Greenwell	HR		John Haskins	JS
Raphael Greenwell	RB		Lawrence Hatter	JJ
Robert Greenwell	IF		Clement Hayden	JI
Stephen Greenwell	RB		William Hayden	JR
Stephen Greenwell	HR		William Hayden of George	JI
Thomas Greenwell	JI		James Haydon	JJ
Thomas Greenwell	RB		Thomas Haywood	BB
William Greenwell	HR		Bennet Hazel	JR
William Greenwell	HR		Edward Hazel	JR
William Greenwell	HR		Jeremiah Hazell	IF
William Greenwell	HR		John Hazell, Jr.	IF
Robert Greeves	BB		Cuthbert Head	HS
Abraham Griffin	BB		Ignatius Heard	JJ
Thomas Griffin	BB		Ignatius Heard	HR
Sabbaston Griggs	BB		James Heard	JJ
Richard Gristy	HS		James Heard of W.	IF
George Guyther	VH		John Heard	JI
			John Heard of Mark	RW
Rodolph Hacket	RB		John Basil Heard	HR
Francis Haden	HR		Luke Heard	HR
George Haden	HR		Matthew Heard	JI
Robert Hagan	IF		William Heard	IF
William Jenkins Hager	RW		William Heard	JI
Aquilla Hall	RW		William Heard, Jr.	JI
Arthur Hall	RW		James Heath	BB
Basil Hall	HS		Caleb Hebb	VH
Ignatius Hall	RW		Jesse Hebb	JS
John Hall	RW		John Hebb	VH
Joseph Hall	RB		Joseph Hebb	VH
Richard Hall	JJ		Thomas Hebb	VH
Thomas Hall	BB		William Hebb	VH
Thomas Hall	JI		Elias Henny	BB
James Hamilton	JR		Martin Henry	JI
William Hamilton	HT		Nathaniel Hickman	BB
Caleb Hammett	RW		John Higdon	JJ

John Baptist Hill	RW	Rodolph Jarboe	BB
Joseph Hill	JR	Stephen Jarboe	BB
Zachariah Hill	HS	Thomas Jarboe	HR
Francis Hilton	RW	John Jeans	JS
Francis Hilton	JS	Thomas Jeans	BB
John Hilton	JS	Whitton Jeffery	RA
William Hilton	RW	Parke Jenifer	RA
Caleb Hinnen	BB	Samuel Jenifer	RW
Judiah Hinnen	BB	Augustin Jenkins of Richard	JI
Nathan Hinnen	BB	Edmund Jenkins	HR
Thomas A. Hinnen	BB	George Jenkins	BB
Henry Hon	JR	Henry Jenkins	RW
Bennett Hopewell	JI	John Jenkins	BB
George Hopewell	RW	Thomas Jenkins	BB
Hugh Hopewell	JT	William Jenkins	RW
James Hopewell	RW	David Johnson	JR
Edward Hopwood	RA	William Johnson	JI
Basil Hopkins	RA	John Jones	HS
Jacob Hopkins	HT	Matthias Jones	RA
Henry Horrell	RB	Morriss Jones	BB
John Horrell	JR	Solomon Jones	RA
Thomas Horrell	JR	Charles Jordan	JJ
Austin Howard	RB	James Jordan	JJ
George Howard	RB	John Jordan	JI
James Howard, Sr.	JI	Samuel Jordan	JS
Jonathan Howard	JI	William Jordan	JJ
Joseph Howard	JI	Justinian Joseph	JR
Leonard Howard	RB	William Joseph	JR
Peter Howard	JS	Athanatius Joy	JR
Peter Howard of Thomas	JI	Charles Joy	IF
Peter Howard of Thomas*	JI	Enoch J. Joy	IF
Thomas Howard	JS	Ignatius Joy, Jr.	IF
William Howard	IF	Ignatius Joy, Sr.	IF
John Hughes	BB	Peter Joy	IF
Bennet Hutchins	HR	Peter Joy	IF
John Hutchins	RB	Thomas Joy	JI
Bennet Hutchinson	HS		
		Timothy Keach	BB
Bennet Jarboe	RB	James Keech	HT
Charles Jarboe, Jr.	IF	John Keech	JR
Henry Jarboe	BB	Thomas Keimer	VH
Henry Jarboe	BB	Joseph Keirk	RA
John Jarboe	HS	Zacharius Kendruk	VH
John Baptist Jarboe	BB	George Kennick	HS
Joshua Jarboe	RB	William Keough	RW
Mark Jarboe	HS	Barton King	HS
Matthew Jarboe	HR	Charles King, Jr.	RW
Peter Jarboe	HR	Francis King (Harford Co.)	IF
Philip Jarboe	HR	George King	JI
Richard Jarboe	RB	Henry King	RW
Robert Jarboe	RW	Henry King, Jr.	BB
Robert Jarboe, Jr.	RB	James King (Harford Co.)	IF

* Bay Side

-77-

James King of John	JI	Ignatius Lowe	JI
John King, Jr.	RW	John Lucas	JR
John King of Thomas	HR	John Lynch	BB
Richard King	RW		
Robert King	JS	Daniel Mackintush	BB
Thomas King	IF	John Mackall	BB
William King	JR	John Maddox	JJ
John Kinnaman	HS	Samuel Maddox	JJ
James Knott	RW	Raphael Magee	IF
John Knott	HS	Basil Mahoney	JR
		John Smith Mahoney	JR
John Lake	JT	James Maiteland	BB
John Lancaster	JI	William Mallehone of Thomas	JI
Raphael Lancaster	JS	John Manley	BB
Josiah Langley	VH	Matthew Manley	BB
William Langley	RA	Rodolph Manley	BB
Henry Langly	JJ	John Manning	RB
Matthew Latham	RB	Joseph Mareman	JI
Thomas Leach	IF	Joshua Mareman	JI
William Leach	JI	William Mareman	JI
James Leake	JS	Zachariah Mareman	JI
John Leaton	JI	William Martin	VH
Charles Lee	BB	Richard Mason	JI
Hance Lee	JJ	Benet Mattingley	JI
John Lee	JR	Benjamin Mattingley	BB
Philip Lee	JS	Clement Mattingley	JJ
Samuel Lee	JJ	Edward Mattingley	JI
Thomas Lee	JS	Francis Mattingley	JI
Christopher Leigh	BB	James Barton Mattingley	JS
George Leigh	BB	Luke Mattingley, Sr.	JI
George H. Leigh	BB	Ignatius Mattingly, Jr.	JI
Joseph Leigh	RA	Robert Mattingly	JI
Joseph Leigh, Jr.	RA	John McClean	HS
William Leigh	BB	Benjamin McKay	BB
Charles Lewellin	JJ	Richard McKay	VH
John Lewellin	JJ	John McLean	RB
Joseph Lewis	BB	Henry McMullin	JJ
William Lilburn	BB	Kenelm McWilliams	JJ
James Lithgow	JJ	Thomas McWilliams	JJ
George Lock	JJ	Enoch Medley	BB
Meveral Lock	JJ	George Medley	RB
Thomas Lock	HS	Henry Medley	HR
Thomas Loker	BB	John Medley	HR
James Long	JJ	Joseph Medley	RB
Jeremiah Long	JJ	Philip Medley	RB
John Long	JJ	William Medley	HR
Perry Long	JJ	Austin Milburn	BB
Robert Long	JJ	Edward Milburn	RW
Samuel Long	JJ	Jeremiah Milburn	RB
John Longson	JJ	Joseph Milburn	BB
John Baptist Low	JS	Richard Milburn	RW
Bennett Lowe	BB	Stephen Milburn	RW

Henry Miles	JR	Zachariah Newton	JI
Philip Miles	JR	Thomas Noakes	JS
Joseph Millard	HR	Joseph Noble	BB
Joshua Millard	HR	George Noe	HT
Ignatius Mills	RB	Richard Nokes	RW
James Mills	JJ	Bennet Norris	HR
James Mills of John	JI	Edmund B. Norris	HR
John Mills of Jesse	RB	Henry Norris	RB
John Mills, 3rd	JJ	Ignatius Norris	JI
Joseph Ignatius Francis Mills	JR	Ignatius Norris	RB
Joshua Mills	JR	James Norris	RB
Justinian Mills	JJ	John Norris	HR
Nicholas Mills	RB	Mackelva Norris	VH
William Mills	JJ	Mark Norris	RB
William Mitchell	RB	Mark Norris, Sr.	RB
Benedict Moore	BB	Matthew Norris	RW
George Moore	HT	Philip Norris	JI
James Moore	IF	Rodolph Norris	HR
Jesse Moore	IF	Thomas Norris	HR
John Moore	BB	Thomas Norris	JI
John Moore	IF	Clement Norriss	RB
Leonard Moore	IF	John Norriss	RB
Benjamin Morgan	HR	William Norriss	BB
James Morgan	JI	Benjamin Nottingham	HR
John Morgan, Sr.	JI	John Basil Nottingham	IF
William Morgan	JI	Philip Nottingham	IF
William Moulds	JJ	Williby Nugent	BB
Thomas Mud	RB		
Joseph Mudd	HT	Bernard O'Niell	JJ
William Muir	JJ	Joseph Owens	JJ
Valentine Murrain	JJ		
		Francis Pain	RB
Bennett Neale	JS	James Pain of Richard	RB
Charles Neale	HS	John Baptist Pain	HR
Henry Neale	JJ	Richard Pain	RB
James Neale, youngest	JJ	Clement Parsons	JR
Jeremiah Neale	JJ	James Parsons	IF
Raphael Neale	JJ	James Payn	JI
Raphael Neale, Jr.	JI	John Payne	JS
Wilfred Neale	JS	Raphael Payne	JI
Senna Nelson	JI	Vincent Payne	RB
James Nevison	JJ	William Payne	JS
John Baptist Nevett	JJ	Ignatius Peacock	IF
Joseph Nevit	JS	Paul Peacock	HR
Charles Nevitt	HS	Augustin Peak	RB
John Nevitt	JJ	John Peak	RB
Joseph Nevitt	JJ	Robert Peak	RB
Bernard Newton	RB	Baptist Peake	RW
Delbert Newton	HR	Ignatius Peake	HR
Gabriel Newton	JI	Peter Peake	JI
Ignatius Newton	IF	Philip Peake	RW
Ignatius Newton	JI	Richard Pearcy	JJ

Bennett Perran	JI	Peregrine Rose	JS
Samuel Phearson	JJ	Lazerous Ross	BB
Henry Phillip	JR	James Russell	IF
Jonathan Phillips	JR	William Russell	RB
Henry Pike	HR	William Russell, Sr.	RB
Richard Pilkinton	IF	Thomas Ryswick	HR
Edmund Plowden	JJ		
Francis G. Plowden	IF	John Sanner	BB
James Plummer	JJ	Joseph Sanner	BB
Bennet Price	BB	John Scissell	HR
John Pusy	BB	John B. Scissell	HR
		William Scissell	RB
Basil Raley	IF	William Scott	HT
Bennett Raley	RW	James Seager	HT
Henry Silvester Raley	IF	Leonard Seale	HS
John Raley of H.	IF	Clement Sewall	RB
John Raley, Jr.	IF	Henry Sewall	JT
John Raley, Sr.	IF	Henry Sewall (L.T.)	RB
John Baptist Raley	RB	N. Lewis Sewall	RW
John W. Raley	IF	Nicholas Sewall	JT
Richard James Rapier	JI	John Shadricks	VH
William Rapour	HR	Joseph Shanks	JJ
John Baptist Read	JI	John Shanks, Sr.	JI
Philip Read	RB	Thomas Shanks	JI
Joshuary Redman	BB	William Shaw	JI
John Reece	BB	Joseph Shercliff	RW
John Reeder, Jr.	VH	Thomas Shercliff	JI
Thomas Attaway Reeder	JR	George Sherley	RW
William Reeder	BB	John Shiercliff	JI
John Reynolds	HR	Joseph Shurbentine	BB
John Reynolds	IF	Anthony Simmes	IF
Abraham Rhodes	RW	Garbiner Simon	BB
Robert Ribbon	HT	Josias Simpson	JJ
Thomas Richardson	RA	Francis Sissell	RB
Thomas Richarson	BB	Ignatius Sissell	RB
Thomas Richarson, Sr.	BB	James Sissell	RB
William Richarson	BB	James Sissell, Jr.	RB
Henry Riley	HR	William Sissell	RB
Bennet Rily	RB	Bartholomew Smith	BB
Wilfred Rishwick	RB	Basil C. Smith	IF
Joseph Riswick	RB	Edward B. Smith	IF
James Ritchie	BB	Elias Smith	RB
James Roach	JI	James Smith	RA
George Roberson	BB	James Smith (S. Master)	BB
Anthony Roberts	JI	John Smith	BB
John Roberts	JI	John Smith	RW
William Rock	JJ	John Smith	RA
Philip Rocke [Rooke?]	JI	John Smith, Jr.	RB
Barnaby Rodes	RW	John Smith of John	B.
John Rodes	RW	Peter Pears Smith	R.
George Rogers	RW	Samuel Smith	B.
William Rooke	BB	Vernon Smith	R

Wat Smith	RW	Moses Tabbs, A.M.	VH
Austin Sanford Smoot	BB	John F. Taney	IF
Cuthbert Smoot	BB	Raphael Taney	IF
John Smoot, Sr.	BB	Bennet Tarlton	BB
Thomas Smoot	BB	James Tarlton	VH
William B. Smoot	VH	John Tarlton	BB
John Somervill	HS	Joshua Tarlton	VH
John I. Sothoron	HT	Thomas Tarlton	BB
Levin Sothoron	HS	William Tarlton	BB
Richard Sothoron	HT	Henry Taylor	RB
Richard Sothoron of Richard	HT	Ignatius Taylor	RB
Richard Sothoron of Samuel	HT	James Taylor	RB
Benedict Spalding	HR	John Taylor	RB
Bennet Spalding	RB	John Taylor, St. Mary's	BB
Edward Spalding	IF	Richard Taylor	RA
Elexs. Spalding	JR	Thomas Taylor	JJ
Henry Spalding	JR	William Taylor	BB
Henry Spalding, Jr.	JR	Jesse Tennison	JI
John Baptist Spalding, Sr.	JR	Jessey Tennison	BB
Joseph Spalding	JI	John Tennison	JI
Michael Spalding	IF	Matthew Tennison	JS
Moses C. Spalding	IF	Samuel Tennison	JS
Peter Spalding	IF	William Tennison	JS
Philip Spalding	BB	James Theobalds	BB
Philip Spalding	JR	Samuel Theobalds	RA
Raphael Spalding	HR	Harbert Thomas	BB
Richard Spalding, Jr.	JR	John A. Thomas	HR
Thomas Spalding	JR	Levy Thomas	BB
William Spalding	JR	Philip Thomas	BB
William Spalding	BB	Robert Thomas	HR
Edward Spink	HR	Tylor Thomas	RA
William Spink	RB	John Thomkins	HR
Enoch Stone	IF	Arron Thompson	JS
Ignatius F. Stone	IF	Arthur Thompson	JI
John Stone	IF	Athanatius Thompson	JI
Joseph Stone	RB	Henry Thompson	JS
Joseph Stone	RB	James Thompson	JS
Joseph Stone, Jr.	IF	James Thompson	RB
William Stone	IF	John Thompson	RB
William H. Stone	RB	John B. Thompson	RB
William Storr	BB	John Baptist Thompson	IF
Benjamin Suit	HT	John Basil Thompson	JI
John Dent Suit	HS	John Gerard Thompson	RB
Dent Suit, Sr.	HS	Joseph Thompson of Thomas	JI
Daniel Sulivan	BB	Peter Thompson	BB
Francis Swales	IF	Raphael Thompson	JI
John Swales	IF	Raphael Thompson	RB
Robert Swales	IF	Richard Thompson	BB
Edward Swan	HR	Robert Thompson	RB
Ignatious Sword	BB	Thomas Thompson	RB
		Thomas Thompson	HR
		Thomas Thompson, Sr.	JI

Thomas Thompson of Thomas	JI	Francis Wheeler	RB
Willifred Thompson	JI	Ignatius Wheeler	JJ
Alexander Thomson	HT	Justinian Wheeler	JI
Bazil Thomson	JR	Abner Wherritt	BB
Joseph Thomson	JR	John Wherritt	BB
Richard Thomson of Edward	JR	Nicholas Wherritt	BB
William Thomson	JR	Thomas Wherritt	VH
Vincent Thornton	HR	Thomas Wherritt	VH
Robert Timms	BB	James White	BB
John Tippett	HS	Cornelius Wildman	JR
John Tippett, Jr.	JJ	John Wildman	JR
Zachariah Tippett	HS	James Wilkinson	IF
John True	HT	William Wilkinson	IF
Joseph Tucker	BB	Benjamin Williams	RA
Charles Turner	JJ	Gabriel Williams	IF
John Turner	JS	George Williams	JJ
Joshua Turner	JS	Henry Williams	JJ
		Hugh Williams	IF
Peter Urquhart	RW	James Williams	RB
Thomas Uzzel	RW	Joseph Williams	JJ
		Simpson Williams	BB
Thomas Vaughan	RA	John Baptist Wimsat	JI
James Vowles	RB	Ignatius Wimsatt	RB
John Vyrmeir	JR	James Wimsatt	RB
		John Wimsatt	RB
John Wakelin	HS	John Wimsatt	HR
Henry Walker	JI	Richard Wimsatt	RB
James Walker	JR	Robert Wimsatt	RB
Joseph Walker	JR	Stephen Wimsatt	RB
Joseph Walker of Thomas	JI	William Wimsatt	RB
Thomas Walls	RB	Adam Wise of Adam	RW
Joseph Walters	JR	Matthew Wise, Sr.	RW
James Walton	JS	Matthew Wise of Matthew	RW
John Watkin	JI	Thomas Wise	RW
Thomas Watt	RW	William Wise	RW
Alexander S.T. Wats	RW	Richard Wiseman	RW
Kenelm B. Watts	RW	John Wood	HT
Thomas Watts	BB	Leonard Wood	HT
William Watts	VH	John Woodard	HR
James Waughop	VH	Daniel Woodburn	HS
Thomas Pal. Waughop	VH	John Woodburn	HT
William C. Waughop	VH	Jonathan Woodburn	HS
Thomas West	JS	William Woodward	JS
Justinian Wharton	JJ	John Wooton	JJ
Francis Wheatley	JI		
Francis Wheatley	HT	Edward Yates	JI
James Wheatley	HR	James Yates	RB
John Wheatley	RB	John Yates	IF
John Wheatley	HT	Martin Yates	RB
Richard Wheatley	HT	Robert Young	RW
Thomas Wheatley	HT		
Francis Wheatly	JI		

SAINT MARY'S COUNTY, MARYLAND

MILITIA, 1794

Original militia list available at the Maryland Historical Society

"An enrollment of the Militia in Saint Mary's County, agreeable to an Act of Assembly as returned by F. Hamersley to the Commissioners of the Tax 1794."

Bennet Abell
Clark Abell
Cuthbert Abell
Elisha Abell
Francis Abell
Henry Abell
John Abell
John Booth Abell
John S. Abell
Joseph Abell
Joseph Abner Abell
Philip Abell
Philip Abell
Samuel Abell
Samuel Abell
Thomas Abell
Abraham Adams
Edmund Adams
James Adams
Moses Adams
Theophilus Adams
William Adams
Jeremiah Adderton
Joseph Aderton
John Aisquith
John Allen
Zachariah Allen
James Alstan
Richard Alstan
Anthony Alvey
Basil Alvey
Bennett Alvey
Clement Alvey
James Alvey

Jeremiah Alvey
John Alvey
Joseph Alvey
William Alvey
Bennet Aprice
Aaron Armsworthy
Bennett Armsworthy
Daniel Armsworthy
John Armsworthy
John Armsworthy
Joshua Armsworthy
Joseph Artis
John Cartwright Ashcome
John Atkinson
William Aud
John Avis
James Bailey
James Bailey
John Bailey
John Bailey
William Baker
Bennet White Barber
Edward Barber
Elias Barber
Hezekiah Barber
Jonathan Barber
Luke Barber, Jr.
Luke White Barber
Philip Barber
Robert Barber
Thomas Barber
James Barnes
George Barnhouse
Rudolph Barnhouse

Edward Baxter
John Baxter
Alexander Bean
Richard Bean
Robert Bean
Alexander Beane
John Beane
John Beane
Robert Beane of Thomas
Thomas Beane
William Beane
Henry Belwood
Hanson Bennet
John Bennet
Joseph Bennet
Joseph Bennet, Jr.
Joseph Bennet of Wm.
Nathan Bennet
Richard Bennet
Thomas Bennet
Gerard Bennett
John Bernard
John Betts
Allen Billingsley
Thomas Billingsley
Basil Biscoe
Bennet Biscoe
Bennet Biscoe of Thos.
James Biscoe
James Biscoe of Geo.
James Biscoe of Joe
Josiah Biscoe
McKay Biscoe
Richard Biscoe

Stephen Biscoe
Thomas Biscoe
James Blair
Joseph Blair
Peter Blair
William Blair
John Blakistone
Nehemiah H. Blakistone
George Bohannon, Jr.
Jonathan Bohannon
Moses Bohannon
John Bond of John
John Bond of Thomas
Peregrine Bond
Richard Bond
Thomas Bond
Richard Booth
Basil Boothe
George Boothe
George Boothe
Henry Boothe
Jesse Boothe
John Boothe
Leonard Boothe
Matthew Boothe
Rodolph Boothe
William Boothe
Thomas Boult
William Boult
Samuel Bowes
Charles Bowling
Francis Bowls
John Bowls
Charles Bradburn
Francis Bradburn
John Bradburn
Matthew Bradburn
William Bradburn
Jonathan Bramhill
Reuben Bramhill
Baptist Branson
Thomas Breeden
John Brewer
Joseph Brewer
Mark Brewer
Thomas Brewer
Charles Bridget
Bennet Bright
John Bright
John Baptist Bright

John Basil Bright
Thomas Bright
John Brinn
Clement Briscoe
Henry Briscoe
John Hanson Briscoe
John Ll. Briscoe
Walter Brook
John Brookbank, Jr.
Francis Brooke
Hooper Broom
Barton Brown
Ignatius Brown
John B. Brown
Joseph Brown
Richard Brown
Thomas Brown
William Brown
John Bruce
John Bruce
William Bruce
Charles Bryan
Philip Bryan
Bennet Buckler
Cornelius Buckler
Joseph Buckman
Charles Bucknam
Clement Bucknam
Francis Bucknam
George Bullock, Jr.
Richard Bullock
Thomas Bullock
William Bullock, Pilot
Jeremiah Burn
Zephaniah Burn
George Burroughs
Gideon Burroughs
Hanson Burroughs
Henry Burroughs
Henry Burroughs
Hezekiah Burroughs
James Burroughs
Joseph Burroughs
Leonard Burroughs
Norman Burroughs
Samuel Burroughs
William Burroughs
Williamson Burroughs
Thomas Cadden
Nathaniel Cahill

James A. Callis
Barnaby Campbell
John Campbell
John Carberry
Thomas Caregin
George Carpenter, Jr.
Turner Carpenter
William Carpenter
Charles John Carroll
John Carter
John Dyson Cartwright
William Cartwright
Aquila Cawood
Stephen Cawood, Jr.
Benjamin Chappelear
John Chappelear
Calestiness Cheseldine
Cyrenius Cheseldine
Kenelm Cheseldine
Senica Cheseldine
William Cheseldine
Charles Chilton
William Chilton
Justinian Chiverall
Austin Cissel, Pilot
Cuthbert Cissel
Ethelbert Cissel
Francis Cissel
Jeremiah Cissel, Pilot
John Cissel
John Cissel
Joseph Cissel
William Cissel
William Cissel
Zachariah Cissel
Bennet Clarke
Caleb Clarke
Charles Clarke
George Clarke
George Clarke, Pilot
Ignatius Clarke, Pilot
James Clarke
James Clarke
James Clarke
John Clarke
Joseph W. Clarke
Matthias Clarke
Richard Clarke
Robert Clarke
Thomas Clarke

William Clarke
William Clarke
William Clarke
Zachariah Clarke
Benjamin Clocker
Daniel Clocker
William Clocker
Joseph Coade
Bennet Cole
Isaac Cole
Isaac Cole
Robert Cole
Valentine Cole
Willougby Cole
Bennet Combs
Charles Combs
Enoch Combs
James Combs
Joseph Combs
Raphael Combs
Thomas H. Combs
William Combs
William Combs
John Coode
Thomas Coode
Donaldson Cook
James Cooke
John U. Cooke
Charles Copsey
Enoch Copsey
John Copsey
Thomas Copsey
Jacob Corby
Isaac Corum
James Corum
John Corum
Theodocius Courtney, Pilot
James Cox
William Coxe
Peter Craig
Reuben Craig
Robert Crain, Pilot
James A. Craine
Ignatius Craycroft
Charles Cullins
George Cullison
John Cullison
George Cusick
James Daffinn
Joseph Daffin
Robert Daffin

John Daft
James Dart
James Dart
Thomas Dart
Anthony Davis
Hezekiah Davis
James Davis
John Davis
Joseph Davis
Kenelm Davis
Leonard Davis
Philemon Davis
Rene Davis
Stephen Davis, Jr.
Thomas Davis
Walter Davis
Baptist Deane
Ignatius Deane
James Deane
John B. Deane
Arthur Delehay
George Dent
Jonathan Dent
Thomas Dent
George Diment
Matthew Diment
Hatton Dixon
Soloman Dixon
Thomas Dixon
William R. Dixon
Cornelius Docherty
John Dorsey
Joseph Dorsey
Walter Dorsey
Jeremiah Downs
Joseph Downs
Aaron Doxey
Jeremiah Doxey
John Doxey
Joseph Doxey
Thomas Doxey
William Doxey, Jr.
Bennett Drury
Bernard Drury
Charles Drury
Edward Drury
Francis D. Drury
Ignatius Drury
Ignatius Drury of Ignatius
Jeremiah Drury
Jesse Drury

John C. Drury
Joseph Drury
Peter Drury
Samuel Drury
William Drury
Joseph Duel
Henry Duk
John U. Duk
John Duke
James Dunbar
Joseph Dunbar
Joseph Dunbar
William Dunbar
Robert Dunkinson
Barton Dyer
Richard Edelen
Benjamin Edwards
Ignatius Edwards
Jesse Edwards
John Edwards
Joseph Edwards
Joseph Edwards
Sturton Edwards
    of Ignatius
Sturton Edwards of John
Thomas Edwards
Charles Calvert Egerton
James Egerton
James Egerton
John Egerton
Philip Ellis
William Ellis
Joseph Estep
William Estep
Ignatius Evans
Jeremiah Evans
John Evans
John Evans
John Evans
Philip Evans
Richard Evans
William Evans
Thomas Everet
Zephaniah Fanning
John Farr
John Bernard Farr
Albion Fenwick
Austin Fenwick
Bennet Fenwick
Bennet Fenwick
Cuthbert Fenwick

Edward Fenwick
Edward Fenwick, Jr.
Francis Fenwick
Francis Fenwick of Ign.
James Fenwick
James Fenwick
Lewis Fenwick
Richard Fenwick, Jr.
William Fenwick
Edward Ferril
William Ferril, Jr.
James A. Fields
Joseph Fields
Barton Fish
Joseph Fish
Francis Fitzgerald
Charles Flower
James Flower
Jeremiah Flower
Joseph Flower
Jesse Floyd
Thomas Foiles
Bennet Ford
Charles Ford
Charles A. Ford
Edward Ford
Henry Ford
Ignatius Ford
Jeremiah Ford
John Gerrard Ford
Joseph Ford
Peter Ford
Philip Ford, Jr.
Robert Ford
Thomas Ford
Thomas Forrest
Charles Fowler
Joseph Fowler
Moses Fowler
Barton French
Benedict French
Ignatius French
Martin French
Peter French
Philip French
Rhodolph French
Henry Gardiner
Henry Gardiner of John
John Gardiner of Clem
John Gardiner of John
Thomas Gardiner of John
William Gardiner

Zephaniah Gardiner
John Garner
John Chun Garner
Edward Gatton
Elias Gatton
James Gatton
John Gatton
Joseph Gatton
Henry Gibbons
John Gibbons
Thomas Gibbons
William Gibon of Josa.
Gerard Gibson
Jeremiah Gibson
Joshua Gibson
Reuben Gibson
Rhody Gibson
Roswell Gibson
Henry Gill
Matthias Gill
Edward Barton Goddard
John B. Goddard
Ignatius Goldsberry
John Baptist Goldsberry
Kelly Goldsberry
William Goldsberry
John Mason Goldsmith
Notley Goldsmith
Wilfred Goodrum
William Goodrum
Richard Goodwin
Samuel Goodwin
Samuel Gormly
Charles Gough
George Gough, Pilot
Ignatius Gough
John Gough, Pilot
Joseph Gough
Thomas Gough, Pilot
William Gough
Elisha Graham
William Gray
James Greaves
Jeremiah Greaves
John Greaves
Joshua Greaves
Bennet Green
Cornelius Green
Nicholas D. Green
Thomas Green
Thomas Greenfield
Albion Greenwell

Andrew Greenwell
Archibald Greenwell
Archibald Greenwell
Austin Greenwell
Austin Greenwell
Barton Greenwell
Bennet Greenwell
Bennet Greenwell
Bernard Greenwell
Edmund Greenwell
Edward Greenwell
Edward B. Greenwell
Elias Greenwell
Henry Greenwell
Ignatius Greenwell
James Greenwell
James Greenwell
Jeremiah Greenwell
John Greenwell
John B. Greenwell
Joseph Greenwell
Joseph Greenwell
  of George
Joseph Greenwell
  of James
Joseph Greenwell
  of Phil
Joshua Greenwell
Joshua Greenwell
Noah Greenwell
Peter Greenwell
Philip Greenwell
Robert Greenwell
Stephen Greenwell
Thomas Greenwell
Wilfred Greenwell
William Greenwell
William Greenwell
William Greenwell
George Greggs
Randolph Grey
Ignatius Griffin
Philip Griffin
James Griggs, Pilot
Joseph Grindall
Josiah B. Grindall,
  Post Master
William Guither
Robert Hagar
Alexander Hall
Basil Hall
Philip Hall

-86-

Reuben Hall
Francis Hamersley
William Hamersley
Bartholomew Hamilton
John Hammit
John Cartwright Hammit
Richard Hammitt
Robert Hammitt
Samuel Hammitt
William Hammit
Zachariah Hammit
Charles Harden
Joseph Harden of Bapts.
Joseph Harden of Joe
Thomas Harden
John Hardisty
Joseph Hardisty
Thomas Hardisty
Reuben Hardy
Richard Harper
Benjamin Harris
James Harris
Robert Harris
Zachariah Harris
Benjamin Harrison
John Harrison
John Harrison
Joseph Harrison
Robert Harrison
William Harrison
Barton Hayden
George Hayden
Gerard Hayden
Ignatius Hayden
John Hayden of Francis
John Hayden of Jona
Joseph Hayden
Peregrine Hayden
Richard Hayden
Thomas Hayden
William Hayden
John H. Hayes
Joseph Hayes
Bennet Hazle
Jeremiah Hazle
Ignatius Heard
James Heard
James Heard
James B. Heard
John Heard
Raphael Heard

Richard Heard
William Heard
James Heathe
Caleb Hebb
George Hebb
William Hebb, Sr.
William Hebb
Peter Yong Hellen
Archibald Henderson
Gabriel Hendley
Israel Hendley
James Hendley
Robert Hendley
Francis Herbert
Joseph Herbert
Joseph Herbert
Philip Herbert
William Herbert, Jr.
John Higginson
James Higgs
Henry Hill
Richard Hill
William Hill
William Hill
William Hill
Thomas Hilton
William Hilton
Bennet Hopewell
Francis Hopewell
George Hopewell
James Hopewell
John Hopewell
Pollard Hopewell
Richard Hopewell
William Hopewell
John Hopkins
Michael Hopkins
William Houlton
William Houlton, Jr.
Bennet Howard
Francis Howard
Gabriel Howard
James Howard
John B. Howard
Jopseph Howard
Leonard Howard
Peregrine Howard
Ignatius Howe
John Howe
Joseph Howe
Richard Howe

Stanislaus Howe
Gladden Huntt
Bennett Hutchens
Samuel Hutchens
Robert Hutchins
Robert Inge
Elijah Jackson
Abner Jarboe
Bennett Jarboe
Bennet Jarboe
Ignatius Jarboe
John Jarboe
John Jarboe
John B. Jarboe
Joseph Jarboe
Joseph Jarboe
Robert Ford Jarboe
Vernon Jarboe
William Jay
Edmund Jenkins
George Jenkins
Joseph Jenkins
William Jenkins
David Johns
Charles Johnson
Elisha Johnson
George Johnson
Ignatius Johnson
James Johnson
James Johnson
John Johnson
John Johnson
Joseph Johnson
Joseph Johnson of Francis
Leonard Johnson
Matthew Johnson
Randolph Johnson
Thomas Johnson
Zachariah Johnson
James Jones
Matthias Jones, Jr.
Stephen Jones
Thomas Jones, Pilot
Vernon Jones
William Jones, Pilot
George Jordan
James Jordan
Jeremiah Jordan
John Jordan
Richard Jordan
Robert Jordan

William Jordan
Edward Joseph, Insane
Edward Joy
Enoch Joy
Ignatius Joy, Jr.
Philip Joy
Thomas Joy
Thomas Joy
William Joy
Benjamin Keech
James Keech
Richard Keech
Samuel Keech
Stephen Keech
Wilson Keech
James Keener
James Keirk
James Keirk, Pilot
George Kennick
Francis Kerby
Francis Kerby
Hopewell Kerby
John Kerby
William Kerby
Edmund Key
Philip Key
Alexander Kilgour
James Kilgour
William Kilgour
James Wilson
Cornelius King
Edmund King
James King
Joshua King
Stpehen King
Elias Knott
Francis Knott
Ignatius Knott
James Knott
James Knott
John Knott
Joseph Knott
William Knott
David Lake
Jonathan Lake
Jeremiah Lancaster
Larkin Lane
James Langley
Walter Langley
William Langley
William Lansdale

James B. Latimer
William Lawrence
William Laythorn
John Leach
Philemon Leach
Thomas Leach
William Leach
Lewis Lee
Richard Lee
William Lee
John Leech, Sr.
Caius Marius Coriolanus
    Leigh
Charles Leigh
Christopher Leigh
Joseph Leigh
Lewis Leigh, Pilot
Richard Leigh
Walter Leigh
George M. Leland
John M. Leland, Pilot
Coveton Lewis
Robert Lilburn
Stephen Lirty
William Lirty
Peter Little
Charles Llewellin
Jesse Locke
George Loker
William Loker
William Loker, Pilot
Charles Long
Peregrine Long
Thomas Long
Charles K. Love
James Low
Bennet Lowe
James Lowry
Barton Lynch, Pilot
James Lynch
John Lynch
Stephen Lynch
Thomas Lynch
Henry Lyon
Henry Lyon
William Lyon
Zachariah Lyon
John Mackall
Edward Maddox
John Maddox
Samuel Maddox

James Mairman
Richard Mairman
Cornelius Manning
Wilfred Manning
John Marman
George Martin
John Martin
Norman Martin
Samuel Martin
Thomas Martin
William Martin
John Mason
Nehemiah Mason
Austin Massey
Austin Mattingley
Charles Mattingley
Edward Mattingley
Gabriel Mattingley
George Mattingley
James Mattingley
James Mattingley
John Mattingley
John Mattingley
John Mattingley
John Mattingley
John Mattingley of Thos.
Joseph Mattingley
Joseph Mattingley
Luke Mattingley
Stephen Mattingley
Thomas Mattingley
William Mattingley
Zachariah Mattingley
John McCowley
Hannon McGee
Raphael McGee
William McGee
Benjamin McKay
Benjamin McKay
George McKay
John McKay
Stephen McKay
Soloman McKinney
Reuben McKinny
Arthur McLearn
William McLearn
Robert McLeland
Alexander McWilliams
George McWilliams
James McWilliams
John McWilliams

Kenelm Medcalf
John Medley
John Medley
William Medley
James Melton
Richard Melton
Thomas Melton
William Merryman
Edward Milburn
John Milburn
Joseph Milburn
Joseph Milburn
Richard Milburn, Jr.
Thomas Milburn
William Milburn, Sr.
William Milburn, Jr.
Henry Miles
Francis Millard
Andrers Mills
Charles Mills
Francis Mills
James A. Mills
John B. Mills
Joseph Mills
Nicholas Mills
William Mills
Benjamin Mitchell
Davis Mitchell
Barnaby Monarch
Edward Monarch
Francis Monarch
Moses Moody
Bennett Moore
Caleb Moore
George Moore
George Moore
Ignatius Moore
James Moore
Stephen Moore
William Moore
Hezekiah Moran
Jonathan Moran
Joseph Moran
Thomas Moran
Ignatius Morgan
James Morgan
Raphael Morgan
William Morgan
Samuel Morton
Peter Mugg
Edward Murphy

Samuel Murphy
Richard Murry
Benoni Neale
Charles Neale
Daniel Neale
Edward Neale
Edward Diggs Neale
Henry Neale
Henry Neale
James Neale
John Neale
Joseph Neale
Raphael Neale
Roswell Neale
William Neale
Joshua Nelson
Obediah Nelson
Thomas Nettle
Francis Nevitt
John Nevitt
Matthew Nevitt
Bennet Newgent
Clement Newton
Ignatius Newton
Basil Norris
Bennet Norris
Ignatius Norris
Ignatius Norris
James Norris
James Norris
John Norris
John Norris
John H. Norris
Joseph Norris
Joseph H. Norris
Matthew Norris
Matthew Norris of Mark
Matthew Norris of Wm.
Philip Norris
Thomas Norris
Thoms Norris
Vincent Norris
William Norris
William Norris
William Norris
Bennett Nottingham
Baptist Nowell
Jeremiah Nowell
James Owings
John Owings
John Ownings

Joseph Owings
Robert Owings
Jeremiah Pantry
Bernard Parsons
John Parsons
Joseph Parsons
Joseph Parsons
James Patterson
Basil Payne
James Payne
James Payne
John Payne
John Payne
Joseph Payne of Basil
Joseph Payne of Vincent
Ignatius Peacock
Stephen Peacock
Thyas Peacock
Zachariah Peacock
Ignatius Peake
James Peake
Joseph Peake
Joshua Peake
Raphael Peake
William Peake
Henry Pike
Richardson Pilkerton
Uriah Pilkerton
Lewis Pilkinton
George Plater
Edmund Plowden
James Poole
Jesse Power
John E. Power
Joseph Power
Philip Power
Thomas Power
Jeremiah Price
John Price
John Price, Pilot
John B. Price
Robert Price, Pilot
John Quiggins
Henry Railey
John B. Railey
Stephen Railey
John Reace
Thomas Reason
Benjamin Redman
John Redman
William Redman

Zachariah Redman
Samuel Reed
George Reeder
Henry Reeder
James Reeder
George Reese, Pilot
Bennet Reiley
Bennett Reiley
Ignatius Reiley
John Reiley
Michael Reiley
Bennett Reilley
George Reintzel
Valentine Reintzel
Ignatius Reynolds
John Reynolds
Bennet Rhodes
James Richardson
Joseph Richardson, Jr.
Joseph Richardson, Sr.
Willongby Richardson
Charles Ridgell
Jonathan Ridgell
John Riley
Zachariah Riley
Basil Riney
Zachariah Riney
Thomas Riswick
Charles Rock
John Rock
Joseph Rock
William Rock
George Rogers
Manning Rogers
Richard Rogers
William Rogers
John Ross
James Russell
John Russell
John Russell
Isaac Sanner, Pilot
Jeremiah Sanner
John Sanner
John Sanner
John Sanner
Jonathan Sanner
Joseph Sanner
Vincent Sanner
Bennett Saxton
Raphael Saxton
Zachariah Saxton

Edward Scott
John Scott
Thomas Scott
Nathaniel Seager
Thomas Seager
Francis Seale
Benjamin Segar
Charles Sewall (dumb)
Clement Sewall
Henry Sewall
Henry Sewall of Nicholas
Nicholas Sewall, Jr.
John Shadrick
Thomas Shadrick
Joseph Shamwell
Henry Shanks
John Shanks
Peter Shanks
William Shaw
Richard Shearley
Bennet Sheirly
Ignatius Sheirly
John Sheirly
Francis X. Sheircliffe
Caleb Shermentine
James Shermentine
John Shermentine
Enoch Silence
William Silence
Matthew W. Simmons
Anthony Simms, Jr.
John Simms
Josias Simpson
Aaron Smith
Anthony Smith
Bartly Smith
Biscoe Smith, Pilot
Edward Smith
Elvily Smith
James Smith
James Smith
Jeremiah Smith
Job Smith
John Smith
John Smith
John Smith
John Smith
  (Ship Carpenter)
Nelson Smith
Richard Smith
Samuel Smith

Hezekiah Smoot
McKay Smoot, Pilot
Thomas Smoot
Thomas Smoot
Thomas Smoot
William Somerville
John Sotherland
Samuel Sotheron
Zachariah Sotheron
Francis Sothoron
Francis Sothoron
Henry Sothoron
John Sothoron
John Sothoron
Augustin Spalding
Bennet Spalding, Pilot
Bernard Spalding
Edward Spalding
Francis Spalding
Henry Spalding
James Spalding
John Spalding
John B. Spalding
Joseph Spalding
Michael Spalding
Stephen Spalding
Thomas Spalding
William Spink
Patrick Starky
Charles Stone of Ed.
Charles Stone of Hatton
Enoch Stone
George Stone
James Stone
John Stone
Joseph Stone
Matthew Stone
Samuel Strong
Benjamin Suit
John Suit
John D. Suit
Stephen Suit
Thomas Suit
Frnacis Suttle
Joseph Sutton, Pilot
Edward B. Swann
Thomas Swann
Thomas Swann, Pilot
William Sweeney
William Sword
Barton Tabbs

George C. Tabbs
Thomas Tabbs
Raphael Taney
Thomas Taney
Elijah Tarleton
Ignatius Tarleton
James Tarleton
Richard Tarleton
Stephen Tarleton
Charles Tarlton
Frederick Tarlton
Joshua Tarlton
Peregrine Tarlton
Thomas Tarlton
Ignatius Tawney
Caleb Taylor
E. Taylor
Ignatius Taylor
James Taylor
Jenifer Taylor
John Taylor
John Taylor
John Taylor, Jr.
Merritt Taylor
Richard Taylor, Pilot
Barton Tear
Augustin Templeman, Pilot
Absalom Tennison
Jesse Tennison
Joshua Tennison
Justinian Tennison
Samuel Tennison
Thomas Tennison
Prior Theobalds
George Thomas
Joshua Thomas
Roger Thomas
Taylor Thomas
Thomas Thomas
William Thomas
William A. Thomas
Zachariah Thomas
Aaron Thompson
Arthur Thompson
Bennett Thompson
Charles Thompson
Elijah Thompson
George Thompson
George Thompson
Ignatius Thompson
James Thompson

James Thompson, Jr.
James Thompson, Pilot
Jesse Thompson
John Thompson
John Thompson of Thomas
John B. Thompson
John B. Thompson
Joseph Thompson
Joseph Thompson
Joseph Thompson
Joseph Thompson
Matthew Thompson
Peter Thompson
Philip Thompson
Raphael Thompson
Richard Thompson
Richard Thompson
Samuel Thompson
Wilfred Thompson
William Thompson
William Thompson
William Thompson
Benjamin Thorn
Vincent Thornton
Benjamin Tippett
Cartwright Tippett
Clement Tippett
Denny Tippett
Dyson Tippett
Henry Tippett
John Tippett
John Tippett of Henry
John Tippett of Wm.
Josiah Tippett
Nelson Tippett
Walker Tippett
Zachariah Tippett
John True
Henry Trusk
Henry Tubman
Alexander Turner
Edmund Turner
Samuel Turner
Jeremiah Underwood
Willian Vironur
Richard Wainright
Enoch Wakelin
Hanson Wakelin
Peregrine Wakelin
Thomas Wakelin
Bennett Walker

Daniel Walker
James Walker
James Walker
John Walker
Joseph Walker
Joseph Walker of James
Joseph Walker of Joseph
Richard Walker
William Walker
William Warren
Thomas Waters
Francis H. Wathen
Hanson Wathen
Henry H. Wathen
Hutson Wathen
John Wathen
Martin Wathen
Thomas Wathen
Henry Watson
John Watson
Joseph Watson
Barton Watts
George Watts
Henry Watts
Richard Watts
Richard Watts, Sr.
Thomas Watts
William Watts
Henry Waughop
Charles Wealch, Pilot
John Welch, Pilot
James West
Jeremiah West
Bennet Wheatley
Elijah Wheatley
Henry Wheatley
Ignatius Wheatley
John Wheatley
John Wheatley
Joseph Wheatley
Raphael Wheatley
Richard Wheatley
William Wheatley
William Wherit, Jr.
James Wherritt
John Wherritt
Robert Wherritt
Thomas Wherritt
William H. Wherritt
James White
Peter White

Tunsil White, Pilot
Vernon White, Pilot
Mark Wilkinson
Ninian Willet
Benjamin Williams
Charles Williams
James Williams
Jesse Williams
John Williams
Bennet Wimsatt
John Wimsatt
John B. Wimsatt
Joseph Wimsatt
Joseph Wimsatt of Baptist
Robert Wimsatt
Samuel Wimsatt
William Wimsatt

Elijah Wise
James Wise
Jeremiah Wise
John Wise
Miel Wise
Richard Wise
Richard Wise
Yonng Wise
George Wiseman
John Wiseman
James Witherington
Thomas Witherington
Gabriel Wood
James Wood
Jeremiah Wood
John Wood
Nathan Wood

Jonathan Woodburn
John Woodward
Joseph Woodward, Jr.
Richard Woodward
Thomas Woodward
John B. Wotton
Joseph Wotton
Richard Wotton
Thomas Wotton
Edward Yates
Ignatius Yates
James Yates
John Yates
Martin Yates
William Yates
William Zachariah, Pilot
Zachariah Zachariah, Pilot

ST. MARY'S CONGREGATION

BRYANTOWN, CHARLES COUNTY, MARYLAND

This list of members with personal worth noted for purposes of assessment is undated but was probably made prior to 1800 for in that year Raphael Hagan moved to Kentucky and Joseph Hagan of Wm. followed in 1803.

Richd. Edelin	Ł2493
Capt. Henry Boarman	1796-10
Jno. Francis Gardiner	609-10
Francis Bowling	505
Charles Boarman	920
Henry Gardiner	790
Charles Gardiner	704
Joseph Gardiner	567
William Gardiner	615
Thomas Boarman Sr.	319
Thomas Boarman Jr.	105
Joseph Boarman	389-10
Raphael Boarman	563
Jane Boarman Widow	470
James Edelin	275
Raphael Hagan	304-10
Joseph Hagan Wm.	415-10
Thomas Osburn Sr.	39
Ann Sanders	1038
William Langley	27
William Mongomery	374
Charles Montgomery	159
Joseph Johnson	180-10
Edward Simms	293
Walter Burch	827
Bennit Mudd	569
Joseph Carter	127
Raphael Jameson	708-10
Thomas Jameson	520-10
Samuel Jameson	568
Sarah Jameson Widow	401-10
Leonard Jameson	100
Henry Jameson	154
Barton Hagan	175
Anthony Levey	30
William Queen	708
Leonard Tench	62
Josias Bryan	20
James Bryan, Sr.	70-10
Basil Bryan	29
Bryan Widow of John	170
Ignatious Bryan	70-10
James Boarman	1135
(John?) Boarman	460
James Carrico Sr.	445

James Carrico Jr.	168
Henry Carrico	120
James Boone	180
John Bowling	182
William Bowling	66
Thomas Bowling	360
Bowling Widow of Jos.	332-10
James Hagan Sr.	97
John Johnson Sr.	402
(Treasia?) Jameson	124
James Johnson Sr.	542
Francis Wheatley Sr.	330
Nicholas Miles	136-10
James Withirington	101-10
Richd. Withirington	33
Barton Wathin	121
Joshua Demar	69
Benjamin Withirington	18
Charles Clemons	25
Alectious Mudd	81
Susanah Hoxton	1367-18-6
Jno. Francis Hardy	275
Stanislaus Hoxton	1090
Doct. Oswald Brook	1540

Not assessed

Richd. Burch
Henry Jameson Jr.
Wm. Jameson Sr.
Walter timson (Simpson?)
Mary Queen
Peggy Queen
(Terea?) Queen
Elizabeth Queen
Sarah Queen
Carrico Widow of Wm.
Igs. Coho
Henry Clemons Jr.
Jerry Neal
Henry (Preter?) Mullato
Thomas (Preter?)
Josias Butler
Jno. Butler
Abraham Carrico
Jno. Tench
Jane Tench
Edward Gates
John Johnson Jr.
(Lorney?) Johnson
Wm. Murry
Hugh Murry
Francis Wheatley Jr.
Duke Boarman
(M---?) Demar
Mary Gates Widow

THE ELECTION OF JANUARY 7, 1789

In this election the voters of St. Mary's County were offered two pairs of slates. The Federalists, those who had supported the adoption of the new Constitution, and the Antifederalists, those who had opposed them, each offered a slate of six for for the six members of the House of Representatives of the United States Congress to which Maryland was entitled. The Federalists offered a slate of eight for the eight Electors of the President to which Maryland was entitled, but the Antifederalists offered a slate of only seven apparently to allow their supporters to vote for George Plater, a prominent resident of St. Mary's County, who was one of the eight Federalist choices. The voters could choose any six names from the twelve candidates for Congress and any eight names from the fifteen candidates for the Electoral College. The following code represents the individual voting preferences:

    F = Federalist
    F1 = Federalist but with one or two from the opposing slate
    A = Antifederalist
    A1 = Antifederalist but with one or two from the opposing slate
          besides Plater
    O = Other, usually no clear preference

THE ELECTION OF OCTOBER 4-7, 1790

In this election for the Second Congress the voters of St. Mary's County were offered a slate of ten candidates, namely:

Philip Key	for the First District
Joshua Seney	for the Second District
William Pinkney	for the Third District
Samuel Sterrett	for the Fourth District
George Gale	for the Fifth District
Daniel Carroll	for the Sixth District
Michael Jenifer Stone	for the First District
James Tilghman	for the Second District
Benjamin Contee	for the Third District
William Vans Murray	for the Fifth District

The six Federalist choices were Sterrett, Gale, Carroll, Stone, Tilghman and Contee. The Antifederalist choices were Key, Seney, Pinkney, Sterrett, Carroll and Murray. There was strong support from both factions for Key, a popular resident of St. Mary's County. The following code represents the individual voting preferences:

    F = Federalist
    F1 = Federalist but for Key instead of Stone
    A = Antifederalist
    A1 = Antifederalist but for Gale instead of Murray
    K = A single vote for Key
    O = Other, usually no clear preference

LIST OF VOTERS

ST. MARY'S COUNTY, MARYLAND

1789

On January 7, 1789, Zachariah Forrest certified that Philip Ford, the sheriff,
and Enoch Millard, Henry Abell, and Augustan Spalding, the clerks, had taken the
oath prescribed by an act of the Maryland Assembly for conducting the first
Federal election (for president and Congress of the United States under the
recently adopted Consitution). On January 10, 1789, Philip Ford certified the
election returns.

Edm. Plowden	F	Phil B. Key	F	William Rapour	F
John Abell, Jr.	F	Edw. Smith	F	Robt. Ford	F
Nich. L. Sewall	F	Henry Trask	F1	Robt. Winsett	F
Henry Neale	F	Matt. Vowls	F	Benj. Abell	F
Justinian Wharton	F	Anth. Simms	F	James Williams	F
George Guyther	F	Zach. Abell	F	Bennett Combs	F
Joseph Ford	F	Ign. Joy, Sr.	F	Henry Abell	A
Henry Sewall, Jr.	F	Thomas Watts	F	William Thomas, Jr.	A1
Robert Chirley	F	Henry King, Jr.	F	John Bradburn, Jr.	F
Elias Smith	F	William Cartwright	F	Ignatius Wheelar	F
George Jenkins	F	Justinian Edwards	F	Wilfred Thompson	A1
Philip Medley	F	Charles Mills	A	Zach. Forrest	A1
Thomas A. Reeder	F	William Tarlton	F	George Plater, Jr.	F
Charles Chilton	F	Leonard Howard	F	Bennoni Neale	F
John A. Thomas	F	John Booth, Jr.	F	John Horrell	A1
William Kelgerer	F	Will Spink	F	Joshua Turner	A1
John B. Thompson	F	Francis Harbert	F	Nicholas Drury	A1
Robert Thompson	F	Richard Smith	F	Ralph Peak	A1
Step. Gough	F	Aug. Spalding	A1	Samuel Abell	F1
Vernon Hebb	F	Thomas Dillon	F	John Bond of John	F
Henry Tubman, Jr.	F	George Fenwick	F	Justinian Thompson	A1
Henry Sotheron	F	Nath. Ewing	O	Frances Abell	A
John Briscoe	F	William Hammett	F	Rubin Craigg	O
John G. Ford	F	James Hammett	F	Joseph Johnson	A1
George Howard	F	Joseph Hebb	F	Bennedict Spalding	F1
John Thompson	F	Benj. Bean	F	Henry J. Carroll	F
John B. Abell	A	John Thompson, Jr.	F	Francis Miller	A1
Edw. Abell	F	Bennett Raley	F	George Jordan	F
James Hopewell	F	Ignatius Hayden	F	Jona. Hayden	A1
George Plater	F	Patrick Kelley	F	Nehem. Masson	F
Coll. Barnes	F	Charles Lewellin	F	James Biscoe	F
George Biscoe	F	James Heard	A1	Bennett Cissell	F
Willm. Greenwell	F	Coll. Jordan	F	John Egerton	A1
Will Bayard	F	Henry Ford	F	John Maddox	A1
John DeButts	F	Joseph Stone, Sr.	F	John E. Greenwell	O
John H. Broome	F	Edmond Heard	F	John Graves	A1
Henry Horrell	F	Joseph Booth	F	Bernard Mills	F
James Gough	F	Ignatius Heard	F	Aug. Medley	F

James Yates   F1
James Morgan   O
Ignat. Morgan   O
Zeph. Forrest   F1
Nich. D. Green   A1
Ignatius Greenwell   F1
James Diveria   A1
Barton Greenwell   F1
Bernard Medley   F1
Leon. Booth   F
Seneca Nelson   A1
William Thomas, Jr. A1
Francis Johnson   F

LIST OF VOTERS

ST. MARY'S COUNTY, MARYLAND

1790

On Monday, October 4, 1790 at Leonardtown, Will. Kilgour and Robert Ware Peacock certified the election returns for candidates to serve from Maryland in the House of Representatives of the Congress of the United States. Philip Ford was the sheriff and Enoch Millard and Henry Abell served as clerks. Reprinted by permission of the Hall of Records, Annapolis, Maryland.

Benj. Edwards	A1	William Manning	F	James Williams	F
J̶o̶h̶n̶/̶W̶a̶t̶s̶o̶n̶*		Mark Brewer	A1	Ben. Combs	F
John N. Dick	A1	Micheal Spalding	A	Edward Gatten	F
Jasper Kennick	A1	Absolum Dickson	A1	Johh McLarran	F
James Kilgour	F	Thomas Dickson	A	Joseph Walker	F
Edward B. Goddard	A1	John Moore	A	George Lock	F
Leond. Johnstone	A1	Leond. Seale	A	Henry H. Wathen	F
Wilfred Thompson	A1	Thomas Reeder of John	F1	John B. Wimsatt	k
John Hardesty	A1	Wm. Woodward	F1	Jeremiah Hazle	
Dent Suit	A1	John B. Thompson	F1	Jeremiah Graves	
Wm. Thompson, Jr.	A	Joseph Greenwell	A	Joseph Hammett	F
John Cartwright of George	A1	Hon. George Plater	F	John Spalding of P.	
John Dent Suit	A1	Charles Chilton	F1	George Biscoe, Esq.	
Benjamin Buckler	A1	John Ross	A	James Neale of Jas.	F
John Basil Jarbeo	A	John Cole St. Georges	F	Edward Smith	F
Benj. Clarke	A	John Abell, Esq.	F	John Baily	
Joseph Waters	A1	Wilfred Neale	F	John B. Browne	
Nehemia Leach	A1	John Smith	F	John Adams	
Cornelius King	A	Thomas A. Reeder	A	Wm. Martin, Sr.	
Zach. Hammett	A	Luke W. Barber	F	Rob. Young	
Edmund Plowden	F	Joseph Dunbar	F	John Corum	
Aron Spalding	K	John Lyon	A1	Rapheal Morgan	
Thomas Edwards	K	Luke Branson	A1	James Hath	
George Dent	K	Benj. McCoy	K	John B. Abell	
Richd. Lyons sadler	A1	Wm. Guither	A	Philip Read	
James Melton	K	MacCoy Biscoe	F	Anthony Baxter	
Philip Spalding	K	Thomas Cissell	A	Bryan Higgins	
Josiah Tippett	A	John Cissell of Thomas	A	David Johnstone	
Jonathan Tippett	A1	John Gibbings	O	John Harris	
Ignas. Hill	K	Francis Spalding	A	Mordicai Jones	
Abraham Davis	A	John B. Goddard	A1	Nathan Harrison	
Joseph Howard, Sr.	A1	John Carpenter	A	Robert Harris	
John Mills, Sr.	A1	James Hayden	A1	Gabriel Howard	
John Tippett	A1	Wm. Somerville, Esq.	F	Henry Sewall P	
Joseph Thompson of Wm.	A1	Ignas. Mattingly	A	Charles King	
Charles Johnstone	A1	Joseph Daffin	F	Joseph Walker, Jr.	
George Kennick	A1	Reuben Craigg	F1	Henry Hill 3d	
Charles Bridgett	A1	Bennoni Neale	F	Nicholas Sewall, Jr.	
Henry Spalding of Peter	A1	Tennison Cheshire	K	Saml. Martin	

*name crossed out in original

Ben. Cusick	A	John Harper	F	John Horrell	F
Thomas Tippett	A	Joseph Smith	A1	Wm. Waters	K
Stephen Tarlton	F	James Seagar	K	Henry Medley	K
Jesse Wharton	F	Ben. Hopewell	K	Thomas Watts	F
Philip Medley	F	Robt. Wimsatt	F1	Wm. Hill	A
Elias Smith	F	Clem. Briscoe	F	Enoch Campbell	O
Ignas. Knott	A	Joseph Turner	F	Jonathan Thorpe	K
Stephen Biscoe	F	Sam. Maddox, Sr.	o	Kenlm B. Watts	K
Clemt. Jarbeo	F	Joseph Riswick	F	John Tarlton, Sr.	K
James Cusick	K	John Abell, Sr.	F	James Gunn	A1
Wm. Smoot	F	Henry Banlay	F	Wm. Wherett	K
James Martin	A	Wm. Morgan	A	Edward Spalding	A
John Lake	A1	James Mattingly	O	Wm. Payne	F
John Ford below	A	Jessy Cartwright	K	Benj. Suit	A1
Josiah Tippett	A	James Gough	F	Thomas Suit	A
Jos. Knott	A	Jessy Alvey	F1	Richd. Sothoron of Sam.	A1
John Hendley	F	Joseph Millard	F	Philip Herbert	A
Adam Wise	A	John Buckler	K	George Guither	F1
Mathias Jones	F1	Wm. Russell	F	Ignatius Joy, Sr.	F
Benj. Buckler	A	Matthew Norriss	F	John B. Buckman	A
George Williams	F	Zacha. Abell	K	John Mattingly	K
Dennis Tippett	A	Rhode Hackett	F	John Thompson joiner	F
Jas. Wise	F	Francis Buckman	F1	James Mills	F1
Henry Spalding, Sr.	F	John Coade, Sr.	F	Seneca Nelson	A1
Calebb Hebb	F	Richd. Smith	F	Mathew Heard	F
Ignas. Edwards	K	Ben. A. Price	F1	Ignas. Raily	F1
Henry Brady	K	Littleton Biscoe	O	John Dunbar	K
Richd. Pool	F	John M. Goldsmith	F	John Bond of Thoms.	O
John Bowlds	K	John Mugg	F	John Mackall, Sr.	O
Francis Knott	A	Thomas Ryney	O	Zach Newton	K
Ben. Price	A1	John Heard of Mk.	F	James Brookebank	K
John Biscoe	F	Jeremiah Nugent	K	John Graves, Jr.	A
Joshua Redman	F1	Peter Jarbeo	F	Bent. Hutchings	K
Micheal Branson	A	Col. Jere. Jordan	F	Enoch Drewry	K
John Smith B side	A1	Ignas. Morgan	K	Stouten Edwards	K
George Buckler	K	Henry Horrell	F	Joshua Tarlton	F
Richd. Hammett	A1	Ben. Fenwick of R.	F	Zacha. Kirby	K
Richd. Millon	A	Jessy Floyd	A	Thomas Clayton	F1
John Hammett, Jr.	A1	Wm. Knott	A	Richd. Watts	K
John Monarch	A1	Amos Chunn	A	John Lynch	K
Henry Hazle	A1	Nehemiah Mason	F	John Tippett, Sr.	A1
Henry Clarke	A	John Brewer	A1	John Cullison	A
James Smoot	F	Roger Clarke	K	Abram Adams	A
Heza. Smoot	F	James Dunbar	A1	Edward Stone	F
Abram Rhodes	F	Wm. Norris	F	Charles Buckman	A
Josha. Poole	F1	John B. Farr	A1	Rapheal McGee	F
Wm. Thompson, Sr.	A1	John Budd	F	Mckelvie Hammett, Jr.	A
Henry Wingate	A1	Bent. Norris	F	Wm. Walker	F
Edward Monarch	A	Rapheal Peake	F	Benj. Nugent	K
Edward Garner	A	John A. Thomas, Esq.	F	Joseph Sanner	A
Ignas. Drewry	F	James Patterson	A	John Stanfield Abell	F
John McClannon	F1	Wm. Kilgour	F	Robt. Thomas	F

George Pembroke	A	John Williams	K	James Alvey	F
Charles Sewall	F	John McCayley	F	Joseph Doneson	F
Charles Bradburne	F	John Hutchins	F	Jessy Hebb	C
Peter Thompson	F	George Hayden	F	Jeremiah Pantry	K
Joshua Millard	F	Daniel Woodburne	K	Rapheal Payne	F
Francis Mills	F1	John Greenwell of Chs.	A	Richd. Jordan	
Johh Bayley	A	Philip Bryan	A1	James Hammett	F
Benja. B. Cheshire	K	Thomas Riswick	F	Wm. Spink	
Bennett Tarlton	A	Benedict Spalding	F	Joseph Thompson	
Walter Davis	F	Joseph Brown	A	Cuthbert Fenwick	
Bent. Nottinghame	F	James A. Mills	A	Wm. Wheatley	
Ben. Norriss	F	Joshua Gibson	F	Wm. Mattingly	
John B. Mattingly	F	James Tarlton	A	Ignas. Shurley	
Hooper Broome	F	Bennett Thompson	F1	Bennett Hazle	
Richard Lewellin	F	Philip Drewry	F	Bennett Cissell	
Henry Taylor	A1	John B. Drewry	F	Joseph Booth	
Wm. Bradburne	F	Raph. Ford	F	James Morgan	
Hon. Richard Barnes	F	James Norris	F	Roswald Gibson	
George Cole St. Georges	F	Henry Spalding of Wm.	F	John Norriss of Thomas	
Isaac Cole	F	Bennett Brown	K	Robert Bean	
James Brewer	A	Thomas Martin	F	Henry Gardiner	F
John Rock	F	Delbert Newton	F	Thomas Weakler	F
Rich. Pierceall	F1	Edmund Heard	F	John Fenwick	F
Joseph Woodward	A	Barton Davis	A	Jeremiah Alvey	A
Ignas. Joy, Jr.	F	Ignas. Heard, Sr.	F	John French	F
Wm. Holton, Jr.	F	Henry Ford	F	Bennett Abell	F
Francis Millard	F1	John Wheatley	F	Bassill Booth	F
Richd. Booth	F	Norman Burroughs	F	Joseph Ford, Jr.	F1
Thomas Power	F1	Barton Smith		Martin Henry	F
Thomas Spalding, Jr.	F	Anthony Davis	F	Francis Cissell	F
Henry Pike	F	Barnaby Monarch	F	Robert Wimsatt, Jr.	F
Wm. Medley	F	Josuha Mermon	F	Thomas Joy, Sr.	F
Joseph Fenwick of Robt.	F	Joseph Ford, Sr.	F	Mathew Norriss	F
Martin Yates	A	Joseph Stone, Sr.	F	Elijah Clarke	F
Ben. Spalding	F	James Yates	F	Wm. Drewry	F
Thomas Wathen	A	Stephen Gough	F	Philip Ford, Jr.	F
James Thompson, Jr.	A1	Thomas Robinson	F	John Norriss of Mark	F
George Booth, Jr.	F	James Mermon	F	Henry Abell	F
Basil Alvey	F1	John R. Plater, Esq.	F	Nicholas Mills	F
Wm. Greenwell	F	Martin French	F	Richard Edelen	F
John Tippett of Jos.	A	Jessy Mills	F	Ignatius Newton	F
George Watts	F1	Wm. Heard, Jr.	F	Ignatius Thompson	F
Strutton Edwards	A	Joseph Howard	F	John E. Greenwell	A
John Bean	F	John Cooke	A	Thomas Greenwell	F
Thomas Tarlton, Sr.	F	Henry Booth	F	Peregrine Bond	F
Archd. Greenwell	F	Peregrine Davis	F	Richd. Bond, Esq.	F1
Arthur Thompson	F1	John B. Wollingham	F1	John Hanson Briscoe	F1
Charles Neale	F	James Callis	F1	John Booth, Jr.	F1
Charles Lewellen	F	Richd. Lee	F	Henry J. Carroll, Esq.	F
Jonathan Hayden	F1	George Martin	K	Thomas Bond, Esq.	K
Rapheal Neale	F	Nathaniel Ewing	O	George Plater, Jr., Esq.	O
Joseph Mattingly	F	John Cartwright Ascum	F	John Downes	F
John Heard	F	Wm. Clarke	F		F

4 Aug 1806, a group of Missouri Catholics residing at The Barrens setttlement in
what is now Perry County wrote to Father Badin in Kentucky asking him to procure
the services of a priest and promising to furnish 200 acres for the pastor.
Most of the signers were born in Maryland. The letter is in the handwriting of
Isidore Moore (1771-1842). In some cases, this letter has the only known
signatures of some individuals.

Joseph Tucker   Michael Burns
Isidore Moore   ----- Coyteux
James Moore, Sr.   Vincent Grenier
Nicholas Tucker   James Burns
Clement Knott   Barnabas Burns
John Layton   James McMillan
Joseph Manning   Bernard Brown
Aquilla Hagan   Bede Moore
Ignatius Layton   James Moore, son of Nicholas
John Layton, Jr.   James Moore, son of James
James Tucker   Clement Hagan
Bernard Layton   William Tucker
Joseph Miles   William Dunn
John Manning   Michael Hagan
William M. Reed   Joseph Hagan
James Manning   Bernard Smith
Henry Riley   Nicholas Moore
Joseph Fenwick   Bernard Cissell
James Hutchins   Peter Tucker
Mark Manning   Simon Duvall
George A. Hamilton   Timothy Celle
Thomas Tucker   Thomas Riney
Walter Fenwick

Reference:

10 D 5,
Archives of the Archdiocese of Baltimore

PARISH CENSUS

ST. MARY OF THE BARRENS

PERRY COUNTY, MISSOURI

1823

This census is included as an illustration of the high percentage of individuals who were either born in Maryland or whose parents were born in Maryland. The surnames of those listed will be familiar to researchers who are interested in the other documents in this volume. A number of the persons listed below will be found in those documents.

The location which is now known as Perry County, Missouri has borne several names. It was originally owned by the French who ceded it to Spain after the French and Indian War. Napoleon later forced Spain to return it to France and sold it to the United States as the Louisiana Purchase. The site was later known as Upper Louisiana, the Sainte Genevieve District and Sainte Genevieve County. After the admission of Missouri to the Union, a portion of Sainte Genevieve County was named Perry County.

William Bell
James Brewer
Charles Brewer
John Brewer
Anthony Brown
Bernard Brown
Joseph Brown

Bernard Cissell
Clement Cissell
John Cissell
Joseph Cissell
Lewis Cissell

Stephen Dolson
Joseph Duffner
William Dunn
John M. Duvall
Simon Duvall

Guy Elder

Stephen Fisher
Joseph French

John Grass

Aquila Hagan
John C. Hagan
Levi Hagan
Michael Hagan
Wilfred Hagan
Frederick C. Hase
Richard Hayden
Sarah Hayden
Thomas Hayden
Christopher Hines
Peter Holster, Jr.
Peter Holster, Sr.
James Hutchings

Joseph James, Jr.
Joseph James, Sr.
Victor Javaux

Clement Knott

Bernard Layton
Hillery Layton
Ignatious Layton
John Layton
John B. Layton
Walter Layton
Wilfred Layton
Zachariah Layton

Elexius Manning
James Manning
Joseph Manning
Joseph Manning, Jr.
Mark Manning
Robert S. Manning
James Mattingly
William Mattingly
John May
Daniel McAtee
Henry McAtee
William McLain
James Michael
Francis Miles
Henry Miles
Nicholas Miles
Bede Moore
Isidore Moore
James C. Moore
James N. Moore
John Moore
Lewis Moore
Martin I. Moore
Nicholas Moore
John B. Moranville

Jeffrey Powers

Benjamin Reed
James Reed
Cornelius Rhodes
Benedict Riley
Henry Riley
Thomas Edward Riney

Cornelius M. Slattery
Bernard Smith
Francis Smith
Richard Spalding
Charles Stewart

Thomas Thompson
Benedict Tucker
Charles Tucker
Francis Tucker
James Tucker
James T. Tucker
John T. Tucker
John T. Tucker
~~Joseph Tucker, Sr.~~
Joseph T. Tucker
Nicholas Tucker
Peter Tucker, Sr.
Thomas Tucker

Delijus Vessells

Michael Warren
James Wimsatt
Joseph Z. Wimsatt
Robert Wimsatt

Ignatious Yates

The middle initial of the first John T. Tucker was crossed out and he is most likely identical with John P. Tucker, son of Peter Tucker, Sr. Joseph Tucker, Sr., whose name is also crossed out, died in 1816.

The following names are of those partly unpaid in their 1822-23 assessment. A few are names not in the previous list. Any names crossed out are as per the original document.

James Brewer
Joseph Brown

John Cissell

Joseph Duffner
William Dunn
John M. Duvall

Guy Elder

Ansel[m] Ferrel

Aquila Hagan
Benedict Hagan
John C. Hagan
Levi Hagan
Michael Hagan
Fredk. C. Hase
Thomas Hayden
Peter Holster, Jr.
Peter Holster, Sr.
Richard Howard
James Hutchins

Joseph James, Jr.
Joseph James, Sr.

C̶l̶e̶m̶e̶n̶t̶/̶K̶n̶o̶t̶t̶

John Layton
John Baptist Layton

Ezekiel Manning
Mark Manning
J̶o̶s̶e̶p̶h̶/̶M̶a̶n̶n̶i̶n̶g̶,̶/̶S̶r̶.̶
Robert S. Manning
Wm. Mattingly
John May
W̶m̶/̶M̶c̶K̶a̶i̶n̶
Edward F. Miles
Nicholas Miles
James N. Moore
Martin I. Moore

James Reed
Cornelius Rhodes
Henry J. Rhodes
Henry Riley

Barnard Smith
Francis Smith

Thomas Tompson
Benedict Tucker
Charles Tucker
Francis Tucker
James Tucker
James T. Tucker
John P. Tucker
Joseph T. Tucker
Peter Tucker

M̶i̶c̶h̶a̶e̶l̶/̶W̶a̶r̶r̶e̶n̶
Joseph Webb
Joseph Z. Wimsatt

Ignatious Yates

INDEX

Baily, (?) 21
  Ann (Mrs.) 21
  John 98
  Mark 39
  Mary 39
  Thomas 36, 39
  Tom 37
  Winifred 37
Bainey, James 42
Baker, William 83
Baley, Edmund 21
  Elizabeth (Mrs.) 21
  John 21
Banfield, Samuel 72
Banlay, Henry 99
Baptist, John 6
Barber, Archibald D. 72
  Bennet White 83
  Cornelius 72
  Dorothy 41
  Edward 83
  Elias 83
  Hezekiah 83
  Jonathan 83
  Luke (Jr.) 83
  Luke W. 98
  Luke White 83
  Philip 83
  Robert 83
  Thomas 83
Barks, Mary 11
  Susan (Mrs.) 11
  Zachariah 11
Barnes, Coll. 96
  James 83
  Richard 71, 100
  Zachariah 33
Barnhouse, George 83
  Richard 72
  Rodolph 72
  Rudolph 83
Barns, Zachariah 72
Barton, John 12, 66
Bassey, Edmund 72
Baxter, Anthony 98
  Edward 83
  John 83
  Joseph 72
Bayard, Will 96
  William 72
Bayley, Johh 100
Bean, Alexander 83
  Ann 21
  Ann (Mrs.) 21

Bean (cont.)
  Barton 54
  Benj. 96
  Bennett 54
  George 54
  John 21, 100
  Margaret (Mrs.) 54
  Richard 83
  Robert 54, 83, 100
Beane, Alexander 83
  John 83
  Robert 83
  Thomas 83
  William 83
Bell, William 102
Bellwood, Ann 26
  Edward 24, 27
  Elizabeth (Mrs.) 29
  Henry 26, 29
  Wm. 10
Belwood, Ann 24, 27
  Elizabeth (Mrs.) 25, 27
  Henry 10, 24, 25, 27,
    83
  Mary 25
  Rebecca 27, 28
  Samuel 4, 6
Benfield, Dorothy (Mrs.)
    7
  Mary Ann 7
  Sam 7
Bennet, (?) (Mrs.) 39
  Hanson 83
  John 83
  Joseph 24, 83
  Joseph (Jr.) 83
  Mary 2
  Nathan 83
  Richard 83
  Thomas 83
  Wm. 83
Bennett, Gerard 83
Berden, Monica 39
Berder, John 39
Bernard, John 83
Betts, John 83
Betty, Edward 39
Billingsley, Allen 83
  Thomas 83
Birchmore, Ann 35
  Margaret (Mrs.) 54
  Rebecca 54
  William 54
Biscoe, Ann Clarke 54

Biscoe (cont.)
  Basil 83
  Benedict 28
  Bennet 83
  Bennett 28, 71
  Eleanor (Mrs.) 54
  Geo. 83
  George 96, 98
  James 83, 96
  James Lewis 54
  Joe 83
  Joseph 83
  Littleton 99
  MacCoy 98
  Mary (Mrs.) 28
  McKay 83
  Richard 54, 83
  Stephen 84, 99
  Thomas 84
  Thos. 83
Blackman, Thomas 44
Blair, James 84
  Joseph 84
  Peter 84
  William 84
Blake, (?) 19
  Ann 19
Blakistone, John 84
  Nehemiah H. 84
Blundell, John 72
Boarman, (John?) 93
  Ann 3, 4, 13
  Ann (Mrs.) 3, 8, 13
  Anne 41
  B. 42
  Batris (Mrs.) 55
  Benedict 42
  Catherine 8, 42
  Catherine (Mrs.) 3
  Charles 93
  Dorothy 7
  Duke 94
  Edward 42
  Frances 3
  Francis 4, 55
  Francis Ignatius 55
  Henrietta 3
  Henry (Cpt.) 93
  James 93
  Jane 41
  Jane (Widow) 93
  Jean 42
  Jean (Jr.) 42
  John 55, 72, 93

Boarman (cont.)
  Joseph 93
  Leonard Benedict 42
  Nicholas 42
  Raphael 93
  Richard 1, 3, 8, 13, 72
  Sarah 55
  Silvester 72
  Thomas (Jr.) 42, 93
  Thomas (Sr.) 93
  Thomas James (Jr.) 42
  Thomas James (Sr.) 42
Bohannon, George (Jr.) 84
  Jonathan 84
  Moses 84
Bolds, John 72
Bond, Jeremiah 72
  John 72, 84, 96, 99
  John (Jr.) 72
  Peregrine 84, 100
  Richard 84
  Richd. 100
  Sam 49
  Samuel 49
  Thomas 72, 84, 100
  Thoms. 99
  William 72
  Zachary 49
Booker, Joseph 72
Boone, James 94
Booth, (?) 3
  Ann 6, 55
  Basil 24, 25, 26, 27,
    28, 29, 36, 72
  Bassill 100
  Eleanor 55
  Elizabeth 26, 29, 55
  Elizabeth (Mrs.) 26,
    28, 29
  George 9, 55, 72
  George (Jr.) 100
  Henry 100
  Ignatius 55
  James 72
  Jane 55
  John 6, 10, 41, 55, 72
  John (Jr.) 96, 100
  John (Sr.) 72
  John Baptist 55
  Joseph 72, 96, 100
  Justinian 55
  Leon. 97
  Leonard 20, 55, 72
  Mary 55

Booth (cont.)
  Mary (Mrs.) 3, 6, 10,
    55
  Matthew 10
  Rebecca 55
  Richard 72, 84
  Richd. 100
  Rodolph 55
  Sarah 55
  Thomas 3, 55
Boothe, Basil 84
  George 84
  Henry 84
  Jesse 84
  John 84
  Leonard 84
  Matthew 84
  Rodolph 84
  William 84
Bothick, John 72
Bould, Catharine 55
  Elizabeth 55
  Henrietta 55
  Jane 55
  John 55
  John Baptist 55
  Mary 55
  Mary (Mrs.) 55
  Mary Ann 55
  Monica (Mrs.) 55
  Susanna 55
  William 55
Boulds, William 72
Boult, Thomas 72, 84
  William 84
Bourn, Mark 72
Bowes, Dorothy 8
  Eleanor 55
  Elizabeth 24
  Joseph 55
  Mary 20
  Mary (Mrs.) 8, 12, 55
  Samuel 12, 84
  Timothy 8, 12, 55
Bowlds, John 99
Bowlen, Mary Ann 5
Bowles, George 47
  Ignatius 36, 72
  Mary 34
Bowling, (?) (Widow) 94
  Charles 84
  Francis 93
  John 94
  Jos. 94

Bowling (cont.)
  Mary A-- 10
  Mary Ann 16
  Thomas 94
  William 72, 94
Bowls, (?) 20
  Catherine (Mrs.) 20
  Elizabeth 16
  Francis 84
  Ignatius 16
  John 12, 35, 84
  John (Jr.) 8
  Mary (Mrs.) 16
  William 16, 19, 20
Boyd, James 72
Bradburn, Anastasia 55
  Ann (Mrs.) 2, 55
  Benjamin 2, 16, 55
  Catharine 55
  Charles 84
  Eleanor (Mrs.) 55
  Elizabeth 16, 55
  Francis 84
  James 55, 72
  John 72, 84
  John (Jr.) 72, 96
  John Baptist 55
  Mark 55
  Mary 55
  Mary (Mrs.) 55
  Mary Ann 55
  Mary Ann (Mrs.) 16
  Matthew 2, 55, 84
  Notley 55
  Sarah 55
  Susanna (Mrs.) 55
  William 14, 36, 72, 84
Bradburne, Charles 100
  Wm. 100
Brady, Henry 99
Bramhill, Jonathan 84
  Reuben 84
Branson, Baptist 84
  Luke 98
  Michael 99
  Susan 6
  Thomas 72
Breding, Arminta 39
Breeden, Enoch 72
  Sarah 50
  Thomas 84
Brent, (?) 42
  Robert 42
Brewer, Ann 14, 35, 37,

Brown (cont.)
14, 15, 20, 35, 56,
73
Peter (Jr.) 8, 15, 73
Peter (Sr.) 18
Raphael 56
Rebecca 2, 56
Richard 56
Rose 18
Sarah 18
Statia (Mrs.) 2
Susan (Mrs.) 2, 14, 15
Susanna 55
Wilfrid 18
William (Jr.) 73
Winifred 9, 56
Browne, Allusia 56
Ann (Mrs.) 56
Chloe 56
Dryden 56
John B. 98
Leander 56
Leonard 56
Lucy 56
Martin 56
Peter 56
Susanna (Mrs.) 56
Bruce, John 84
William 84
Brumbaugh, (?) 51
Bryan, (?) (Widow) 93
Basil 93
Charles 84
Elenor 46
Hellen 41
Henry 1, 41, 46
Ignatious 93
Ignatius 46, 51, 73
James (Sr.) 93
John 93
Josias 93
Monica 41
Philip 73, 84, 100
William 46, 73
Buchman, John 1
Buchmore, William 1
Buckler, Benj. 99
Benjamin 98
Bennet 84
Cornelius 84
George 99
John 99
Robert 73
Buckman, Charles 73, 99

Buckman (cont.)
Francis 99
Ignatius 73
John B. 99
Joseph 84
Bucknam, Charles 84
Clement 84
Francis 84
Budd, John 99
Joseph 73
Bullock, Ann 21, 26
El-- 26
Elizabeth 21
George 73
George (Jr.) 84
Richard 84
Susan 26, 27
Thomas 84
William 84
Burch, Richd. 94
Walter 93
Burn, Jeremiah 84
John 42
Walter 41
Zephaniah 84
Burns, Barnabas 101
James 101
Michael 39, 101
Burroughs, Benjamin 73
Benjamin (Jr.) 73
George 73, 84
Gideon 84
Hanson 84
Henry 84
Hezekiah 73, 84
James 73, 84
John (Jr.) 73
John (Sr.) 73
Joseph 73, 84
Leonard 84
Matthew 73
Norman 84, 100
Richard 73
Samuel 84
Samuel (Jr.) 73
William 73, 84
Williamson 73, 84
Butler, Jno. 94
Josias 94
Byrn, Enoch 4
Mary (Mrs.) 4
Nicholas 4, 73
Byrne, Elizabeth 21, 22
Ignatius 23

Byrne (cont.)
Michael 23, 73
Nicholas 23
Priscilla (Mrs.) 23
Rebecca 24
Cadden, Thomas 84
Caen, Mary 41
Cahill, Nathaniel 84
Cain, Thomas 73
Callis, James 100
James A. 84
Campbell, (?) 18
Ann 23
Ann (Mrs.) 15, 17, 18,
22
Archibald 73
Barnaby 84
Bernard 15
Edward 11, 12, 15, 16,
17, 18, 73
Eleanor 2, 4, 6, 9, 45
Eleanor (Mrs.) 7, 11
Elizabeth (Mrs.) 11,
15, 23
Enoch 11, 15, 22, 23,
34, 73, 99
Ignatius 7, 10, 15, 18
Jane 15
Jane (Mrs.) 11, 12
Jinny 7
John 45, 84
Jonathan 11
Mary 10
Mildred (Mrs.) 10, 15,
18
Canning, Andrew 16
Mary 16
Winifred (Mrs.) 16
Carberry, John 84
Joseph 73
Peter 1
Carbery, John 23
Joseph 16, 18
Martha 19
Patrick 73
Peter 73
Sarah (Mrs.) 23
Thomas 19, 23
Carburey, John (Jr.) 1
Card, Justinian 73
William 73
Caregin, Thomas 84
Carpenter, Barbara 22
Eleanor 24, 26, 29

110

Carpenter (cont.)
Elizabeth 22, 24, 37, 39
Ellen 37, 39
George 20, 73
George (Jr.) 84
John 73, 98
John (Sr.) 73
Lydia (Mrs.) 20
Marian 39
Priscilla 39
Turner 84
William 20, 37, 39, 73, 84
Carr, Ambrose 18, 73
Eleanor (Mrs.) 18
Francis Xavier 18
Carrico, Abraham 94
Henry 94
James (Jr.) 94
James (Sr.) 93
Carroll, Charles John 84
Daniel 95
Henry J. 96, 100
Ignatius 14
Ignatius (Widower) 34
Winifred (Mrs.) 14
Carter, Eliz. (Mrs.) 24
Elizabeth 24
Henry 24
James 73
John 84
Joseph 93
Cartwright, George 98
Jessy 99
John 73, 98
John Dyson 84
William 84, 96
Cawley, Ellen 39
Cawood, Aquila 84
Stephen (Jr.) 84
Cecell, Sarah 46
Cecil, (?) 16, 18, 26
(?) (Mrs.) 26
Anastasia 16, 34
Ann 23, 37, 39
Baptist 16
Benedict 26
Bernard 6
Dorothy 28, 36
Eleanor 12, 16
Eleanor (Mrs.) 18
Elizabeth 28, 37, 39
Francis 28

Cecil (cont.)
Ignatius 6, 12, 14, 16
Jane 16, 18, 25
John 8, 16, 18, 21, 23, 24, 25
John Baptist 18
Mary 6, 18
Mary (Mrs.) 6, 16, 18
Mildred (Mrs.) 12
Rachel 6, 18, 19
Statia 4
Susan 16, 18, 21
Susan (Mrs.) 8, 21, 23, 24, 25, 28
Thomas 50
Zachariah 8
Celle, Timothy 101
Cesell, Ann 46
Thomas 46
Cessell, John 46
Chamberlain, Eleanor 45
Ignatius 7, 18, 73
Mary 45
Chappelear, Benjamin 84
John 84
Cheseldine, Calestiness 84
Cyrenius 84
Gerard 73
Kenelm 73, 84
Senica 84
William 73, 84
Cheshire, Benja. B. 100
Tennison 98
Chesley, John 73
Chezeldine, Senica 73
Chilton, Charles 84, 96, 98
George 73
William 84
Chirley, Robert 96
Chittim, James 73
Chiverall, Justinian 84
Chiverill, Jessey 73
Chrisman, Elizabeth (Mrs.) 56
John 56
Luke 56
Chrysostom, (?) (Mrs.) 24
John 24, 27, 28, 29
Chunn, Amos 99
Susanna 70
Cicel, John 13
Lydya 13

Cicel (cont.)
Susan (Mrs.) 13
Cicil, Susanna 3
Cissel, Austin 84
Cuthbert 84
Ethelbert 84
Francis 84
Jeremiah 84
John 84
Joseph 84
William 84
Zachariah 84
Cissell, Anastasia 56
Ann 57
Ann (Mrs.) 57
Augustine 27
Barton 73
Bennet 73
Bennett 96, 100
Bernard 56, 73, 101, 102
Catherine (Mrs.) 57
Clement 102
Delbert 56
Dorothy 27, 29, 56
Dorothy (Mrs.) 29
Edmund Barton 56
Eleanor 56
Eleanor (Mrs.) 29
Elizabeth (Mrs.) 56
Francis 100
Henrietta (Mrs.) 56
Ignatius 56
James 56
James Rodolph 56
Jeremiah 29, 57
John 27, 56, 98, 102, 104
John Baptist 57, 73
Joseph 29, 56, 102
Lewis 102
Margaret (Mrs.) 56
Mary 56, 57
Mary (Mrs.) 56
Matthew 57
Peter 56
Raphael 73
Rebecca (Mrs.) 57
Shedrick 56
Susan (Mrs.) 27
Susanna 56
Thomas 57, 98
Wilford 56
William 57

112

113

Daft (cont.)
Elizabeth (Mrs.) 57
Ignatius 74
John 36, 74, 85
John Baptist 57
Mary 57
William 57, 74
Dagbon, Elizabeth 39
Daley, Charles 58
Daniel 58
Susanna 58
Dant, Anne 41
Charles 3, 7, 14, 74
John Baptist 74
Joseph 42
Mary 36, 64
Mary Ann 7
Dart, James 85
John 74
Mary 41
Thomas 85
Davis, (Monica?) 6
Abraham 98
Ann 16
Ann (Mrs.) 14
Anthony 85, 100
Barton 6, 9, 100
Eleanor 19
Elizabeth 15
Hezekiah 85
James 12, 74, 85
Jemima (Mrs.) 12, 15,
16
John 74, 85
Joseph 6, 9, 10, 12,
15, 16, 19, 34, 74,
85
Kenelm 85
Leonard 85
Mary 8, 11, 34
Mima (Mrs.) 19
Monica 6
Moses 74
Peregrine 100
Philemon 85
Rene 85
Sarah (Mrs.) 6, 9, 12,
14
Stephen 14, 74
Stephen (Jr.) 85
Thomas 85
Walter 4, 6, 9, 12, 14,
16, 74, 85, 100
Dawsey, Minta 35

DeButts, John 96
Dean, Alley 7
James 74
John 33, 74
John (Widower) 35
Margaret (Mrs.) 7
Thomas 7, 74
William 74
Deane, Baptist 85
Ignatius 85
James 85
John B. 85
Delahay, Ann 12, 13
Ann (Mrs.) 6
Elizabeth (Mrs.) 6, 13
Frances 8
John 8, 9, 12
John Baptist 13
Mary Ann 8
Rhod. 6
Rodulphus 13
Thomas 6
Winifred 12
Winifred (Mrs.) 8, 9,
12
Delehay, Arthur 85
Demar, (M--?) 94
Joshua 94
M-- 94
Denike, Samuel 36
Dennis, (?) (Widow) 27
William 27
Dennison, Thomas 74
Dent, Charles 74
George 74, 85, 98
John 74
John Bap. 41
Jonathan 85
Tabitha 44
Thomas 85
Denyk, John 27
Devaul, John Miles 74
Dick, John N. 98
Dickson, Absolum 98
Thomas 98
Diddle, Francis 74
Diegs, Mary (Mrs.) 6
Sarah 6
William 6
Digges, Edward 1
Diggs, Ann 33
Charles 21
John 7, 33
Sarah 21

Diggs (cont.)
Sarah (Mrs.) 21
Dillahay, John 74
Road 74
Thomas 74
Dillehay, John 58
Joseph 58
Stephen 58
Winifred (Mrs.) 58
Dillen, Thomas 74
Dillion, Anne 54
Dillon, Thomas 96
Diment, George 85
Matthew 85
Diveria, James 97
Dixon, Hatton 85
Henry 74
Peter 74
Soloman 85
Thomas 85
William R. 85
William Rooke 74
Docherty, Cornelius 85
Dogan, Ann (Mrs.) 58
Eleanor 58
James 58
Jeremiah 58
John 58
Monica (Mrs.) 58
Thomas 58
William 58
Dogin, Thomas 50
Dolson, Stephen 102
Doneson, Joseph 100
Doran, Ann 22, 25
Dorsey, John 44, 85
Joseph 85
Walter 85
Dorsy, Ann 35
Dorothy 20
James 16
John 16
Winifred (Mrs.) 16
Dosse, Ann (Mrs.) 14
Dorothy 17
John 2, 8, 12
John Baptist 12
Joseph 14
Mildred 2
Winifred 9
Winifred (Mrs.) 2, 12
Dossey, John 6, 74
Winifred (Mrs.) 6
Downes, Ann 58

Downes (cont.)
  Ann (Mrs.) 58
  Elizabeth 58
  Ignatius 58
  John 58, 100
  Joseph 58
  Mary 58
Downs, Ann (Mrs.) 8, 13
  Jeremiah 13, 85
  Joseph 8, 13, 74, 85
Doxey, Aaron 85
  Austin S. 74
  James 74
  Jeremiah 85
  John 74, 85
  Joseph 85
  Thomas 85
  William 74
  William (Jr.) 85
Drewry, Enoch 99
  Ignas. 99
  John B. 100
  Philip 100
  Robert 74
  Thomas 74
  Wm. 100
Drudge, John 29, 35, 74
Drury, (?) (Mrs.) 8, 39
  (Henrietta?) 22
  Alethar 14
  Aloysia 8
  Anastasia (Mrs.) 8, 13
  Ann 10, 39
  Ann (Mrs.) 9, 14, 17,
    18, 20
  Anne 41
  Baptist 7, 16
  Bennet 4
  Bennett 85
  Bernard 8, 42, 85
  Bibiana (Mrs.) 11, 15
  Catherine 8, 9, 15, 17,
    19
  Catherine (Mrs.) 12,
    16, 20
  Charles 16, 85
  Dorothy 6, 8, 17
  Edward 9, 85
  Eleanor 6, 14
  Eleanor (Mrs.) 8, 17,
    20
  Eliz. (Mrs.) 22
  Elizabeth 2, 7, 11, 33,
    34, 39, 42

Drury (cont.)
  Elizabeth (Mrs.) 2, 9,
    24, 27
  Ellen 39
  Emerentiana 18
  Emerentiana (Mrs.) 20
  Ena (Mrs.) 18
  Enoch 8, 11, 14, 16,
    18, 74
  Enoch (Jr.) 19
  Enoch (Sr.) 74
  Fran. 2
  Francis 24, 39
  Francis D. 85
  Francis Xavier 24
  Henrietta 22
  Ignatius 8, 9, 12, 13,
    16, 20, 27, 29, 33,
    41, 74, 85
  James 4, 9, 14, 16, 39,
    45, 74
  Jeremiah 19, 85
  Jesse 17, 85
  John 2, 3, 4, 20, 21,
    24, 39
  John (Jr.) 39
  John (Sr.) 74
  John -- 23
  John B. 74
  John Baptist 2, 4, 18
  John C. 85
  John Chrysostom 24
  Joseph 7, 22, 27, 39,
    85
  Joshua 14
  Margaret 6
  Mary 4, 7, 18, 29, 37
  Mary (Mrs.) 2, 4, 6, 7,
    10
  Mary Anne 41
  Matthew 37, 39
  Michael 2, 7, 8, 9, 14,
    17, 20, 33, 74
  Mildred 8
  Monica 2, 11, 18, 28
  Monica (Mrs.) 2, 4, 7,
    11, 29
  Nicholas 4, 7, 11, 46,
    96
  Peter 4, 8, 9, 10, 14,
    17, 20, 46, 85
  Philip 8, 10, 11, 12,
    15, 18, 20, 33, 74
  Richard 9

Drury (cont.)
  Robert 6, 10, 27
  Samuel 15, 85
  Sarah (Mrs.) 9, 14, 20
  Susan 36, 39
  Tabitha 12
  Tabitha (Mrs.) 8, 11,
    14, 16
  Teresa 39
  Thecla 11
  Thomas 4, 14, 37
  Wilfred 20
  William 41, 46, 85
Duel, Joseph 85
Duffner, Joseph 102, 104
Dugent, Monica 16
Duk, Henry 85
  John U. 85
Duke, Ann 28
  John 85
Dunbar, James 85, 99
  Jane 37, 39
  John 37, 39, 74, 99
  Joseph 74, 85, 98
  William 85
Duncaster, John 74
Dunkinson, Robert 85
Dunn, Ann 20
  William 101, 102, 104
Dunnard, John 74
Duval, John 29
Duvall, John M. 102, 104
  Senet 74
  Simon 101, 102
Duvol, Alisia (Mrs.) 11
  Gabriel 22
  Harpi (Mrs.) 22
  John 11
  Mary 11
  Miles 22
Dyal, (?) 24
  Elva (Mrs.) 24
  John 29
  Joshua 24
Dyer, Ann 13
  Barton 85
  James 13
  Mary (Mrs.) 13
Dyne, (?) 2
  Dorothy 18
  Eleanor (Mrs.) 18, 19,
    20
  Elizabeth 2, 13
  George 16

Fenwick (cont.)
34, 39, 58, 75, 100
John (Jr.) 39, 75
Joseph 6, 11, 28, 75,
  100, 101
Lewis 86
M. 39
Margaret 28
Marian 39
Mary 11, 15, 26, 28,
  37, 39
Mary (Mrs.) 4, 12
Mary Anna 37
Monica 6, 15
Monica (Mrs.) 6, 58
Nancy 39
Nelly (Mrs.) 10
Nicholas 6
P. 75
Philip 4, 8, 9, 11, 13,
  15, 33, 75
Priscilla 24
R. 99
Rebecca (Mrs.) 6, 9,
  13, 15
Richard 4, 14, 18, 21,
  24, 26, 28, 29, 37,
  39, 75
Richard (Jr.) 29, 86
Robert 4, 6, 9, 12, 13,
  14, 24, 39
Robert (Jr.) 6
Robt. 100
Sarah 4, 13
Sarah (Mrs.) 24, 26
Susan (Mrs.) 6, 14
Thomas 15, 16, 18, 35,
  75
Walter 101
William 3, 6, 9, 12,
  13, 58, 75, 86
Ferrel, Ansel(m) 104
Ferril, Edward 86
  William (Jr.) 86
Ferrill, Thomas 75
  William (Jr.) 75
  William (Sr.) 75
Field, (?) 6
  Allison 28
  Catherine 41
  Dorothy 6
Fielder, Nicholas 75
Fields, James A. 86
  Joseph 86

Fields (cont.)
  Leonard 75
  Sarah 35
  William 75
Finwick, Benjamin 1
  Cudbert 1
  Ignatious 1
Fish, Ann 21
  Barton 86
  Francis 28
  James 25, 36
  Joseph 21, 24, 25, 27,
    28, 86
  Lydia (Mrs.) 21, 24,
    25, 27, 28
  Margaret 27
Fisher, Ben. 10
  Christopher 75
  Eleanor 29
  Elizabeth 10
  Elizabeth (Mrs.) 10
  James 10
  Stephen 102
Fitzgerald, Francis 86
  Thomas 36
Fitzgiffard, Sara 37
Fitzgo, William 75
Fitzjeffery, Charles 75
  Joseph 75
  Richard 75
Fletcher, Ann 28, 37
  Henry 75
Flood, Joseph 75
Flower, Charles 86
  James 86
  Jeremiah 75, 86
  Joseph 86
  Thomas 75
Floyd, (?) 15
  Ann 20
  Jesse 15, 20, 35, 75,
    86
  Jesse (Widower) 36
  Jessy 99
  Justinian 14
  Mary (Mrs.) 20
Foard, Raphael 75
Foiles, Thomas 86
Ford, (?) 2, 14
  Anastasia (Mrs.) 58
  Ann 2, 12, 18, 33
  Ann (Jr.) 8
  Ann (Mrs.) 2, 7, 8, 10
  Athanatius 2, 8, 10,

Ford (cont.)
  15, 20, 46
  Barbara 4
  Bennet 86
  Bernard 21
  Bibiana 8, 12, 13, 15
  Bibiana (Mrs.) 6, 15
  Catherine 6, 15, 17, 36
  Charles 18, 58, 86
  Charles A. 86
  Clara 58
  Dorothy 4
  Dorothy (Mrs.) 8, 18,
    21
  Dorothy (Widow) 8
  Edward 12, 86
  Eleanor 8
  Eleanor (Mrs.) 58
  Eliz. (Mrs.) 18
  Elizabeth 8, 9, 12, 35
  Elizabeth (Mrs.) 4, 17,
    19, 20
  Gerard 20
  Henrietta (Mrs.) 12
  Henry 6, 10, 11, 15,
    18, 20, 75, 86, 96,
    100
  Ignatius 3, 6, 8, 16,
    20, 58, 86
  James 6
  Jane 14, 16, 18, 19
  Jeremiah 86
  Jesse 16
  John 4, 12, 18, 19, 46,
    75, 99
  John (Jr.) 19, 46, 75
  John (Sr.) 2
  John Francis 58
  John G. 96
  John Gerrard 86
  Joseph 2, 4, 6, 11, 12,
    14, 36, 86, 96
  Joseph (Jr.) 100
  Joseph (Sr.) 100
  Lucy 2
  Margaret 36
  Mary 8, 14
  Mary (Mrs.) 20
  Michael 7
  Peter 12, 15, 18, 36,
    58, 75, 86
  Phil 18
  Philip 4, 10, 13, 15,
    17, 20, 35, 58, 75,

119

Greenwell (cont.)
Eliz. 14
Eliz. (Mrs.) 6
Elizabaeth (Mrs.) 59
Elizabeth 5, 7, 10, 14,
16, 25, 59, 60
Elizabeth (Mrs.) 4, 7,
10, 15
Emerentiana 10, 59
Enoch 6, 76
Eunie (?) Ranseau Anna
59
Frances (Mrs.) 59
George 7, 59, 76, 86
Hannah (Mrs.) 59
Henrietta 6, 10, 12
Henry 20, 45, 48, 59,
76, 86
Ignatius 4, 5, 6, 8,
10, 15, 16, 18, 20,
28, 45, 48, 59, 76,
86, 97
Ignatius (Jr.) 76
James 7, 10, 14, 46,
59, 76, 86
Jane 59
Jane (Mrs.) 8, 10, 15,
59
Jeremiah 60, 86
Jesse 6, 9, 11
John 2, 5, 8, 12, 16,
59, 76, 86, 100
John (Jr.) 8, 9, 76
John (Sr.) 76
John B. 86
John Baptist 6, 12, 14,
59
John Basil 59
John E. 76, 96, 100
John Wiseman 6
Jos. 8, 100
Joseph 6, 8, 10, 11,
15, 24, 59, 76, 86,
98
Joshua 10, 15, 23, 24,
25, 27, 35, 76, 86
Joshua Leonard 59
Juliana 23
Justin 7
Justinian 10, 14, 59,
60, 76
Leonard 76
Mary 10, 11, 12, 13,
24, 33, 60

Greenwell (cont.)
Mary (Mrs.) 6, 11, 15,
20, 60
Mary Ann 6, 59
Mary Ann (Mrs.) 8
Mildred 6
Mildred (Mrs.) 8, 12
Monica 6, 34
Nicholas 8, 10, 13, 76
Noah 60, 86
Peter 4, 86
Phil 86
Philip 7, 8, 11, 60, 86
Ralph 15
Raphael 13, 35, 76
Rebecca 6, 13, 33
Rebecca (Mrs.) 24
Richard 59
Robert 6, 14, 17, 76,
86
Rodulphus 8, 18
Rose 8
Sarah 8, 16
Stephen 10, 76, 86
Susan 6, 13
Susan (Mrs.) 5, 6, 8,
10, 12, 16, 20, 25
Susanna (Mrs.) 59
Thomas 6, 10, 17, 60,
76, 86, 100
Ursula 14
Wilfred 18, 86
William 8, 12, 16, 59,
76, 86
Willm. 96
Winifred (Mrs.) 7, 8,
11, 60
Wm. 100
Greeves, Robert 76
Greggs, Elizabeth 37
George 86
Margaret 28
Sebastian 39
Gregs, Elizabeth 39
Grenier, Vincent 101
Grey, Randolph 86
Griffin, (?) 42
Abraham 76
Ignatius 86
John 41, 42
Philip 86
Sarah 41
Thomas 76
Griggs, (?) 21

Griggs (cont.)
James 86
Lydia 24
Mary 21
Sabbaston 76
Grindall, Joseph 86
Josiah B. 86
Grinwell, Hellen 41
Gristy, Richard 76
Guida, Jane 37
John 37
Guido, John 33
Guither, George 99
Jane 39
John 39
Jon. 39
William 86
Wm. 98
Guleson, Elizabeth 37
Gunn, James 99
Guyther, George 76, 96
Hacket, Henrietta 12
Rodolph 76
Rodolphus 9
Hackett, Rhode 99
Haddester, Thomas 42
Haden, Clement 1
Francis 12, 14, 76
George 14, 76
Joseph 14
Mary (Mrs.) 14
Mary Ann (Mrs.) 12
Hagan, Aquila 102, 104
Aquilla 101
Barton 93
Benedict 104
Clement 101
James (Sr.) 94
John C. 102, 104
Joseph 93, 101
Levi 102, 104
Michael 101, 102, 104
Raphael 93
Robert 76
Wilfred 102
Wm. 93
Hagar, Elizabeth 28
Mathew 49
Matthew 28
Robert 86
Hager, (?) 25
Eleanor 6
Eleanor (Mrs.) 6
Matthew 6

121

125

128

Mc--, John 25
  Susan 25
  Susan (Mrs.) 25
McAtee, Daniel 102
  Henry 102
McCawley, Nelly 37
  William 37
McCayley, John 100
McClannon, John 99
McClean, John 78
McCowley, John 88
McCoy, Benj. 98
McGee, Hannon 88
  Raphael 88
  Rapheal 99
  William 88
McGill, Arthur 36
  Susan 6
  Susan (Mrs.) 6, 11
  Susanna (Mrs.) 4
  Thomas 4, 6, 11
McGui(re?), Henrietta 10
McGuire, Henrietta 10
McKain, Wm. 104
McKay, Benjamin 78, 88
  George 88
  John 88
  Richard 78
  Stephen 88
McKinney, Soloman 88
McKinny, Joseph 24
  Priscilla (Mrs.) 24, 28
  Reuben 88
  Ruben 24, 28
  Solomon 28
McLain, William 102
McLarran, Johh 98
McLean, (?) 27
  (?) (Mrs.) 25, 27
  Ann 28
  Arthur 25
  Elizabeth 25
  Elizabeth (Mrs.) 28
  John 78
  Richard 27, 28
McLearn, Arthur 88
  William 88
McLeland, Robert 88
McMillan, James 101
McMullin, Henry 78
McWilliams, Alexander 88
  George 88
  James 88
  John 88

McWilliams (cont.)
  Kelly 16
  Kenelm 78
  Sarah 16
  Thomas 78
Medcalf, (?) 4, 6
  Elizabeth (Mrs.) 4, 6,
    9, 12
  Ignatius 63
  James 9
  John 4, 6, 9
  John Kenelm 63
  Kenelm 89
  Martin 12
  Sarah (Mrs.) 63
  Sarah (Widow) 33
Medley, Anastasia 12
  Anastasia (Mrs.) 27
  Anastatia (Mrs.) 63
  Ann 8, 9, 63
  Ann (Mrs.) 11, 63
  Ann Elizabeth 63
  Aug. 96
  Augustine 63
  Ben. 10
  Bennet 8
  Bernard 18, 63, 97
  Catharine 63
  Clement 6, 63
  Eleanor 63
  Elizabeth 10
  Elizabeth (Mrs.) 10
  Enoch 78
  Frances 8
  Frances (Mrs.) 13
  George 63, 78
  Henry 13, 15, 36, 78,
    99
  Ignatius 11, 13
  Jane 8
  John 8, 13, 78, 89
  Joseph 11, 27, 63, 78
  Margaret 17, 18
  Mary 6, 7, 34, 63
  Mary (Mrs.) 6, 13, 63
  Mary Ann (Mrs.) 63
  Matthew 63
  Nancy 8
  Philip 78, 96, 99
  Sarah 63
  William 63, 78, 89
  Wm. 100
Meekins, Agnes 24
  Dorothy 21

Meekins (cont.)
  Elizabeth (Mrs.) 21, 25
  Henry 21, 25
  Henry (Sr.) 21, 24
  Joshua 24
  Mary 25
  Matthew 21
  Priscilla (Mrs.) 21
  Rachel (Mrs.) 24
  Sarah 21, 24
  Stephen 21
  Susan 25
Megrs, Mary 29
Mehoney, Joseph 6
Meken, Augustine 64
  Margaret 64
  Margaret (Mrs.) 64
  Susanna 64
Mekins, Abraham 42
  Elizabeth 42
  Mary 41, 42
  Teresa 41
  Thomas 42
Melton, James 89, 98
  John 41
  Joshua 34
  Richard 89
  Susan 34
  Thomas 89
Mermon, James 100
  Josuha 100
Merryman, William 89
Michael, Ann 37
  James 102
Michaels, James 21
Middleton, (?) (Mrs.) 42
  Charity 42
  Elisabeth 42
  Gutherick 42
  Guthlack 42
  Ignatius 42
  Martha 42
  Samuel 42
Milborn, Elizabeth 34
  Frances 12
Milbourn, Elizabeth 40
  John 50, 51
  Joseph 50
Milbourne, Anne 33
  Elizabeth 37
Milburn, Ann 50, 51
  Austin 78
  Edward 78, 89
  Eleanor 64

More (cont.)
  Nicholas 47
  Nicholas (Jr.) 37
  Nicholas (Sr.) 37
  Richard 18
  Stephen 10
  Susan 6
  William 24, 47
Morgan, Benedict 18
  Benjamin 79
  Eleanor 18
  Ignas. 99
  Ignat. 97
  Ignatius 89
  James 79, 89, 97, 100
  John (Sr.) 79
  Raphael 89
  Rapheal 98
  William 79, 89
  Winifred (Mrs.) 18
  Wm. 99
Morris, (?) 26
  Ann (Mrs.) 26
  John 26
Morton, Samuel 89
Mosely, Joseph 41
Mosley, Joseph 1, 41, 42
  Joseph (Rev.) 41
Moulds, William 79
Mud, Thomas 79
Mudd, Alectious 94
  Bennit 93
  Joseph 79
Mugg, John 45, 99
  Peter 45, 89
  Peter (Jr.) 45
  Thomas 45
  Walter 45
Muir, William 79
Mulanny, Andrew 16
Murphy, Edward 89
  Samuel 89
Murray, William Vans 95
Murrein, James 7, 12, 33
  John 12
  Mary (Mrs.) 7, 12
  Sarah 7
Murrian, Valentine 79
Murry, Hugh 94
  Richard 89
  Wm. 94
Neal, Jerry 94
Neale, (?) (Mrs.) 41
  Ann 7

Neale (cont.)
  Bennet 1
  Bennett 79
  Bennoni 96, 98
  Benoni 89
  Charles 79, 89, 100
  Daniel 89
  Edward 89
  Edward Diggs 89
  Elizabeth (Mrs.) 7
  H. 1
  Henry 79, 89, 96
  James 79, 89, 98
  Jas. 98
  Jeremiah 1, 79
  John 89
  Joseph 89
  Raphael 79, 89
  Raphael (Jr.) 79
  Rapheal 100
  Roswell 89
  Sarah 10
  Wilford 1, 7
  Wilfred 79, 98
  William 89
Nelson, Joshua 89
  Obediah 89
  Seneca 97, 99
  Senna 79
Nettle, Thomas 89
Nevett, John 47
  John Baptist 79
Nevison, James 79
Nevit, John 47
  John Baptist 47
  Joseph 79
  Mary 47
Nevitt, Charles 79
  Francis 89
  John 79, 89
  Joseph 18, 79
  Mary (Mrs.) 18
  Matthew 89
Newgent, Bennet 89
Newton, (?) 7
  Agatha 14
  Alban 14, 34
  Ann 33
  Bernard 8, 18, 33, 35,
    64, 79
  Bibiana 4
  Clement 7, 89
  Delbert 15, 79, 100
  Elizabeth 8, 35, 64

Newton (cont.)
  Gabriel 7, 8, 35, 79
  Gilbert 11
  Ignatius 79, 89, 100
  James 64
  Jane 18
  Jeremiah 9
  John Shadrach 64
  Joseph 9, 64
  Mary 16, 18
  Mary (Mrs.) 7, 8
  Mary Ann (Mrs.) 14, 18,
    64
  Mildred (Mrs.) 9, 64
  Rhodolph 64
  Sarah 5, 9, 10, 16
  Sarah (Mrs.) 4, 23
  Susan 34
  Thomas 4, 23
  William 10
  Zach 99
  Zachariah 79
Nivet, Joseph 3
  Rachel 3
Noakes, Thomas 79
Noble, Henry 41
  Joseph 38, 40, 79
  Lydia 40
Noe, George 79
Nokes, Richard 79
Norris, Ann 12
  Ann (Mrs.) 65
  Ann Dresden 10
  Arnold 64
  Baptist 8, 12
  Barbara 64
  Basil 89
  Benedict 13
  Bennet 6, 10, 79, 89
  Bennett 64
  Bent. 99
  Bibiana 64
  Catherine 11
  Clement 10, 64
  Cuthbert 10, 64
  Dorothy 13, 65
  Dorothy (Mrs.) 8, 10,
    11, 12, 14, 65
  Dresden (Mrs.) 6, 10
  Edmund 20
  Edmund B. 79
  Eleanor 65
  Elizabeth 13, 65
  Elizabeth (Mrs.) 12, 64

Norris (cont.)
Enoch 64
Frances (Mrs.) 6, 10,
64
George 4
Henrietta 64, 65
Henry 79
Henry Elijah 64
Ignatius 8, 11, 14, 33,
79, 89
James 12, 34, 79, 89,
100
John 6, 8, 10, 51, 64,
79, 89
John Baptist 13, 33
John H. 89
Joseph 6, 64, 65, 89
Joseph H. 89
Lucy (Mrs.) 8, 11, 14
Luke 64
M. 4
Mackelva 79
Margaret 14
Mark 7, 12, 14, 64, 79,
89
Mark (Jr.) 7, 12
Mark (Sr.) 79
Mary 6, 8, 35, 64, 65
Mary (Mrs.) 4, 8, 12,
64, 65
Mary Ann 65
Mary Ann (Mrs.) 13, 65
Matthew 79, 89
Matthias 64
Monica 8
Monica (Mrs.) 7, 12,
13, 65
Philip 6, 7, 13, 64,
65, 79, 89
Priscilla 36
Rebecca 65
Rhodolph 65
Rodolph 79
Rodulphus 8, 10, 11,
12, 14
Sarah 12
Stephen 8
Susanna 64, 65
Thomas 7, 12, 13, 64,
65, 79, 89
Vincent 64, 89
William 7, 65, 89
Winifred 64
Wm. 89, 99

Norriss, Ben. 100
Clement 79
John 79, 100
Mark 100
Mathew 100
Matthew 99
Thomas 100
William 79
Nottingham, Ann 65
Athanasius 65
Basil 10, 18, 35
Benjamin 79
Bennett 89
Catherine 13
Eleanor 12
Eleanor (Mrs.) 10
Elizabeth 65
Elizabeth (Mrs.) 16
Enoch 65
Ignatius 65
Jane 8
Jane (Mrs.) 18
John 16
John Basil 79
Mary 8, 34, 65
Mary (Mrs.) 65
Mary (Widow) 13
Mary Ann 65
Matthias 65
Monica 13
Philip 6, 19, 79
Raphael Ignatius 65
Nottinghame, Bent. 100
Novice, Mary 38
Nowell, Baptist 89
Jeremiah 89
Nugent, Benj. 99
Elizabeth 10
Henry 18
Jeremiah 99
Rebecca (Mrs.) 10, 18
Thomas 15
Williby 79
Willoughby 10, 15, 18
O'Bryan, Eleanor 53
O'Niell, Bernard 79
Oneile, Bernard 40
Osburn, Thomas (Sr.) 93
Owens, Joseph 79
Owings, James 89
John 89
Joseph 89
Robert 89
Ownings, John 89

Pain, Ann (Mrs.) 4
Baptist 4
Elizabeth 4
Francis 79
James 79
John 25
John Baptist 79
Richard 79
Paine, Leonard 1
Pane, Frances 3
Leonard 3
Pantry, Jeremiah 89, 100
Parnham, Jane 42
Parsons, Bernard 89
Clement 1, 42, 79
Elizabeth (Mrs.) 6, 9,
12
James 6, 9, 12, 33, 79
Jeremiah 6
John 89
Joseph 9, 89
Mary 42
Peter 12
Patterson, James 89, 99
Payn, (?) 19
Aloysia 18
Ann 8
Ann (Mrs.) 8
Baptist 8, 14
Basil 17
Cloe 35
Eleanor 8
Eleanor (Mrs.) 10
Elizabeth 35
Elizabeth (Mrs.) 16
Henrietta (Mrs.) 10, 18
James 10, 20, 79
John 33
Leonard 18
Margaret (Mrs.) 17
Mary 33
Mary Ann (Mrs.) 16
Priscilla 34
Susan 8, 16
Veincent 16
Vincent 14
William 10, 18
Payne, Allelusia 65
Anastasia 66
Ann 65
Ann (Mrs.) 65
Basil 89
Bernard 65
Charles 65

132

134

135

Sanson (cont.)
William 67
Saunders, Ann (Mrs.) 8,
  67
  Elizabeth 67
  Sinnet 8
  Sinnott 67
  Susan 8
Saxon, Eleanor 10
  Elizabeth (Mrs.) 10
  Robert 10
Saxton, Bennett 90
  Elizabeth (Mrs.) 13
  Raphael 90
  Robert 13
  Zachariah 13, 90
Schafer, (?) 24
  (?) (Mrs.) 24
  Thomas 24
Scherclift, Eliz. 41
  Francis Xaverius 41
  Richard 41
Scissell, John 80
  John B. 80
  William 80
Scot, Elizabeth (Mrs.) 8
  James 8
  Thomas 8
Scott, Edward 90
  John 90
  Thomas 90
  William 80
Seagar, James 99
Seager, James 80
  Nathaniel 90
  Thomas 90
Seale, (?) 47
  Francis 90
  Jonathan 43, 44, 49
  Leonard 80
  Leond. 98
  Lidia 49
  Lydia 47
  Mary 47
  Monaca 49
Seall, Ann 43
  Elizabeth 44
Seaton, John 71
Secill, Sarah 46
Segar, Benjamin 90
Semmes, Ann 6
  Anthony 6, 7, 9, 10,
  12, 15, 16, 18
  Elizabeth 6, 18

Semmes (cont.)
  Henrietta 42
  Ignatius 12
  John 7
  Mary (Mrs.) 6, 7, 10,
  12, 15
  Sarah 7
Seney, Joshua 95
Sewall, Charles 90, 100
  Clement 80, 90
  Dorothy 7
  Ellen (Mrs.) 4
  Henry 4, 7, 80, 90, 98
  Henry (Jr.) 96
  Letitia 24
  Mary 36
  Mary (Mrs.) 7, 29
  N. Lewis 80
  Nich. L. 96
  Nicholas 29, 80, 90
  Nicholas (Jr.) 29, 90,
  98
Sewel, (?) 2
  Henry 2
  Mary (Mrs.) 2
Sewell, Charles 67
  Clement 67
  Henry 67
  Letitia 24
  Mary (Mrs.) 67
  Mary Smith 67
Shadrick, John 90
  Thomas 90
Shadricks, John 80
Shamwell, Joseph 90
Shange, Anastasia (Mrs.)
  8
  Philip 8
  Sylvester 8
Shanks, Henry 90
  John 71, 90
  John (Sr.) 80
  Joseph 34, 80
  Margaret 19
  Peter 90
  Susan 12
  Thomas 80
Sharpe, Horatio (Gov.) 1
Shaw, William 80, 90
Shearley, Richard 90
Shehawn, Helen 41
  Mary 42
  Mason 42
Sheircliffe, Francis X.

Sheircliffe (cont.)
  90
Sheirly, Bennet 90
  Ignatius 90
  John 90
Shenton, Joseph 41, 42
  Mary 42
Sher(cl?)if, Esther 29
Sherclif, Esther 29
Shercliff, John 1
  Joseph 80
  Thomas 80
Sherley, Elizabeth 29
  George 80
Sherly, Mary 41
Shermentine, Caleb 90
  James 90
  John 90
Shiercliff, John 80
Shinton, (?) 22
  Anastasia 25
  J-- (Sr.) 22
  John 41
  Mary 41
  Rachel (Mrs.) 25
  Raymond 41
  Rebecca (Mrs.) 22
  William 25
Shircliff, Ann 35
Shirden, Sarah 16
Shirkley, Eleanor 2
Shirley, Anastasia 25
  Benedict 25
  Mary 6, 10
  Mary (Mrs.) 25
Shirly, Ignatius 35
Shurbentine, Joseph 80
Shurley, Ignas. 100
Siford, Elizabeth 10, 29,
  34
  Joseph 2
  Mary Ann 2
Silence, Enoch 90
  William 90
Simmes, Anthony 80
Simmons, Matthew W. 90
Simms, Anth. 96
  Anthony (Jr.) 90
  Edward 93
  John 90
Simon, Garbiner 80
Simpson, Josias 80, 90
  Walter 94
Sims, Anthony 49, 67

136

137

Sword, Ignatious 81
  William 90
Tabbs, Barton 90
  George C. 91
  Moses 81
  Thomas 91
Tailton, James 49, 50
  John 50
Taney, Charles 41
  Eleanor 68
  Eleanor (Mrs.) 12, 68
  Elizabeth (Mrs.) 7
  Francis 7, 41
  Henrietta 7
  Henry 7
  James 7
  Jane 13
  John 68
  John F. 81
  Joseph 7
  Mary 12, 41
  Michael 34
  Raphael 48, 81, 91
  Rodulphus 12
  Sarah 68
  Thomas 41, 48, 91
Tanner, Elizabeth 24
Tarleton, Charles 91
  Elijah 91
  Frederick 91
  Ignatius 91
  James 91
  Joshua 91
  Peregrine 91
  Richard 91
  Stephen 91
  Thomas 91
Tarlton, (?) (Mrs.) 26
  Bennet 81
  Bennett 100
  Cloa 35
  Cloe 12, 29
  Dorothy 28
  Dorothy (Mrs.) 29
  El-- 29
  Eleanor (Mrs.) 7, 8, 22
  Elijah 68
  Enoch 14
  Enora (Mrs.) 12
  Ignatius 68
  James 49, 50, 68, 81,
    100
  Jane (Mrs.) 68
  Jeremiah 68

Tarlton (cont.)
  John 50, 51, 68, 81
  John (Sr.) 99
  Joshua 81, 99
  Mary (Mrs.) 28
  Mary Ann (Mrs.) 68
  Moses 7, 8, 10, 12, 13,
    14, 22, 26
  Richard 29
  Stephen 14, 99
  Susan (Mrs.) 13, 14
  Teresa 7
  Thomas 11, 14, 29, 81
  Thomas (Sr.) 100
  William 68, 81, 96
  Zachariah 12, 28
Tawney, Eleanor (Mrs.) 4
  Elizabeth (Mrs.) 4
  Francis 4
  Ignatius 4, 91
  Mary 4
  Rodulphus 4
Taylor, Anastasia 18
  Ann 68
  Barbara 18
  Caleb 91
  Dorothy 21
  E. 91
  Eleanor 25
  Elizabeth 14, 15, 23
  Henrietta 68
  Henry 81, 100
  Ignatius 16, 68, 81, 91
  James 4, 19, 25, 81, 91
  Jane 16
  Jenifer 71, 91
  John 81, 91
  John (Jr.) 91
  Mary 68
  Mary (Mrs.) 16
  Mary Ann 4
  Merritt 91
  Monica 40
  Richard 81, 91
  Statia 53
  Thomas 81
  William 40, 81
Tear, Barton 91
  John 40
  John (Jr.) 40
  John (Mrs.) 22
  Mary 40
  Monica 40
  William 40

Templeman, Augustin 91
Tench, Jane 94
  Jno. 94
  Leonard 93
Tennison, Absalom 91
  Jesse 81, 91
  Jessey 81
  John 81
  Joshua 91
  Justinian 91
  Matthew 81
  Samuel 81, 91
  Thomas 91
  William 81
Tewkes, Joseph 71
Theobalds, James 81
  Prior 91
  Samuel 81
Thomas, Abell 68
  Ann 68
  Dorothy 8
  Dorothy (Mrs.) 8, 14,
    68
  Edward 68
  Eleanor (Mrs.) 29
  Eliza 29
  Elizabeth 68
  Elizabeth (Mrs.) 68
  Elizabeth (Widow) 35
  George 91
  Harbert 81
  James 68
  Jamima 68
  John 8, 14, 68
  John A. 81, 96, 99
  Joshua 91
  Levy 81
  Luke 68
  Mark 68
  Mary 25, 26, 68
  Mary Ann 14
  Philip 29, 81
  Robert 68, 81
  Robt. 99
  Roger 91
  Samuel 68
  Sarah (Mrs.) 68
  Taylor 91
  Thomas 8, 91
  Tylor 81
  William 91
  William (Jr.) 96, 97
  William A. 91
  Zachariah 91

Wimsatt (cont.)
  Joseph Z. 103, 104
  Mary (Mrs.) 15
  Richard 1, 5, 10, 47,
    82
  Robert 6, 10, 47, 82,
    92, 103
  Robert (Jr.) 100
  Robt. 99
  Samuel 92
  Stephen 15, 21, 82
  Tenison 47
  William 47, 82, 92
Windder, Athanasius 42
Wingate, Henry 99
Wingatt, John 41
Winsatt, Ann 2
  Stephen 33
Winsett, Robt. 96
Wise, Adam 82, 99
  Elijah 92
  James 92
  Jas. 99
  Jeremiah 92
  John 92
  Mathew 51
  Matthew 51
  Matthew (Sr.) 82
  Miel 92
  Richard 51, 92
  Thomas 82
  William 82
  Yonng 92
Wiseman, George 92
  John 4, 92
  Richard 82
Witfield, Ann 10
Witherington, James 92
  Thomas 92
Withirington, Benjamin 94
  James 94
  Richd. 94
Wm., Joseph Hagan 93
Wollingham, John B. 100
Wood, Gabriel 92
  James 92
  Jeremiah 92
  John 82, 92
  Leonard 82
  Nathan 92
Woodard, John 82
Woodburn, Daniel 82
  John 82
  Jonathan 82, 92

Woodburne, Chs. 100
  Daniel 100
Woodward, John 92
  Joseph 100
  Joseph (Jr.) 92
  Mary 33
  Richard 92
  Thomas 92
  William 82
  Wm. 98
Wooten, Ann (Mrs.) 28
  Eleanor (Mrs.) 28
  Joseph 28
  Susan 28
  Thomas 9, 28
Wooton, (?) 27
  Charles 13
  Eleanor (Mrs.) 26
  Elizabeth (Mrs.) 10,
    18, 26
  James 6
  John 13, 82
  Joseph 6, 13, 26
  Mary 26
  Mary (Mrs.) 6, 13
  Richard 26
  Susan (Mrs.) 13
  Thomas 10, 12, 13, 14,
    18, 27
  Thomas (Jr.) 26
Wotten, John 42
Wotton, John B. 92
  Joseph 92
  Richard 92
  Thomas 92
Wright, Joseph 41
Yates, Aloysia (Mrs.) 20
  Ann (Mrs.) 11
  Bernard 7
  Dorothy 17
  Edward 45, 82, 92
  Enoch 7
  Francis 1
  Ignatious 103, 104
  Ignatius 6, 92
  James 82, 92, 97, 100
  John 7, 82, 92
  Martin 11, 45, 82, 92,
    100
  Martin (Jr.) 45
  Mary (Mrs.) 7
  Thomas 1
  William 11, 92
  Zachariah 20

Yeates, Martin 45
Yets, (?) (Mrs.) 21
  Aloysia 18
  Ann 6, 33
  Ann (Mrs.) 15, 17
  Bartholomew 14, 15
  Catherine 17
  Dorothy 9
  Edward 4, 6
  Ignatius 15
  James 9, 21, 36
  John 6, 12, 17
  Martin 15, 17
  Mary (Mrs.) 4, 6, 12,
    17
  Monica 8
  Monica (Mrs.) 14
  Priscilla 21
  Rebecca 6, 10, 11, 14,
    15, 16, 18
  Susan 33
Young, Rob. 98
  Robert 82
Zachariah, William 92
  Zachariah 92

143